ENOCH'S JOURNEY

Enoch's Journey

Seven Steps to "Was Not"

Earl A. Jones

RESOURCE *Publications* • Eugene, Oregon

ENOCH'S JOURNEY
Seven Steps to "Was Not"

Copyright © 2018 Earl A. Jones. All rights reserved. Except for brief quotations in critical publications or reviews, no part of this book may be reproduced in any manner without prior written permission from the publisher. Write: Permissions, Wipf and Stock Publishers, 199 W. 8th Ave., Suite 3, Eugene, OR 97401.

Resource Publications
An Imprint of Wipf and Stock Publishers
199 W. 8th Ave., Suite 3
Eugene, OR 97401

www.wipfandstock.com

PAPERBACK ISBN: 978-1-5326-6407-6
HARDCOVER ISBN: 978-1-5326-6408-3
EBOOK ISBN: 978-1-5326-6409-0

Manufactured in the U.S.A.   12/17/18

Contents

Prologue | vii

1. Enoch's Journey: Seven Steps to "Was Not" | 1
2. Enoch's Journey: What We Know | 14
3. Step One: Faith | 52
4. Step Two: Pleasing God | 73
5. Step Three: The Dream | 89
6. Step Four: Obedience & Submission | 112
7. Step Five: Endurance, Perseverance, & Seeking Diligently | 138
8. Step Six: The Reward & the Rewarder | 172
9. Step Seven: "Was Not" | 198
10. The End & the Beginning of the Journey: The Promised Land of "Was Not" | 233

Epilogue | 259

Prologue

What's past may indeed become prologue.

Which can lead you to a good, or a bad place,

depending on where your past is located

in the present . . .

ADAPTED FROM SHAKESPEARE
"WHAT'S PAST IS PROLOGUE"
SPOKEN BY ANTONIO IN ACT II, SCENE I OF *THE TEMPEST*

1

Enoch's Journey: Seven Steps to "Was Not"

AN UNUSUAL FEELING

YESTERDAY EVENING I HAD a strange occurrence transpire, which led to an unusual feeling for me. I am not an insecure person. Not at all. Incorrectly, some people would probably call me cocky, overconfident, intellectually arrogant, etc. Those people of course, do not know me as well as they think they do, as I am actually none of those things.[1]

Please believe me, I do not say this to sound cocky or overly self-assured. However, I often say, particularly to one friend and brother of mine (whose cage I enjoy rattling because of his negative and shrinking perception of my, seemingly to him, outsized level of self-confidence) that, "I do not sit around wondering if I am wrong."

If I am wrong, it is usually due to a lack of information. But, for the most part, I trust the analysis process by which I have arrived at an opinion or decision. I am who I am, and I embrace this person.

I am typically very sure of myself, and comfortable in my own skin. I have some things that I do not like, such as the occasional pimple. However, I work on those immediately, assiduously, and relentlessly, until I correct them. Oh, by the way, did I mention that I am a perfectionist? Much to my mother's chagrin.

---

1. 2 Cor 12:7.

I know what I know, and I know those things quite well. However, I also love and enjoy being around people who know things that I do not know. Those who can do things based out of their gifts and callings that I cannot do, like art—also, in some circumstances, and with some people (though not others), medicine.

However, I will intentionally often remain silent in group conversations. I do this because I believe that I tend to dominate conversations. And I do not want to do that to some of the people who are at the table. I prefer that they share their ideas before I inevitably, and often regrettably, turn and "take over" the conversation.

A TRYING FAITH JOURNEY

Anyway, yesterday I emailed three of my professional references regarding uploading letters of recommendation for a lecturer position that I applied for. Now, I am amid a pretty serious and trying faith journey as I write this book, one that has lasted far too long for my taste and preference.

I have only shared the specifics of this particular journey with a very select group of people. Those who God has told me to share it with, or those with who he has inevitably placed me in contact, or in close quarters. And in those latter cases, I could not avoid telling them about *only some* parts of this journey.

I am also an intensely private person. I treat most people like "mushrooms," as Chuck Noll, the former coach of the Pittsburgh Steelers used to say. "Keep the media in the dark and feed them fertilizer."[2]

My mentor, Doc, was the only one of the three professional references that decided to immediately follow-up and reply to my email reminder. However, he will accommodate pretty much any request that I make. And he is generally very responsive relative to professional emails, received from any university, when I list him as a reference.

He informed me that he had already followed up with the university and submitted his letter of recommendation. I thanked him and told him that I figured he had already completed the upload. The email was primarily intended for the other two. And it was sent, by me, at the behest

---

2. Bouchette, Ed. "Memories of Chuck Noll." *Pittsburgh Post-Gazette* (blog) *Post-gazette.com*, April 6, 2016. https://www.post-gazette.com/sports/Steelers-Blog/2014/06/14/Memories-of-Chuck-Noll/stories/201406140177.

of the university where I applied. These other two references are not at all "sketchy" people. However, some people need reminders to follow up. But not Doc.

IF MY GOAL WAS POPULARITY . . .

I only come off to some (I say insecure) people as "cocky" or "intellectually arrogant." Most often, only to that one specific "brother" of mine. Maybe to a few others. However, I only present in that way to that very select group of people when I intend to come off that way. In those instances, I call it "throwing my shoe (or the dead fish) on the table." During those times, their perception, largely generated by my intentional actions, may not be so far from the truth, if I am being completely honest.

This occurs because I do not care, at all, what 99 percent of people think of me. Most people like me. Yet, very few people know the real me.

For a person who comes off, at times, as "intellectually arrogant," I not-so-secretly abhor when others try to mask their insecurities by making others feel intellectually inferior. That is when I "throw my shoe, or the dead fish" on the table. I usually do this by saying something that will checkmate their "actual" display of intellectual arrogance. This verse describes me very well, during those times:

> Do you think I speak this strongly in order to manipulate crowds?
> Or (to) curry favor with God?
> Or (to) get popular applause? . . .
> . . . If my goal was popularity, I wouldn't bother being Christ's slave.[3]

The Liberian Ninja

One person, and the *only* person who has *ever* gotten past my filters, walls, and psychoanalytical deflectors, was so good, so stealth, that she was "in there" like a Liberian ninja. I had absolutely no idea that she was already so deeply and firmly entrenched behind my guards and walls.

She had completely worked her way into the core of my being, my heart, and my soul. She protected me when I needed it; at that time I could not do it for myself. She cared for me, and I needed that too. I am usually pretty adept at doing those things for myself.

---

3. Gal 1:10.

However, for the most part, sans Doc and the Liberian Ninja, I do not care what most people think of me. Most people like me. The few who do not might have good reason. I can be an anarchist, at times.

Or, they might be insecure. And I seem to exacerbate that fear in the few people who fit that particular personality portrait. Who's to say? I am generally detached by profession, training, and habit. Again, as I said, most people like me.

AN UNUSUAL STORM

So, when Doc replied to my email, I was washed over with these overwhelming feelings of insecurity. I care what he thinks of me. Yet I knew the general parameters of this unusual storm in my life, which seemingly came out of nowhere.[4] This storm, which has plagued my life for far too long to narrate by my accounting, would be incredibly difficult for me to explain to him. Specifically, regarding why I was applying for that particular job in the first place.

As I said, he is one of a select few. Probably two, including him, who I care what they think of me. At times I hide certain information from him, because I know how protective he is of me. Guess that's over, huh?

So, when unusual storms arise on my job, in my church, or during my educational journey, I have hidden many of those things from him. I knew, during those very difficult and challenging times, that God had a larger purpose, a higher calling, and a very unusual calling on my life, which requires these strange and sudden storms to form on the horizon of my life.

They come to prepare and train me. Sadly, I still resist them to a certain extent. But I am getting better at that. Getting better, as a result of submitting to them, instead of constantly fighting them. By learning obedience to God through the things that I have suffered through, now I resist less often. I just allow them to play all the way out.[5]

These unusual storms are very difficult to explain, even to most Christians. They are also extremely difficult to endure. However, I have seen enough of them to be able to distinguish: what type of storm this one is, why it has come, as well as, how tough it will be to explain. How do you tell someone, whose opinion that you care about, that yes, all of

---

4. Mark 4:35–38.
5. Heb 5:8.

ENOCH'S JOURNEY: SEVEN STEPS TO "WAS NOT"

a sudden, people I once considered family, mother-figures, a close and trusted confidant, or a professional or academic mentor, suddenly turned on me?

They quickly pivoted and did not just put a knife in my back. Rather, they put a rather powerful gun to my head and pulled the trigger. And, but for the grace of God, I would not have survived. Again, I have learned, and I knew that this was all a part of the process. Like Job, I was recommended to face this trial and betrayal, by my Father.[6]

Jesus had his "son of perdition" who he had to tell, "Do what you must and betray me, but do it quickly." Similarly, I have encountered many personal betrayals.[7] Specifically, people who I have been very close to emotionally, spiritually, professionally, or a combination of those. These are people who suddenly, like that unusual storm, turned on me, and tried to blow my head off.

Joseph, too, had more than enough of his own. Such that he could spare a few unusual storms. He had his brothers, Potiphar's wife, and the butler/advisor/wine steward in prison, to name a few.[8] Knowing something of how God works in our lives, I am sure that you have had similar experiences with your own version of Lady Potiphar.

Where's Jesus?

However, one of the main things to remain mindful of when you see the storm is to ask, "Where is Jesus in all of this?" Please do not just ask yourself, ask him. See if Jesus is somewhere sleeping in the back of the boat of your life while the shingles on the roof of your life are blowing in the wind, and you are taking on water. Then the thought that should come to mind should be, "If Jesus is seemingly asleep, and not lifting a finger to help me, then everything must be OK."[9]

It is true that he is the Prince of Peace, and we walk by faith and not by sight.[10] Therefore, the thing *not* to do in those seasons of unusual storm is to do like the disciples. Please do not run to where Jesus is

---

6. Job 1:8, 2:3.
7. John 13:27, 17:12.
8. Gen 37–41.
9. Ps 121:2–4; Mark 4:35–38.
10. Isa 9:6; 2 Cor 5:7.

sleeping, wake him, and say, "Don't you, who created me, care if I die in this storm?"[11]

I am sure you already know that God does not take vacations. He knows your "going out, from your coming in. And he has counted the hairs on your head."[12] Even if you shave them off like I do.

The book of Job comes to mind. For thirty-seven chapters, Job had no clue. He had no idea that God and the enemy had made side deals to essentially wreck his life with these unusual storms. He looked up and one day, all of his family, save his wife, who told him to "curse God and die," had actually died by violent and unusual storms. Then he broke out in boils and illnesses that he had never faced, prior to this point in his life.[13]

Yet, the ever-inspiring Job, never doubted God. And he, unwaveringly, during those same thirty-seven chapters, asked God, "What in the world are you doing?" He would say, "Even if he kills me, I will ask my questions."[14]

The reason that you do not want to "wake Jesus up," and you want to just assume that he already knows and cares, begins in chapter thirty-eight in the "where were you Job, when . . ." section of the Book of Job, as I call it.[15] You see, the God-reply can be so humbling, when Jesus finally wakes up from his intentional slumber, that you will be left, as my mother used to say, feeling like "a penny waiting on change." The idea is to let the Lord sleep if he must, and to stop fighting the unusual storms that come into your life.

If Jesus is asleep in the back of the boat of your life, then learn to trust that if he is at rest, and if I am one of his beloved then, as horrible as this experience may be for me to go through, he also gave me rest. So I should rest.[16] But I know me. Also, I think that I know how Job felt. And most likely, I know how you feel. This particular skill relative to finding peace amidst an "unusual storm" takes a lot of practice.

---

11. Mark 4:38.
12. Ps 121:8; Luke 12:7.
13. Job 1–2.
14. Job 13:15.
15. Job 38–42.
16. Ps 127:2.

WHERE WAS ENOCH GOING DURING HIS THREE-HUNDRED-YEAR WALK?

Have you ever wondered, as I have, why it took Enoch three hundred years' worth of walking with God before he "Was Not"? Enoch lived a total of three hundred and sixty-five years. The Bible states that after his son was born, Enoch walked with God (age sixty-five). Thus, presumably it took all of sixty-five years of living to get into the condition where he would have to purge himself of that sixty-five years, over the next three hundred years, taking a long walk with God.[17] The Bible says that "Enoch walked with God," and he "Was Not," because God had taken him out of the earthly realm to be with Elohim, in glory.[18] Now we also know that God is a Spirit, though he took on flesh in order to become the Savior of the world, known as Jesus.[19]

Thus, according to Scripture, Enoch lived for sixty-five years, having one son named Methuselah, whose name in Hebrew means a "man who was shot out, or thrown hard, like a dart toward a dartboard."[20] Enoch's name means to be "initiated" or to be inducted into the "God-Club." This induction is a result of his dedication and the faithfully unwavering way that he would come to follow God. So, Enoch was destined to face an "unusual storm" from birth.[21]

The Bible seems to separate Enoch's life into portions. For the first sixty-five years, the most significant reporting done on Enoch's life was that he became the father of Methuselah, i.e., the father who threw the dart, Methuselah, into the world, as one might say.[22] After he became a father, he presumably began a life of walking in close and intimate fellowship. If I proceed with one of the themes of this book, Enoch began to accept the unusual storms to follow.

We never find out why it took sixty-five years for Enoch to begin his journey, walking with God, in earnest. The Bible does not tell us. As I stated earlier, Enoch began walking with God after the birth of his son Methuselah. Thus, I propose that the balance of Enoch's journey, walking

17. Gen 5:24.
18. Gen 5:21–24; Heb 11:5.
19. John 1:14; 4:24.
20. "Chanowk," King James Bible: Strong's Hebrew Dictionary, http://www.html-bible.com/sacrednamebiblecom/kjvstrongs/STRHEB25.htm#S2585.
21. Gen 5:21.
22. Gen 5:22.

with God, took the next three hundred years to complete. Prior to getting close with God, and embracing every storm and trial to such an extent that Enoch "forced" the hand of God, such that God had no choice other than to "disappear" him.[23]

God had to take Enoch into the heavenly realm without seeing death, because he had walked such a great distance with God. Allowing his spirit-man to take over to such an extent to the diminishment of his fleshly existence, that he did not see death. This was similar to some accounts of Moses based on his appearance with Jesus on the Mount of Transfiguration with Elijah.[24]

NO ONE WILL EVER KNOW FOR SURE

No one will ever know exactly why God waited until Enoch was sixty-five in order to begin their time of close fellowship. However, often times in our lives, it occurs in a similar fashion. We can all remember a time, as we were born in sin, when we behaved unabashedly out of that nature.[25] If you have turned your life over to Christ, this is nothing to condemn yourself about, because you are now free from behaving primarily out of your sin nature. Besides, those sins of the past occurred by choice, and as a result of the fallen state of man.[26]

Hopefully, a turn occurred in your life when you began to walk with Christ as both your Lord and Savior. He died so you might be saved or redeemed. But he also desires to be the Lord of your life.[27]

However, there is a difference between walking with God, and walking as Enoch did: in close fellowship with God.[28] God not only wants to have a relationship with each one of us as friends. He desires an intimate relationship with each one of us, similar to the one that he had with Enoch.

Now, in order to become as close to God as Enoch was, maybe it will take each of us three hundred years. But I do not believe that we have that

---

23. Gen 5:23–24.
24. 2 Kings 2:11; Luke 9:28–36; Rom 8:5; Heb 11:5.
25. Ps 51:5.
26. Rom 5:12; Rom 8:1.
27. Rom 5:8–11.
28. Heb 11:5.

long. During Enoch's time, people lived, as did his son Methuselah, for nine hundred plus years at a time.

Enoch's time on earth was cut short because of the depth of intimacy in his particular relationship with God. God wanted to use Enoch as an aspirational example for the rest of us. However, to get that close to God, we will be required to submit ourselves after accepting Christ as our Savior. And we will be required to make him the Lord of our entire life.[29]

That means every time God chooses to break us out in boils, as he did with Job; take us on a windy sea and then go to sleep when the unusual storm arises, as occurred with the disciples; or have us encounter a situation where our own brothers plot to kill us, we have to "buck up," dedicate ourself, and go with the flow. We have to know that God is just initiating us into the God-club, as he did with Enoch.

Maybe your trial will not be anywhere near as severe as all of that. That all depends on the call on your life. However, you cannot convince anyone who is in the middle of a trial that their specific storm is *not* the most boisterous, troublesome, and frightful storm that they have ever seen or experienced in their life. That occurs with godly intention, as well.

However, remember this, if nothing else: God only allowed Satan to test Job because he knew that, no matter how Job might ultimately question the logic and intelligence of God, as well as query his purpose for allowing such things to befall him, Job would never curse his name. God knew that Job would ultimately pass every test.[30]

God desires intimate fellowship with all of us. He died so we might enter into that type of relationship with him. As a result of that intimate relationship, we might arrive at a place where we are not only prepared for his purpose, but where we are ready for complete and consistent submission to his perfect will.

Abraham was called the friend of God. However, God could not fully reveal himself to Moses, the meekest man who lived. He had to pass by Moses with his "back" to Moses. And even then, Moses' countenance radiated, because God's Glory remained on Moses, based on their encounters and intimate fellowship.[31] God reveals himself to his Friends.[32] However, we have to humbly submit to his will for our lives, trusting in

---

29. Matt 7:21.
30. Job 1–2.
31. Exod 33:18–34:9; Num 12:3; 2 Chr 20:7; Isa 41:8; Jas 2:23.
32. John 14:21–23.

God's great intentions. I know that all of this is more easily said than done.

MANY TWISTS AND TURNS

Each of our individual Journey's to "Was Not," as I am calling it, will take many different twists and turns. We have to learn through submission, obedience, practice, patience, endurance, humility, and, yes, suffering, to trust God all the way. The journey will likely occur in stages, just as it did with Enoch. The first step will begin with us knowing that God is out there, and yet, not really knowing who he is.

Then, as we proceed, taking the succeeding steps in lockstep with God, hopefully we will learn much more about him. Prayerfully, we will have a steady series of true encounters that will continuously change our lives in such a way that we not only recognize him as Savior, but we submit ourselves to him as Lord of our entire being and existence. That second stage, where we begin to submit, is still only the beginning.[33] Thus, one might say that Enoch started living at age sixty-five.

EACH PERSON'S JOURNEY TO "WAS NOT" WILL DIFFER BASED ON GOD'S PURPOSE & CALLING

As I mentioned, our individual journey toward "Was Not" will be very different based on purpose and calling once we decide to humbly submit ourselves, as well as our lives, to the will of God. Once we do that, he begins the process of shaping and molding us into the person who can fulfill those callings and purposes. At the same time, he begins to simply, though at times, painstakingly, develop that intimate relationship with each of us as individuals just as he did with Enoch.

This process will occur in stages and via repeated trials. It takes a lot, as well as a long time, to develop intimacy with God. It also takes a long time to burn off your past habits and submit your free will to God's sovereign will, as well as to his plan and purpose for our lives.

If you are like most people, you think, or at least I did, that you are ready for it all right now. I can say that Joseph likely thought that he was ready to have his brothers, father, and mother bow down to him, such

---

33. Rom 12:1.

that he could, at seventeen years old, take over his daddy's business.[34] I say "likely," because the Bible never directly states that Joseph was being verbose or full of hubris when he told his brothers and father about his two dreams. I do not believe that was the case at all as I describe in detail in another book that I wrote.[35]

Rather, I considered his discussion to be an extension of his personality, which God gave him and planned to use in a stepwise and dependent fashion. This was to get Joseph prepared, via intimate fellowship and submission, to walk in and fully execute the calling on his life. This calling was not designed to make him take over his daddy's farm.

I only say that because that is what I would have thought when God gave him two dreams where his eleven brothers, as well as his mother and father, were all bowing down to him. He, to date, did not know anything else. Little did he know, that he was being prepared for intimacy, and equipped for purpose.

STEPWISE-DEPENDENT PROGRESSION

We cannot know and will never know exactly what happened on Enoch's Journey to "Was Not." The Bible does not tell us. It does, however, provide us with some of the dramatic results of intimacy with God. It also reveals to us some things that must occur, as well as some things that we must know and believe in order to get to a place of total intimacy with God, things to fulfill the callings that he has placed on our lives, as well as to discover and fulfill the divine purpose for our lives.[36]

Now I personally believe that we have many gifts, talents, and callings on our lives.[37] I once told one of my former students, the one who coined the phrase, "You are my advisor for life," to "attack each gift, talent, and calling with an intensity previously unknown to mankind."

However, I also know that there is likely one overarching purpose and plan for us which is designed for us to step forward and fulfill. This is that overarching purpose for which God takes us through a stepwise progression where each step, stage, and trial is completely dependent on

---

34. Gen 37.

35. Jones, Earl A. *A Personality Portrait: Sixteen Biblical Leaders Who Identify Your Traits.* Eugene, OR: Wipf & Stock, 2018.

36. Heb 11:5–7.

37. 1 Cor 12:4–11.

the previous step, stage, and trial. Each must be completed before we can move on to the next phase. This occurs while God is also teaching us to trust in and to learn to depend on him for everything.

This definitely transpired in Joseph's life, where the preparation, planning, calling, refining, intimacy, and the dependency phases occurred all in sequential stepwise order.[38] Those training phases most likely looked nothing like Joseph thought that they would. However, the culminating result of all of the trials, difficulty, betrayal, losses, incarceration, enslavement, and pain. All the while, somehow, God poured all that bad stuff into a pot and stirred in a bunch of intimacy, obedience, and submission. Out came a Joseph, having followed a stepwise-dependent progression to an intimate relationship with God, which enabled him to "save many,"[39] and to fulfill the overarching purpose and calling that God had placed on his life.[40]

That calling, and purpose required a very intense and shocking thirteen years for Joseph. I am not sure exactly how long it took Job because the Bible does not tell us. We know that it took Enoch three hundred years to arrive at "Was Not." While we may not know what happened during that three-hundred-year journey, we do learn something about the calling, which was one of the outcomes of the submissive obedience of Enoch.[41]

Personally, the final stage of my preparation journey, has taken a few years and still counting. I had to hide parts of it from some of the few people that I truly care about—people whose opinion of me matters to me.

But, how could I explain these boils on my skin, my four trips to the hospital in one year, my brothers wanting to kill me (but settling for selling me into slavery)? And we wont even talk about Potiphar's scandalous wife and what she wanted to do to and with me. We will also not discuss being forgotten by those who I had helped, while I was personally imprisoned for a crime that I did not commit. No, really, all of that stuff happened to me, in some form or another, just like similar trials occurred in the lives of Joseph and "them boys."

---

38. Gen 37–41.
39. Gen 50:20.
40. Gen 45:1–8.
41. Gen 5:18–24; Heb 11:5–6; Jude 1:14–16.

Painfully, though not at all regrettably, it all comes, part and parcel, with the call, plan, and purpose of God. But I know that I have reaped the benefits of a profoundly more intimate relationship, as a result of submitting to the unusual storms that arose on the horizon of my life, and have continued to stay.

I have, or God has, wrung two books so far (with more to come) out of this rag. It's not bad for a man who never wanted to write a book, be an author, and who does not (much at all) like to read. And as for Enoch, yep, it took three hundred years of "glorious living" in order for him to get to the promised land of "Was Not."

So, what exactly do we know about Enoch's Walk?

2

Enoch's Journey: What We Know

OVERLAY: BECAUSE WE WILL NEVER KNOW SPECIFICS

I RECENTLY PLACED A C.S. Lewis quote on my personal Facebook page. Let me correct that: I actually recreated the quote which was overlaid by someone on the internet on top of a very dark green forest picture. The picture obscured the words, in my opinion. Also, I prefer pictures of water and oceans as a background, as opposed to a forest. So, I decided to recreate it. Using a very simple program, I turned it into a .jpg file, for easy upload onto Facebook, serving as my cover photo.

I have many photos from fishing trips. The ones that I take while leaving the dock in the morning are the best. The horizon in the background of the photo that I used looks black. The rest is amber-colored sky mixed with reflective water. I just typed the words over top of the photo, in black font, and placed them in the appropriate spot, using the appropriately sized font, so my profile photo would not block the quote or the reference to the author.

We will never know exactly what happened to Enoch during his three-hundred-year journey to "Was Not." The Bible chose not to tell us. However, we all have had personal experiences with trials and tribulations. I continue to acknowledge, irrespective of their comparable pain relative to someone else's trial, that our personal trials and tribulations seem to be the worst, most devastating, tumultuous torture that we could ever endure.

Now, if we have developed enough of an intimate relationship with the Lord by this point in our life, then we can distinguish the differences between trials and tribulations which we encounter because of our own human failing and human error, and "unusual storms" that arise in our lives to test us. The storms are what God will use to prepare us for purpose, calling, and promotion. Then we will know that, in spite of the pain, and irrespective of the fact that God *never* tells us how long the storm will last, we remain assured that we are being trained and prepared by God the Father for "such a time as . . . that."[1]

WHAT IS A TEST?

Thus, when you proceed through your individual journey, you develop an assurance, within your spirit. This assurance lets you know that, even though you cannot see how this trial will help you, nor can you see the end of the road, you know that Emmanuel, God with us, is with you the whole way.[2]

My pastor says that, "The teacher always goes silent during the test." I know I do. I love test days more than any others, because I have absolutely nothing to prepare for class that day. I sit there and look at ESPN on the internet. Like a hockey goalie, I kick away questions from students who are trying to get me to give them the correct answers to my "difficult" test questions.

A test is a measuring instrument that is used by teachers. It assesses the ability of a student to learn, memorize, and apply knowledge acquired during a previous level, stage, or step. We use the test to ensure that the students have not only acquired and retained the requisite knowledge, but that they can apply it to real life situations. All of this occurs prior to moving forward to the next step, grade, level, or portion of the semester.

This is how we separate the God-sent unusual storms from those that we incur because of our disobedience. Hopefully, we are also learning not to behave disobediently, i.e., he must increase in our lives as we,

---

1. Esth 4:14.
2. Matt 1:23.

meaning our flesh, free will, and poor decision-making apparatus, must decrease.[3]

When they are God-sent storms, we know that this present suffering cannot be compared to the next place of promised purpose that God has prepared for us. I try to convince people, with varying levels of success, that the whole earth, or at least some specific part of it, is groaning in travail as a mother with the labor pains of childbirth, waiting for you to get through the present trouble and trial that you are facing. God is waiting for you to get into the position, as a person, so he can release you into that called place of purpose that he has destined for you to fill in his kingdom. All of this occurs such that, through you, he might "save many."[4]

The Vision Will Not Make Sense

The primary point of this filibuster is to tell us that we have no idea what happened to Enoch during the three hundred years when he walked with God, because then he disappeared from the earthly realm when God took him.[5] The Bible also chooses not to disclose how long Job's trial lasted. We do know, through the employment of a little math, how long Joseph's trial season lasted. It basically lasted thirteen years before he was able to enter into service essentially as Prime Minister of Egypt.[6]

Following his trial, he would witness and understand the unfolding of the vision that God had shown him, twice via dreams, thirteen years prior to the day that he was brought before Pharaoh in his royal court. That's kind of how this works.

God will show you a vision. Trust me, the vision will not make any sense to you. Though you will try to make sense of it, via your human filters.[7] He will show you this plan and purpose through a dream, through his word, or through an unquenchable passion that drives you toward a particular end.

As long as you are currently walking in fellowship with him, you can rest with some reasonable certainty that it is the Holy Spirit, who

---

3. John 3:30.
4. Gen 45:5; Rom 8:18–22, 23–39.
5. Heb 11:5.
6. Gen 37–41.
7. Hab 2:1–3.

is pushing you and revealing the vision to you.[8] Otherwise the dream, vision, or spiritual impression will disturb you and will bring no internal peace or assurance. Now you must still go to God in prayer through the entire process in order to receive stepwise guidance relative to your journey. However, know this: you are entering a season of preparation and trial. You will not fully understand the vision that was revealed to and birthed inside of you.

Just be ready to walk a winding road replete with many blind alleys and, rest assured, during the most difficult times, the road and journey will end. It will end with all of it working together, not only for your good because this really ain't about you, as I always say. It will work together for the good of the kingdom.[9] You will end up in the promised land of "Was Not," fully prepared, well-trained, well-seasoned, and quite capable of fulfilling the call on your life. You will also gain an understanding relative to the ever unfolding vision that you received in the beginning when all of this started.

STEPPING OUT

The actual title to this book was or could have been *Enoch's Stepwise Dependent Progressive Journey: Seven Steps to "Was Not."* For reasons that should be obvious as I progressed through the personal editing and revising stages. Prior to finding a publisher, I decided to make the title more concise. Now, as for the matter of the often alluded to stepwise-dependent-progression, this is an integral and essential part of the entire journey as well. However, at the moment of presentation, it is equally as obscure as the vision itself until it all comes together.

We have no idea what happens to Enoch during his three-hundred-year journey, and while we do know what happened to Job, we actually have no idea how long his journey lasts.

We do know the answers to both of these questions when it comes to Joseph. Thus, we will overlay the life of Joseph as the primary template for the methodology which we will use to undergird or support what a stepwise dependent journey to "Was Not" actually looks like.

At this juncture, my encouragement to you is that you compare, contrast, and then overlay your personal journey, atop the journeys of all

---

8. 1 Sam 3:1–14.
9. Rom 8:28–39.

three of these characters, as well as any others that God lays on your heart, and all of the others present in the succeeding chapters in this book.

Everyone's journey is different, but God provides us with comparable similarities so we do not give up halfway through the journey. Under the ever-false assumption that Emmanuel has now left us, he will never do that because he promised to be with us always.[10]

JOSEPH & JESUS: WHY THEY HAD TO TELL

I listen to others, mostly ministers, discuss, in particular, the life of Joseph. I generally disagree with major parts of their self-extrapolated analysis of Joseph's journey. My primary contention with them is regarding the things that they attribute to his personality, which simply are not true. Those things are true of that specific minister's personality. However, they overlay their sensibilities and attribute their behavioral motivations on to Joseph.

This happens when ministers discuss Joseph's rationale and motivation regarding the reason that he chose to tell his brothers, as well as father the second time, about his dreams. They call him "a verbose braggart who should have kept his mouth shut." The fact is that Joseph (and Jesus) was compelled to discuss the revelations, directives, or dreams with their target audience, so that they could not state that they were not aware of what was coming. Also, the Bible states that the brothers hated Joseph even more after he told them of his first dream, implying that they hated him long before he ever had a dream.[11] In the next sentence during their sermons on Joseph, those same ministers will compare his life and times to Jesus, based on a similar stepwise-dependent progression.

I believe I know who should in fact keep their mouths shut, and keep their personality, typology-based psychoanalyses to themselves, but I will not be any more rude than I have already been by insinuation. Also, I discuss Joseph, the ENTJ and his personality type, in my other book previously mentioned—one that you should read if you have not already procured a copy.

But if you believe that Joseph, "the oft accused braggart," should have kept his mouth shut and not have told his brothers about his dreams, then you also believe, by some miracle of a change of nature, that

---

10. Isa 7:14; Matt 28:20; 1 Pet 3:9.
11. Gen 37:8; 11.

his wonderful older brothers would not have wanted to kill him for the horrific and intemperate act of sharing two dreams with them. These are dreams where God showed Joseph that he would ultimately end up in a leadership position relative, specifically, to those ten brothers. Additionally, you believe that his same wonderful brothers would become eagerly subservient to him and, in some way, willingly become dependent on him.

Now these are the same guys who wiped out an entire village through more than duplicitous means, because the men in that village violated their sister, but those same men in that village wanted to make amends by offering to marry the women in Israel's household.[12] Then when dear ole dad rebuked them for their actions and informed them (particularly Levi and Simeon) that the consequences of their actions would become his responsibility, the brothers angrily replied to dad and essentially told him that, "We don't suffer fools lightly, particularly those fools who we think are trying to take advantage of us."

Then the ministers, compare Joseph's journey, life, and the things that he suffered to those of Jesus Christ. It does not wash. If they are correct that Joseph should have kept his mouth shut, then I assume that they also believe that Jesus should have never called the Pharisees a "brood of vipers,"[13] nor should the Savior have behaved so brutishly, as to presume to tell the people that, "He and the Father are one. He is the temple that they will destroy. But, in three days, God will raise him up again from the dead."[14] Again, as my pastor says, "Stay in your lane."

However, they do, in my opinion, get a few things right regarding their comparisons, relative to Joseph and Jesus. Both were tasked by God to discuss the vision and calling that God had placed on their lives. Dreams, during Joseph's time, were very culturally significant; people discussed them openly.

When Pharaoh had a dream that he could not resolve, he knew that it came from a higher power than he, and he desperately wanted to learn exactly what this strange dream meant. See the entire book of Daniel, for comparison, as well as the entire book of Nehemiah. The point is that

---

12. Gen 34, 37.
13. Matt 3:1–32, 33, 34–39.
14. John 2:18–19, 20–22, 10:22–29, 30, 31–42.

people openly discussed dreams during those times, particularly when they knew them to contain revelation from God.[15]

In addition to Joseph, relative to his personality, never considering *not* sharing his dream, I will ever contend that he did so because he assumed that they were already well aware of the leadership mantle that he was born wearing. Not because he was trying to rub their noses in it. Well maybe a little, but that is his personality too. He shared the dreams because they were mandates from God which he was compelled to share, because he was given the divine dreams by God in the first place. Jesus had to warn the people, so he shared realities with them. Though those realities were prophetic in nature at the time he shared them.

STEPWISE-DEPENDENT-PROGRESSION & THE KINGDOM OF THE DIGI-BRAINS

The ministers who discuss Joseph get at least one other thing right when they arrive at the parts in the sermon where they discuss Joseph's stepwise-dependent-progression. Although they do not call it that. I created that term through a series of random things that I was familiar with relative to statistical equations and mathematical modeling. Fear not, I will not drive you nuts with explanations in relation to that stuff. Though I have done it many times, I cannot actually explain it very well. But the idea fits what happened to Joseph, and what happens to us, very well.

Joseph's journey occurred in stages. Thus, one can assume that Enoch's journey also went in stages. Along a dark winding road, with many twists, turns, and blind alleys ahead, including stuff popping out at him unexpectedly. We are made aware of some of the pop-out items that occurred in Job's life, as well as in Joseph's life.

Stepwise, is defined as a gradual and progressive series of events, tests, trials, or stages, as if moving and proceeding, step by step.[16] Consider this progression opposite to flowing water like that in a river. That flow is continuous, assuming that the river is not drying up. Now, relative to music theory, stepwise occurs as the musician moves from one tone or note to the adjacent note on a music sheet or scale.[17]

---

15. Gen 37:11.
16. https://en.oxforddictionaries.com/definition/stepwise.
17. http://www.yourdictionary.com/stepwise.

I am sure that you now understand why I chose the term stepwise when referring to Enoch's journey. Or maybe not. Here is the reason: Joseph's trial season progressed from stage to stage. These stages or steps occur such that some people may not have thought that they were linked to each other in any way.

I know during most trial seasons in my life, at least until I became fully aware and assured that a specific and unusual storm had actually come from God, I believed that these Job-like tragedies that had befallen my life could not be related. I was awakened to the notion that the storm would not end or cease in intensity until his appointed time.

However, as I progressed through each storm, I began to comprehend the idea I had when this present storm first began. I later understood that they had all started because I said something or made a promise to God. This was a promise which God made me, or tricked me, into uttering aloud. He tricked me by frustrating me into thinking that it was all my idea in the first place.

On one particular occasion recently, after I had learned to respect the storms as well as begin to understand their point of origin, I said something unexpected on a seemingly normal morning, after many preceding mornings of seeing the same digi-brains as I walked through the parking garage into my office. This is my pet name for my fellow administrative assistant and administrative faculty colleagues—all who perform the same Borg drone-like activities.

We were performing the exact same activities yesterday, as we did, today, as we would again tomorrow, and so on. Ad nauseum and ad infinitum. What he tricked me into saying was, "God if you put me back into the classroom, I will never come out again, for anything."

Now implicit in the previous declaration, both in my mind and, I believe, in divine accordance with the overarching purpose of God, he tricked me into making it so that whenever I became a full-time or teaching-only faculty member, I would never come back out of the classroom.[18] Either way, little could I know what he had in store for me, at that mere utterance, in the succeeding months and years.

I was frustrated with the current state of affairs. (Though it was a separate stepwise series of events that led me to that specific parking garage—where I made that true declarative confession). Prior to becoming

---

18. John 15:7; Rom 4:16–22.

chief of the digi-brained people at that university with the parking garage, I was an underling chief digi-brain at a previous university.

However, I was also a classroom lecturer there. I had these jobs, though all I ever really wanted to be, as I left graduate school and my master's program, was an academic advisor for academically, as well as generally, at-risk students. I simply wanted to teach related one credit courses, relative to aiding and facilitating the plight of the students in those populations. However, now that I think about it, the series of events that led me to graduate school in the first place were also a part of God's stepwise setup.

By this point, I was familiar with the setup move of God. Thus I knew to ride it out. Also, I had learned obedience through the things that I had suffered at each stage or step[19] when I was the underling chief digi-brain and lecturer who, originally, never wanted to teach a three credit course, much less two of them. I always remember that it was the aforementioned Doc, my mentor, who wanted me to finish my doctorate immediately after my master's program and bypass the digi-brain life altogether.

He wanted me to enter directly into the classroom. I did not want to take that route, preferring to actualize my goal of helping students through advising and teaching. I could have done both had I done it his way #sadface. But God had a plan.

While I was underling chief of the digi-brain people, God used my entire personality portrait, the one that I share with Joseph, which serves as a major impetus regarding why he is the subplot of, as well as, the secondary main character in this book. As an aside, we do not know enough of the major parts of Enoch's life. Thus, we cannot know what his personality type is with any level of certainty.

Anyway, while serving as a lecturer and underling chief digi-brain, I faced some really bad actors among the narcissistic, ruling clan of the digi-brain kingdom. They were not interested in helping students. Rather, they were far more interested in helping themselves as well as building a larger digi-brain kingdom than that of any other university. This typically occurred to the detriment of my students. In short, they were Joseph's older brothers as well as Job's fateful, doubting, and ill-informed, blasphemous friends.

---

19. Heb 5:8.

Well, being the hero in this story, I could not and would not stand for any of that nonsense. I had to reveal the dreams to those self-centered, ruling class digi-brains with whom I served in the comparatively meager, yet powerful enough, capacity of underling chief digi-brain and lecturer. I was fully prepared to fight the good fight,[20] knowing that I was doing the Lord's work and being completely aware that God was in charge of how this entire phase would turn out.

I knew this because he had opened the door for me to get the specific job, or parts of it anyway. He was also simultaneously training and instilling within me a passion and love for lecture-style teaching that would supersede and suborn the appetite for advising and teaching one credit, academic skill-set development-style courses.

He would also guide me toward a doctoral program, which I always desired to obtain. However, once he ignited the teaching fire in me, he began preparing me to take the next steps with a clearer sense of purpose.

I will not bore you with all of the specific details. Suffice it to say that when I revealed the dream to the digi-brained nobility, it was received about as well as it was when Joseph revealed his two dreams to his duplicitous and murderous brothers, or as well as it was when Jesus revealed his true purpose and calling to his fellow rabbinical brethren of the Sanhedrin.

They wanted to kill me, but they settled for plotting, concocting, and scheming up evermore imaginative ways designed to simply getting rid of me. Each plot would be rendered completely impotent until the omnipotent had completely fulfilled his purpose for me at that step and when his timing for me to move on to the next step had fully come. Yet I faced many a traitorous pit, and an Ishmaelite broker, bent on purchasing me from the digi-brained ruling class, and selling me into a life of slavery—or worse.[21]

However, that season of testing served as my entrance exam and graduation ticket to the next stage. At the next stage, I would become high chief of the digi-brained kingdom. However, I never received an actual teaching assignment during my tenure at that university. Although I did serve as a part of the digi-brained faculty and I had to attend departmental faculty meetings for the department I was assigned to.

---

20. 1 Tim 6:12.
21. Gen 37.

What was happening in my life regarding all of these tests and stabs in the back? Simply because I revealed my dream of developing and advancing all of my students to graduation and maturity[22] irrespective of how the digi-brained nobility might concurrently try to use me, in order to advance their duplicitous cause of self-aggrandizement. Those digi-brained King Ahabs and Jezebels.

Too harsh? I think not. I understood and was given insight into the underlying motivations relative to the digi-brains.[23] Also, I was moving to the next step in this stepwise-dependent-progression.

I call it a dependent-progression, having previously defined the term stepwise, for our purposes because I learned to depend on God for absolutely everything along the way. From pre-master's to dreaming of a career at the only thing that I was ever good at: people. "What kind of people?" A friend of mine once asked me, pre-master's. During my post-bachelor's wilderness phase, I replied, "College student people."

At that time, I had no idea that I could not only get a master's degree in "college people," but a doctorate, too, as well as many jobs that involve working with those college people: advising them and teaching them. God had set my end from the beginning.[24]

God knew that each phase was a step, but God also knew that each step would include a trial. A great many tests and trials at each level would all ultimately prepare me to fulfill his purpose.

This was a larger purpose that I was internally compelled to actualize because I knew he would be inside of me, pushing me to fulfill the dream. He showed me the dream during my bachelor's program when I first met him via a confluence of circumstances that I would take seriously for the rest of my life. These are circumstances that would cause me to submit my will to his.

Stepwise: a series of, or a gradual progression of, events, tests, trials, and/or stages that occur in a continuous state as if moving and proceeding from step-to-step.

---

22. Matt 11:12.
23. 1 Kgs 21:25.
24. Isa 46:10.

THE DEPENDENT

The dependent portion of this actual book title comes from learning to depend on him for everything. The longer the road gets, the darker it becomes, and the more blind alleys come with that phase in the journey. The good news (just kidding, of course, because none of that about the dark road sounds good) is that you are only experiencing this long, dark road filled with betrayal and calamity while in *one* of the steps, which occur within an overarching journey.

I can joke about all of it now, acknowledging that at the time that I am writing this, pre-promised land and Pharaoh's palace, I have become settled enough to do so. Also, because I am at peace in my spirit and soul, I also know and deeply experience the fact that, "It is well." I never wanted to write about this because I *only* like to reveal to people what I want them to see and know about me.

However, I am at peace and I have stopped, awhile ago, in fact, trying to snatch the steering wheel from God. I have even stopped asking people, as Joseph did, to "remember me," or asking the King to get me out of this horrible and undeserved dungeon, place, and season.[25]

See, I have also been forgotten by the butler, who I helped by using the gifts that God placed inside of me. These gifts were refined in the fires in each step,[26] such that I could learn to allow him to give me things to say in books[27] even if it remains my personal preference to remain an elusive, anonymous, extrovert. I have learned to depend on him, and I have learned to do only what I have seen my Father do. Also, to say, as well as do, only what he releases me to write, say, and do.[28] It is his play, I am just the actor.

STEPWISE-DEPENDENT PROGRESSION

At this point, we have defined stepwise. We have also briefly discussed how I became God's dependent son, as well as why I included dependent in the "true" title of this book. I am attempting to describe the overarching occurrence of a series of trials that lead to and prepare us for God's

---

25. Gen 40:1–13, 14–15, 16–23.

26. 1 Pet 1:7.

27. C.S. Lewis: "I never exactly made a book." https://www.goodreads.com/quotes/16985-i-never-exactly-made-a-book-it-s-rather-like-taking.

28. Heb 5:8; John 5:19.

purpose and calling designed exclusively for our lives. Now we will discuss the stepwise progression.

A stepwise progression actually came to mind, as I mentioned, because of the stepwise regression, which is a mathematical term. I decided to use the word progression instead of regression due to the negative connotation that regression carries in general usage. Also, I have heard the term stepwise progression somewhere in my travels through the kingdom of the digi-brains.

A stepwise progression is actually a term related to the field of medical science. It describes an occurrence in dementia patients where their symptoms of dementia may remain the same for a certain period of time then, all of a sudden, they, out of nowhere, move to a new step or stage in their dementia. I am sure, regrettably speaking, that we have all experienced this phenomena with a cherished relative or loved one.[29]

As it turns out, that is not as positive a phrase as I had hoped when I initially decided to include it. However, it gets the job done in this case in very clear, if also unfortunate, terms.

This series of trials that we must face if we decide to take the journey with God by submitting ourselves to his leadership and overarching plan. The plan that he decided to reveal to us through dreams, visions, his word, and an internal passion.[30] These series of trials faced along the journey occur as a stepwise-dependent progression.

On this journey, we move from step-to-step, stage-to-stage, until we reach a portion of the long, dark, winding road fraught with blind alleys and unexpectedly harmful betrayals, where circumstances can change without notice. Yet, we decide to take the walk, just like Enoch did, just like Job did, when he comported himself as a man who would never curse God, come what may.[31] We decide to take the walk like Joseph did when he, against the advice of the misguided ministers, decided to tell his family about the dreams that God had placed in his heart. These are the dreams that internally compelled him forward and would not let him go until he actualized the full measure of their purpose.

He would wrestle and fight with the angel just like his Father did.[32] Joseph would not be able to let go of his integrity, nor his pursuit of the

---

29. Dementia Care Central, "Symptoms of Vascular Dementia," https://www.dementiacarecentral.com/aboutdementia/vasculardementia/symptoms/.

30. Jer 20:9; 29:11.

31. Job 1–2.

32. Gen 32:22–32.

dream until he fulfilled the purpose for which God had destined him. Joseph would take this walk, this stepwise progressive journey with God, becoming ever-more dependent on the God of the dreams and journey. Joseph would learn obedience, submission, pace, diligence, and faith in God through every trial.

He would do this in order to pass each trial and test in one step, then progress to the next step. Joseph would learn that his life and the lives of many others would depend on his success at each stage, as is the case in this stepwise-dependent progressive journey toward the fulfillment of purpose and destiny.

PUTTING ONE FOOT IN FRONT OF THE OTHER: STEPWISE

There is a method to God's maddeningly orchestrated stepwise-dependent progression. To clear one thing up: you learn to depend on God as you proceed on the journey with him, or else you do not get very far. Without depending on God, you kind of end up walking, stumbling, and wandering around the same mountain. You then realize that this mountain, which seemingly, or actually, has taken you forty years to make a forty-day journey. Going from the parted Red Sea, you first experienced a "Miraculous Occurrence" orchestrated only by the hand of God that helped you reach the Jericho River and the promised land via dream. This is the same promised land which the children of Israel were destined and purposed to enter on the west side. This has been spoken by Abraham, Isaac, Jacob, Joseph, and Moses at different times.[33]

As I mentioned, each step includes its requisite trials, tests, and tribulations designed by God for training purposes at that level and stage. Then you take the next step, where awaits another set of training modules. Only God, line upon line, step after step, one step at a time will choreograph, as well as orchestrate, a symphony. This symphony, at first, makes sense only to him. To you, it seems like random noises, like stumbling buffalo crashing down a Midwestern plain.

It looks even worse to those who may be observing the course of your life. While you have some, or even a complete, sense of what is transpiring, other just see random chaos which some assume must not have come from God, as did Job's falsely accusatory friends. That's why I

---

33. Josh 1.

hide these things, particularly from Doc. Though he might understand. They look completely strange to those looking at you from a safe distance while you try to keep pace and remain in lockstep with God on this journey.[34]

I feel compelled by the Master Orchestra Conductor to use highlights from Enoch's journey, Joseph's stepwise-dependent progression, Job's tests and trials, my personal journey, and the steps of many others mentioned in this book. All of these people are discussed in order to illustrate how God brings it all together at his divinely appointed time. He does this both for your good, remembering that it ain't about you, and for the good of the Kingdom to fulfill purpose, so that, through your efforts following preparation, he might use you to help him "save many." That is, once you learn how to play the horn.

LEARNING TO PLAY THE CLARINET

When I was in middle school I learned to play the clarinet. I played it all of the way through high school. Although my mother had to bribe me during my senior year to stick with it. My brother chose the much cooler alto saxophone so, obviously, I couldn't choose that. I couldn't even select a tenor or soprano version of the same instrument.

Thus, I had to decide if I wanted to play the trumpet, which would have made life much easier when we were marching in those horribly cold parades and on freezing fall football fields in Pittsburgh.

I could read music, but I was far from the person who could learn to play by ear. That was not my gift. I did not choose the trumpet because everyone told me, and by everyone I mean my brother and father, that I would get a corn on my upper lip from tightening my embouchure. As I got older I found out that seemed to be a complete falsehood and an old wives' tale.

Then there was the piano. My father really advocated for that. Why? I have no idea. He was not the most church attending person, nor was he willing to admit, at all, to ever having entered one. I later learned of his church days when I asked my mother. She replied, "Do you think I would have married him if he wasn't?" Good point, knowing her.

Anyway, he said, "You can play the piano at parties that you attend." Now I was only in the sixth grade or so but, man, I had never attended a

---

34. Isa 28:10; Matt 28:20.

party where some genius was sitting down at the piano to play and entertain the assembled masses. It seemed so corny to me. So, that was nixed.

I wish, in retrospect, considering my future in the church, that he had just said, "You need to develop this skill because every church that you attend will have at its center someone skilled in playing the piano and organ, for the choir and for soloists. It will also help you to learn to sing." But he was kind of corny and did not want to discuss church. So he failed himself and me.

Thus, I was left with the clarinet, and left with Benny Goodman as my only role model. Later, I fell in love with the music of the Big band era orchestra that played at the 1930s Cotton Club in Harlem. Oh yeah, I forget why I did not choose the drums?

I was pretty, or even very, good at the clarinet through middle school. If I actually took it seriously, I would have played in a higher chair in the honor's band, which assembled students from all over the city who attended private schools like mine. However, I never took it very seriously. I would learn the pieces at home until I could get through them by reading the music. I would never touch them again until rehearsal.

Once, in middle school, we had to do solos accompanied by the music teacher. I had memorized the piece. It was easy when I was familiar with the song. Though not so much when it was a song that I had never heard.

I was overconfident as usual and ready for my solo, a solo that I was, of course, not taking very seriously. It was probably my first solo, but who cared? I had it. This particular piece had many pages, verses, and a refrain which you had to flip back a few pages in order to play.

Long story short: I think the pages fell on the ground and I lost my place while the music teacher followed the master. I stumbled and stopped but, being the ever-elusive Jones the eighth-grader, I recovered pretty quickly. Mrs. Pruz caught up with my improvisation and we stumbled a bit before we finished strong.

I learned two things that day. First, it's not a good thing not to be nervous before a performance. Overconfidence is a killer. Performance anxiety is a good thing. But, honestly, that lesson never stuck with me. I am who I am.

The second thing I learned was to come to understand what Paul was talking about when he said that athletes cannot win the prize unless they follow the rules. Thus, we must all learn to endure the full measure of suffering that comes with each test and performance. We must follow all of the rules of engagement at each level and step like good soldiers. That is if we expect to win both the battle and the war.[35]

FIGHTS, DOCTORAL PROGRAMS, & JAMES EARL

Now this will likely not surprise you: I like to fight. Probably a little too much. God made me, and he trained me. He knows my personality and through many fires, he has refined and tested me so that I could, as Job said, emerge from that fire as pure gold.[36]

Verbal sparring sessions are fun for me. I no longer have any desire to engage in pugilistic fights. I left that life behind long ago. One reason was my mother's only standing orders to me, "Don't you let nobody mess up your face, Earl." I could usually talk my way out of a fistfight or I was facing such an underwhelmingly inferior opponent that I could easily win (and not have to break my mom's prime mandate).

I let my boys go to the parties and handle all of that heavy lifting. They enjoyed it. God intentionally snatched me from that environment at the exact time when I was coming of age and could have, not only been compelled to join in the weekly "gang fights," actually led the charge. I was a natural born leader with a still, at times, hair-trigger temper.

To that end, as I was recently reminded, I was born in sin and my old nature can quickly rise up and take hold.[37] I was under the false impression, after many years of walking with God, that all of those Muhammad Ali style imbroglio related activities were long ago burnt out of me. Regrettably, they were not. Not by a destructive long shot, in one specific instance. The journey continues . . .

God still has to restrain me from fighting certain verbal and intellectual battles. As my favorite head coach, Mike Tomlin, of the Steelers says, "I'd rather have to say whoa than sic 'em."[38] God rarely has to say "sic 'em" to me. "Whoa" is another story.

I was seemingly close to completion of a particular step. This Step preceded me getting into a doctoral program at a university. Upon being

---

35. 2 Tim 2:3–7.
36. Job 23:10.
37. Ps 51:5.
38. Gorman, Kevin. "Tomlin preaches discipline." *Sports* (blog) *Triblive.com*, August 31, 2010. https://triblive.com/x/pittsburghtrib/sports/steelers/s_697196.html.

rejected, for about the third time overall from different schools, I asked God, "When will I get in and finish this terminal degree that I know you are calling me to complete?"

He said, "When I need it." That was, what they call, a mic-drop situation. I had not an arrow left in my quiver, and I am rarely left speechless.

This conversation occurred at a time when my life was in upheaval. However, I was happy for much of that upheaval because I was moving on from a bad marriage to become the most happily divorced man on the planet.

I was trying to understand everything. I am a perfectionist, after all. That divorce was a blight on my record. It was one that I did not cause and one where I was on a scripturally solid foundation, regarding my specific role.

Yet, of course, I was required by my personality portrait and obsessive need to achieve perfection. I was required to obtain all of the cheat codes and memorize everything on this step. I could then master the test and swiftly move to the next level. When I actually applied myself, I could pass any test by memorizing all of the material.

It's a gift I always knew that I had. It could have only come from God. I never took credit for it, but I used it to my advantage and on my whim.

Once, I got 147 out of 150 on a tenth grade Civilization's History test. I had spent the entire semester not applying myself. However, I had to ace the final exam in order to pass the class and avoid summer school. I intentionally missed three questions so the teacher would not think I cheated. He called me James Earl. Beyond the name similarities, I guess I looked like a younger version of James Earl Jones with glasses.

UPSLID

As I got older and "finally upslid," as my mother called the day that I, genuinely, decided to dedicate my life to the Lord with no turning back. The steps and stages became more difficult to traverse using my old quiver full of customary arrows. I could not rely on my old tricks like memorizing the test to get me by, not in the kingdom. I was being trained to do his will.

God gets to make up the tests. And as I learned during the final phase, only God can make a test and set a trap that I cannot quickly master and memorize my way out of! On this final step for Joseph, it would take a full two years to get out of his unwarranted prison sentence, even after he translated the dreams of the baker and the butler in prison, after asking the butler to remember him and mention him to Pharaoh. Alas, the butler forgot all about him.[39]

It took that butler two full years before the confluence of situation and circumstances, orchestrated and choreographed by God, would allow Joseph to get out of jail. In other words, paraphrasing 2 Timothy (2:3), you must play by all of the rules if you want to win the game. I was not going to be able to cheat the test this time. I had to wait until he needed me to get out of that jail step. No Earlism or Jones Jedi-Mind-Memorization-Trick would get me out of this one.

But there is a good side to learning to submit to the teacher and to the tests, which will come at each step in the dependent progression. Only God can orchestrate and choreograph things in such a way that everything works together. Such that, you show up in Pharaoh's court at just the right time. This is possible because two years earlier, the butler and advisor to the king finally remembered you and told the king that you were the prepared and gifted person for the job.

As a matter of fact, Pharaoh and his advisors would agree that no one in the kingdom was as wise, intelligent, gifted, or anointed by God to handle the job of prime minister in this kingdom as Joseph. He was ready, prepared, tested, and fully capable of handling everything that encompassed the task for which he had been destined, prepared, and purposed by God to fulfill.[40]

JOSEPH'S STEPWISE ORCHESTRATION

What the ministers are right about regarding their repristination of the story of Joseph is that the next step in Joseph's life was completely dependent on his ability to humbly submit to God, learn obedience, learn that God was in control, and then be willing to take the next step without prearranging the outcome. Joseph and I love to fix the outcome. Joseph and I are fully capable of fixing all of the outcomes—or so we think. That is only when God is not creating, orchestrating, and choreographing the tests—and he keeps the answer sheets.

39. Gen 40:1–41, 41:1.
40. Gen 41:37–40.

The ministers are correct when they note that, for example, if Joseph had never told his brothers and father about his dreams (yep, the very dreams that led to being accused of being too full of himself for telling his family), then his brothers would have never been exposed as the murderously duplicitous bunch of villains that they were. Subsequently, they would not have tried to kill Joseph. Rather, they would have been willing to settle for selling him into slavery to some Midianite traders headed for Egypt. After throwing him into a pit, they planned to leave him for dead.

This, after Ruben, the first born of the bunch, tried to rescue Joseph, in order to cut a side deal and get back in Daddy's good graces. This, after sleeping with one of Dad's wives. This, after throwing him into a pit, planning to leave him for dead.

And Judah. That guy. He suggested, "Why should we kill Joseph such that we could then see what comes (or does not come) of his dreams?" We can just sell him for a profit, rip his coat, dip it in the blood of one of dad's lambs, and take it to dad to cover our tracks. If all of that never happened, then Joseph didn't get sold into slavery in Egypt.[41]

If Joseph never gets sold to Pharaoh's chief executioner and the general in charge of the royal body guard, named Potiphar, then the next step is disrupted.

However, Joseph does get sold to Potiphar because of his duplicitous brothers, and because it just so happens that when the brothers were being talked down from killing him. Rather, they settled on slavery as the future for their younger brother, via a band of Ishmaelite traders, who were also their distant cousins. They just so happened to be passing by, taking goods, as well as people, to Egypt for trading.

Dad reacted more favorably toward Joseph by giving him a beautiful coat, representing Joseph's favor with his father, Israel, as well as representing Joseph's prominent leadership within the family, despite Joseph being the second-youngest brother. He was also the first-born son of the only wife that Jacob wanted (and worked on his uncle Laban's farm) to marry, Rachel.

Joseph was a leader from the outset, and his father placed him in a leadership position. Joseph was sent by Dad to report on his misguided older brothers. Although, at first, he worked under his brothers who were the sons of Israel's bondservant wives, Bilhah and Zilpah.[42] After the

---

41. Gen 37.
42. Gen 37:2–14.

second dream, when his father wondered what Joseph's dreams meant, the older brothers grew murderously resentful of him. Israel sent Joseph to check on his brothers and report back to him. Thus, placing him in the role of family supervisor or underling chief of the homicidal digi-brains.

Now, if Joseph was not sold into slavery and did not end up with the right distant relatives, then Joseph would have never learned to manage and lead a house in Egypt for one of Pharaoh's most important military officers and cabinet members. Joseph was placed by God in the next step in this unfolding stepwise-dependent progression. He was being prepared for an entirely new set of tests and trials—tests and trials equally as severe as, yet different from, those he faced in his dad's house with his brothers.

He had obviously passed all of those taken at Dad's house, including telling them about the dreams that God had given him. Thus, he was able to step to the next level, albeit as a slave. He was chief in charge of the entire house. The head of the digi-brains now . . . and a slave. While Joseph was leading the troops, his master, Potiphar, only had to think of what he wanted others to make him for dinner.[43] Joseph's Gifts made room for him.[44]

Then comes the test in this step. Potiphar had a dissatisfied and rather duplicitously and licentiously lascivious wife. She was also bold. She said to the rather attractive young man known as Joseph, "Sleep with me."[45] He was able to pass this daily test, too.

He probably thought that this would be the only test he would face at this level while he likely tried to figure out how he could buy his freedom. He told the good Lady Potiphar, "My master has given me access to, and leadership over, everything in his house except for you. Why? Because you are his wife. How could I sin against my God and betray him by doing as you are requesting?"[46] Joseph was demonstrating the development of his dependence in this step as he makes progress toward the actualization of what must have certainly become a fading dream for him at this point.

Lady Potiphar would not take no for an answer. She basically attacked the man when they were home alone. But he passed that test and ran away from her leaving his second torn robe, symbolizing tattered

---

43. Gen 39:6, 23–24.
44. Prov 18:16.
45. Gen 39:6–12.
46. Gen 39:8–9.

authority, once again rent from a man who still had done nothing save dream God's dreams.

"Hell hath no fury like a Lady Potiphar scorned." She quickly played the betrayed and spurned victim of Joseph's advances. And she held the torn robe, the robe that she tore trying to get at Joseph, as evidence for the arrival of her husband, the executioner.

When Potiphar got home, quite naturally, he was furious. Though, he was likely not that surprised, and he probably saw through his wife's subterfuge. I say that because the penalty during that time for attempted and forced adultery was death. And, after all, he was the Chief Executioner. The fact that he decided to throw Joseph in Pharaoh's dungeon may be evidence that he knew of his wife's duplicitous and scandalous intentions.[47]

So, Joseph was off to jail, for only and simply passing a test, for doing an excellent job using the gifts that God gave him as he searched for the manifestation of a tattered and fading dream at this, the next step's end.

However, if Joseph had not been sold to Potiphar, and if he had not been allowed to become a business leader in Egypt, then he would not have been prepared for the next step. Joseph became the translation and manifestation of his own dream, and he never even knew it.

He became a farming and sheep herding industry leader in his father's house. Then he became a business industry titan and managerial leader, serving as a slave in Potiphar's house in Egypt which was the largest economic power in the region.

Now he gets thrown into the next step of this progression: learning to depend on the God of the dreams. In jail, he is placed in charge again. This time as a slave prisoner and, falsely accused, "philandering attacker" of his master's wife. The warden places Joseph in a leadership position in Pharaoh's dungeon. On this step, Joseph would also gain some active practice in dream interpretation. He meets two members of Pharaoh's household staff.[48] One of whom, if not both, were chief advisors to Pharaoh.

How do we know this? See the book of Nehemiah once again. Nehemiah held the exact same position as the advisor, butler, and wine steward.[49] This same butler just so happened to be present in Pharaoh's royal

---

47. Gen 39.
48. Gen 40.
49. Gen 40:21; Neh 1:11.

court two years later when Pharaoh was given two of his own dreams by God.

Have you also noticed that the dreams in this stepwise-dependent progression seem to come in pairs?[50] This is according to that, as yet to be established, Levitical Law. This is another reason that Joseph was not executed by Potiphar. You will get it ... just think about it.

Joseph had two dreams. The baker and the butler from Pharaoh's court had one dream each. Pharaoh had two dreams. When Joseph would interpret the dreams, he would tell Pharaoh that your two dreams mean that this thing has been declared by God, and it will happen very shortly.[51] Joseph was developing a more profound dependence on his God with every passing test on every separate, but dependent, preceding level or step.

If the steps on the staircase or ladder are not connected, then they are just a bunch of random pieces of oblong wood.[52] God connects them, then he leads us on the journey, testing us on each level, in order to prepare and purify us. This is so that when we reach the afore-revealed and -promised top, we will be fully equipped and capably ready for him to use us to "save many."

Anyway, Joseph gets to run the jail now, and gets some additional dream interpretation practice in. During a previous season and step, he likely misinterpreted or under-interpreted his own dreams. He likely aimed too low and thought that they meant that his brothers and father would come to work for him, surreptitiously bowing down to him.

His father asked him, upon hearing the second dream, "Will me and your mother and your brothers really come to bow down before you?"[53] He never refuted dad, or his brothers when they queried him about the meaning of the dreams. I will not be as brazen as my mistaken ministerial brethren by presuming that I know this to be fact. But Joseph did tell the butler I was sold into slavery, stolen from my father's homeland, and did nothing to deserve a prison sentence.[54]

As the underling chief warden in charge of prison digi-brains, he was placed as caretaker over the incarcerated men from Pharaoh's staff,

50. Deut 19:15.
51. Gen 41:32.
52. Isa 28:10.
53. Gen 37.
54. Gen 40.

i.e., the baker and the butler. They looked troubled one morning, so he asked them about their state of being.

They told him that they each had a disturbing dream the night before, and they had no one to interpret the dreams. Joseph, demonstrating his developing dependence, told them that interpreting dreams is God's business. Then, demonstrating his understanding of his developing and clarifying role in the kingdom, he told them to "Tell God's business to me, the one who he has gifted to interpret his business."[55]

Joseph started to understand his role in the kingdom, as well as his gifts. He understood, as demonstrated by this statement, that he had many gifts and talents, all given to him by God.[56] He just had to learn how to use each one.

By now, after being placed in a leadership position at every trying step and stage, it could not have been a surprise to him that one of his areas of gifting must have been in the area of administrative leadership. I will refrain from making my digi-brain reference here. Joseph was an excellent leader, in the latter tradition of excellence demonstrated by Daniel 5:7 and 6:3.

The butler went first. He told Joseph his dream. Joseph appropriately interpreted the dream for him. Joseph told him that, in three days, his dream revealed that he would be released from prison and restored to his former position as an advisor and wine steward in Pharaoh's palace.

Joseph also took this occasion to request the assistance of the butler. He asked the butler to remember him when he returned to his position in Pharaoh's court. Essentially, "Please remember how God used me to help you, and to put your mind at ease."

I was stolen from my homeland, the land of the Hebrews, sold into slavery, and then placed in this dungeon. All of this, for never having committed a crime any more serious than having a couple of dreams, displaying exemplary leadership at each stop, and being too attractive to the lusty Lady Potiphar. Such is the fate of those who are taking a stepwise-dependent progressive journey with God.

The baker, having seen how well the dream interpretation process went for the butler, felt pretty good about telling Joseph his dream. Joseph was pretty matter-of-fact in dispensing the interpretation of the baker's dream. He told the baker, "In three days, Pharaoh will have you

---

55. Gen 40:7–8, 41:15–16.
56. Rom 12:6.

decapitated. Furthermore, you will be impaled on a pole, where buzzards and dirty bird ravens will eat your flesh." Fundamentally filthy and useless creatures are those purple and black hued ravens.

Things happened exactly as interpreted by Joseph. The baker was decapitated and impaled with a pole. I wonder what he did. The butler was restored to his former position. His troubles were over. His trial at this step in his progression was over.

Happy days were there again for the butler who quickly, and summarily, forgot all about the interpreter. The man who had set his heart and mind at ease, while apparently being imprisoned for a crime that he obviously did not commit. Yep, the butler forgot all about Joseph, and would not remember him for two years.[57]

Each person who chooses to begin the stepwise-dependent journey with God, toward the fulfillment of their purposed destiny and calling, will follow a different path. The tests on each step and level in the journey will be different. The length will be different. The severity will be different. Although not to the individual test taker. This is all because the steps and the final destination are different for each person. However, they are all ordered by God.[58]

God is the one who orders every step. He brings together every test taken during each semester, at each academic level and step along the journey. God assigns the homework, designed to prepare you for the tests.

God selects the test dates, and God most definitely, and liberally, dispenses the pop quizzes. They are not "signature quizzes" based on timely attendance, as I used to give my marketing students (when I wanted to jam some of the perpetually late students out of an extra ten points). God does not give many "signature quizzes." He may give one or two.

He does these things like the perfect Symphony Orchestra Conductor that he is, understanding the intricately essential nature of each and every assignment and what the successful completion of each will mean. Not only during that semester, but when you are finally ready to graduate into your promised land . . .

---

57. Gen 40:1–41:1.

58. Ps 37:23.

Thanks, Pete

He fixes up the internships and co-ops too. You gotta get that real-life work experience in there, just like Joseph when he practiced his leadership skills and sharpened his skill set related to dream interpretation. All students eventually ask the professor, "Is this gonna be on the test?" Worst question ever.

We assume that if the professor says no, then we do not need to study that useless junk. I tried that once on my comprehensive exams (comps) for my master's program. Thank you, Pete.

He begged me to study the answers to that one question (one which I was most certain would never appear on comps). I doubled back in my preparation and reviewed that material.

The next day, as we sat in that room at our individual computers, Pete was right in front of me. Sure enough . . . that question . . . the one that I refused to study was there.

Pete, who was seated directly in front of me, turned around, and smiled. I think he knew, by the relieved look on my face, that I had heeded his warning. Thanks again, Pete. You saved me on that one.

. . . And the Mighty Clarinets

Only God can bring all of these seemingly disparate parts, tests, assignments, tasks, betrayals, lies, pains, trials, and difficulties together to make beautiful, preparatory music, just like the conductor brings together the trumpets, saxophones, flutes, drums, stringed instruments, and yes, the mighty clarinets. He brings them all together to symphonically play the Ukrainian Bell Carol for Christmas.

God orchestrates each test, at each step, during each semester, linking each step in the staircase. When we reach the top, we are ready to play like never before. We become the proverbial thornbird. (Look it up; it was an excellent mini-series too.) Such that we do what no one else can do, we are fully prepared to be used to handle "God's Business" for the King. Then we are to be placed in the position which we were always destined for: our true calling, which is to aid, assist, help, bless, and "save many."

For Joseph this meant that he was able to translate Pharaoh's dream, a dream that none of his other advisors in the entire kingdom could translate.⁵⁹ Why? Because Joseph, and Joseph alone, had been tested by God.

He kept the pace, along the dark winding road, passing all of the pop quizzes given in each step. Joseph let God drive the car, and his humble submission allowed God to bring all of the semesters together, by doing his job of just keeping pace. He finished the degree, "when God needed it," and when God said that his required time of study and testing was fully complete.⁶⁰

For Joseph, he transacted God's business for Pharaoh and placed the King's troubled mind at ease. He was also prepared to save the entire kingdom of Egypt, as well as every surrounding country and land in that region. Egypt was the superpower of that day and age. Everyone would experience the famine. Joseph was used to structure and led the market economy of Egypt for the next fourteen years and well beyond; such that Egypt would not just survive, but prosper during a famine, and "save many lives."⁶¹

Pharaoh and his top advisors, including the butler who was present for the discussion of Pharaoh's dreams, immediately recognized that Joseph had God's hand and anointing on his life. No one was wiser nor more well-prepared than Joseph to lead the country as second in command to Pharaoh. Pharaoh knew it. His advisors knew it. Everyone in the kingdom would soon know it.

Also, Joseph got himself a new robe, one of penultimate authority in all of Egypt, as well as everywhere that would become beholden to Egypt for food during the impending famine. In Genesis 47, it describes how Egypt prospered and flourished under the administrative leadership of Joseph throughout the seasons of both bull and bear markets. This means that they prospered during the seven years of abundant harvests in Egypt, as well as during the seven years of famine and crop failure that Joseph correctly interpreted from Pharaoh's dreams. The surrounding chapters also demonstrate the full manifestation of those two dreams that Joseph had, some twenty-two years prior.

His brothers would bow down to him on two occasions, just as the dream revealed. His father would also become dependent on Joseph, just as Joseph dreamed.

---

59. Gen 41.
60. 2 Tim 4:7.
61. Gen 41–50.

Thank God He Told Everyone the Dreams

Brother ministers, he told everyone. Thank God he "Was Not" quiet nor did he keep his mouth shut. He could have gotten off course in that first step had he listened to you folks.

Joseph learned to become dependent on God for everything that he did, and would do, for the rest of his life. All of this occurred because the stepwise-dependent progression, requires complete surrender to the Good Master Teacher.[62]

ME & THE KINGDOM OF THE DIGI-BRAINS

I hate spotlights that I do not shine on myself. Again, I am, and love to remain, an elusive, obscure extrovert when it comes to revealing personal parts of my life save to the two aforementioned people, Doc and the Liberian Ninja, who are insiders by their own gifting and grace. Maybe a very select few others. I feel compelled to overlay some significant and relevant parts of my stepwise-dependent progression toward the fulfillment of purpose and calling in order to clarify the point. This, before we proceed to the discussion of the actual seven steps to "Was Not."

In addition to the many steps that have brought about a great many tests, trials, betrayals, and difficulties during my personal journey. My steps can be measured by many measuring sticks including, in part, by university. Granted, there were a great many tests at each university stop for me. They were not all related to my educational journey, church service, or to my kingdom work assignments.

It was a journey that encompassed many years, beginning from the time that I "upslid," as my mother deemed my process of confessing and believing in Jesus as my Lord and personal Savior on that Friday night, February 14. It took me on travels through many states and too many universities to count. At first, I was located along the eastern seaboard. Eventually, I would work with and for universities all throughout the country.

---

62. John 13:13; Luke 18:18.

Reading & Writing

One specific group of tests stands out, at one specific stage. It relates to a career that I never sought: writing. I quite famously do not read. Therefore, the thought of becoming a writer and author was, to put it mildly, a nonstarter for me. Someone long ago, while in church, told me via a dream or prophetic revelation that "You're going to begin to write."

I worked as a sound technician for that church, among many other things. I shared these different prophetic visions and utterances with members of that congregation on individual cassette tapes. This team was brought by a pastor during that weekend's conference. I never forgot that she said that to me. Although I never wanted to write, much less become an author.

Fast forward to my work as lecturer and underling chief in charge of the digi-brains. During this time, I was musing my next planned steps to reach my proposed destiny. I was preparing God to "need" my doctorate, so I could finally enroll in a program and get out of that university, which did not offer a suitable doctorate program at the time.

Also, as I remember, I wanted to move more full-time into the classroom and advise students secondarily. Now, when I say I was "preparing God," he was actually preparing me.

I remember telling one of my favorite students that I always wanted to write a book, but not an academic book. Rather, I wanted to write one that the "humans" would enjoy. I would float some rudimentary concepts past her based on personality typology, which was taught in one of her favorite business classes. I imagined it one way, but I had to wait on the steps and tests at each level.

I ultimately wrote that book. Then I was tasked to get it published. Also, by this point, I had finally finished my doctorate. I assumed that finishing that degree meant that God, *finally*, according to my logic and timing, "needed" it. So, when I finished it, I concurrently misassumed that God would wondrously turn me loose on the full-time professorate and deliver me from the kingdom of the digi-brains. After all, I had the degree so he must have needed it, right?

Wrong again, of course. I had more tests, trials, pop quizzes and one *long*, last step that was just beginning. I was delivered from the kingdom of the digi-brains, all right. Just not how I thought I would be—of course.

By now having learned obedience through the many things that I suffered, when God told me this time, "Don't fight. Don't sic 'em. Rather, I want you to open not your mouth."[63] I, actually happily, quickly submitted and obliged. I misinterpreted the step, stage, and the dream, but not the command of God.

I figured, hey, "He needed the doctorate." I was set to defend my dissertation exactly one month from the point when Lady Potiphar, ultimate queen of the digi-brained fiefdom, and her head underling noble in that fiefdom (and my boss) blew everything up. This was likely only by God's permission and suggestion in the heavenlies.[64] Besides, I knew that I was right regarding the disputed issue.

Furthermore, the ultimate queen digi-brain that I worked for as lecturer in name only and chief of the digi-brains. The latter mother-betrayer, who at one time had been like a genuine mother figure to me, had now betrayed me for Lady Potiphar, the new ultimate queen digi-brain who I helped hire. My betraying mother, at the behest of Lady Potiphar, threw me at the fastest moving bus that she could find. She knew that I was being falsely accused.

So, I figured: obey the Lord; "Open not your mouth"; defend the dissertation. My dissertation was based on work with academically at-risk students, largely completed while at my previous university stop.

Thus, entering my promised land, I also kept my previously spoken promise, the one that God tricked me into making. You remember that one, don't you? "Once you get me back into the classroom, I will never come out for anything." Meaning, I will never come out, no matter who offers me what kingdom of the digi-brains job to go along with any teaching assignment. Doc always said, "Don't nobody want that job." (They had offered it to him on multiple occasions.)

Dr. I Like to Fight

Of course, I successfully defended the dissertation and donned a title that would take some getting used to: Dr. EA Jones. I still don't much care for it, but he "needs" it. So I live with it. From my perspective, I got that degree because I enjoyed the fight.

---

63. Isa 53:7.
64. Job 1:8.

I just wanted to walk into that dissertation defense room like a knight of the Jedi Order, slay all of my opponents, who were also my dissertation committee members. All but one really helped me every step of the way, all to who I am eternally grateful. For me, it was the thrill of the hunt.

The fight itself was the most satisfying portion of this step. I like to fight. I, as Doc once said about me in reference to a grad school entrance exam, "slayed the dragon." After my defense, I walked out victorious. I was ready to hang their ceremonial pelts on my trophy wall.

The truth is that I actually used to keep my college degrees in a bookbag in my closet. Once, I used that bag for fishing, but I took 'em out before leaving. Subsequently, it smelled too bad to bring it back home. So I threw it away.

I will fight until, as Alexander the Great who has been erroneously given credit for saying and doing, "I wept, for I have no more worlds left to conquer."[65] Truer words have never been spoken (or misattributed).

Of course, God had other plans—one more huge step replete with many tests and diverse, as well as painful, trials and betrayals. I encountered the first one month prior to my dissertation defense. But I passed the first and second tests. I "opened not my mouth," easily resisting the urge to fight or defend myself. In the face of bald-faced lies and incomprehensible, yet pervasive, stupidity.

See these people were not on the list of the people who I cared what they thought of me, anyway. And I knew that they, particularly the Ultimate Queen-Mother-Betrayer thought a lot of me anyway. She threw me at that bus to save someone else's hide as the Jack in that Fiefdom, and a very good man, as well as an excellent digi-brain, told me later. Thus, I knew that she knew the truth. I knew what she actually thought of me, particularly, prior to the hire of the ultimate queen of the digi-brain fiefdom. I knew why she had so seemingly easily betrayed me.

Many trials later, God finally released me to write my first book. I had accepted that I would also have to write more academic-based articles, but I already had a few things of that sort published by then.

In my heart and mind, I was still linking my career in academia to my writing. However, I wanted to write one book for the "regular humans." One and only one, mind you.

---

65. The origins of this quote have been largely disputed. https://en.wikiquote.org/wiki/Alexander_the_Great#Disputed.

Although I accepted the fact that I had to write for the digi-brains in academia, the "big-heads" as I call them, or us, I still never considered myself a Christian author, one who also has a career in academia as a professor. Also, I never stopped teaching in the university classroom. I just happened to do so in unforeseen classrooms. I was being given practice at dream translation, by continuing to teach, but the promise of "once I enter full time ..." had yet to fully manifest.

But the first book was written. I binge wrote the first draft in four days. As C.S. Lewis said, "I never exactly made a book. It's rather like taking dictation. I was given things to say." Now I had to get it published. Later, I accepted that it would "have to" be published by a Christian publishing house. Remember, I had no idea that I was a Christian author, so why would I publish my book with a Christian publisher? I eventually discovered the place for that book within the publishing arena. Oh yeah, God also told me, "Do not self-publish. The book will be published by a traditional publishing house."

So, now I had my marching orders. I received a lot of rejection letters, but that did not matter. I never wanted to be an author, anyway. God told me what to say, so it was his job to get it published.

It really did not matter to me. This was not my fight. I had bombs going off all over the place in the other areas of my life. Tests, too many to count, with more betrayals by more "mothers" mounting and those yet to come.

I finally got a few positive replies and one referral to a vanity publisher. Then, awhile later, after being thrown into a pit, forgotten, sold into slavery, falsely accused again, thrown in jail, promoted while simultaneously being demoted, forgotten, and kicked out again, I got a tacit offer from a reputable publishing house. Finally. The happy days are here again. (Insert loser gameshow music here.)

I would not hear back from them for six months. During that time, I had one more displacing betrayal, by another "mother." However, I was simultaneously rescued by my own Reubens, who had no agendas, as did Joseph's eldest brother. Then I got another offer and was ready to go with it.

Instead, I sought to use it to leverage and motivate the first reputable publisher to action. That is, if I could. It was all up to the Good Master Teacher. I actually had little personal investment in this fight. I just knew that he ordained it to be so.

Ultimately, I signed with a reputable publishing house. Well, remember, I do not read, so I have no idea who is reputable and who is not, at least not in the world of Christian publishing. A friend told me that she had heard of them, so I researched them a few weeks after submitting my manuscript. Go figure.

Still, on this last step, a very long while later, things with my last publishing house went bad because they had changed something that would potentially cause us legal trouble. And they refused to change it back. They did this while ignoring me and my requests. They also disregarded the appeals and demands of my newly obtained (but old friend) attorney. So now what, God?

While writing this, I am still being tested. I am quite dependent now and very submissive, but I am seemingly making no progress. Why do we now have to find a new publisher? Should I consider the self-publishing option that you told me that we were not to pursue?

Professor Christian Author

I learned on this step, through the things that I suffered—yep all of the things suffered, including the new things that I suffered in the publishing world with my Christian Publisher—that I had to go through this, with them, in order to convince Dr. EA Jones (yuck) to use that as his "nom de plume." I otherwise forbid anyone other than my students to ever use that moniker.

I had to be persuaded to embrace, and become accustomed to, the Dr. EA Jones title, as both an earned designation and as a persona. I still have not completely arrived in this area. However, I love to fight and I am an extrovert. I am also secretly a very humble person who shies away from spotlights that I do not shine on myself. Don't tell anyone, OK?[66]

I had to learn that Dr. EA Jones was an academic and a professor who also had finally learned what he has in his house.[67] I am also a Christian author. It is very uncomfortable for me to admit all of this stuff in print.

I learned from the things that I suffered, specifically with the first publishing house, that I was both, and that they were separate callings. I

---

66. 2 Cor 12:7.

67. 2 Kgs 4:1–7.

could do both as God led me to do them, on the stages that he placed me on to perform, to play my instruments in his symphony.

Once I accepted those things I was released to write this book, one of many that I had completed outlines for but had never been released to write. This one: a fully Christian book. I wrote it while I continued to pursue my career in secular academia.

Staircase

If I had not passed all of the steps at university kingdom number one, then I am never released to go to university kingdom number two. If I do not finish and pass every test on step two at university kingdom number two, and graduate, I am not released to university kingdoms number three, four, five, etc.

Just like Joseph moving from Daddy's house to the pit, then to slavery and the dungeon inside of the prison, and, ultimately, to Pharaoh's palace. Fight on, win, pass every test, and take the next step. Only God knew how long Job's journey would last and only God knew what happened during Enoch's stepwise-dependent progression toward the fulfillment of purpose.

More on this story at the end of this book.

You, my friend, are on your own stepwise-dependent progression. Keep the pace. Pass each of the tests one at a time, and you will graduate to the next step on the journey.

SUMMARY OF THE STEPWISE DEPENDENT JOURNEY

Stepwise

We need to conclude this discussion by summarizing what the stepwise-dependent progressive journey actually means. It means that we must begin by accepting that there is a God, one who wants us to join him on the journey through life. We also have to accept that he has destined a journey for us to take. He wants us to join him on that journey because he made us with free will.

So we are free to choose to believe that there is a God. Although I personally doubt that we, as humans, are ever capable of achieving such a level of doubt and deference toward God, because we know that "God has apportioned to each a degree of faith (and a purpose designed for service)."[68] This is in order to keep us from thinking too much of ourselves.

So in order to take this journey, you have to choose to believe that God actually exists. Then you have to accept that he has a Purpose for your life. This requires you to begin the process of submitting your free will to choose to do and be whatever you want. Submit those to the will of God—who you either recognize as, or are beginning to recognize as, God and creator with power and a plan that far exceeds yours. You are presently saying that, "You know better than I because you have been here longer. You are smarter and wiser than I." Because you are, *I am*.

There are some other minor assumptions, but those are the biggies required to begin the journey with God. If you have these down, you can start the journey. The stepwise portion requires faith, which comes through intimate fellowship with God. Then, as you travel, you begin to learn that this will not be a flat walk. It has levels, as well as steps or plateaus involved. The faith, patience, and diligence required to travel to the end of level one will need to be elevated as you begin to recognize that you are now on a new level of testing.

Ultimately, you recognize that God is the only one who could make, create, and spontaneously generate all of the things that you learned and did on level one. You will then connect those things to level two and so on. You will begin to absorb and understand that he was planning and interconnecting, or enmeshing, each trial together with each plateau. He was also combining all of the tests that you have taken on each level, plotting the course to lead to one large place with many facets.

This multifaceted place, like a diamond, is a place that you cannot look directly through like a piece of translucent glass or a window. It has many different pieces inside, all reflecting off each other, refracting or breaking down the light in a manner, such that when the one level, at the top of purpose and promise, shines light on another, it creates many different brilliant rainbows. You have to be fully prepared to help and play your part in this complex maze that is the metaphorical diamond. In other words, you are being prepared to play your part in the kingdom of heaven.

---

68. Rom 12:3.

Only God knows all parts, facets, and levels in the kingdom. He knows where you fit. He knows who will need you, and when they will need you. He also knows how to prepare you to fulfill those needs of the many people that you will encounter along the way and at that time. Such that, the entire kingdom can advance forcefully.[69]

Thus, he knows exactly when he will need to use you, and exactly who you need to be regarding your training and preparation. He also knows exactly what you will need to know when you get to that place of purpose on the final level of this stepwise progression. This level is one that only God can properly orchestrate. All you need to do for now is to keep walking in lockstep with God, allowing him to lead. He brings it all together.

Dependent

That's the stepwise part, in a nutshell. The next part is the learning to depend on God for everything. That comes as the journey progresses toward "Was Not." The closer you get to God on this journey, the more you will learn to trust him, his voice, and his direction. You will ultimately learn, if you keep walking, to depend completely on God for everything in every situation.[70]

That seems a lofty goal. However, I assume that this may be what took Enoch three hundred years to learn: to die to self and selfish desires. He then was able to learn to relinquish control of his life, placing it and himself in full submission to God.[71]

A Progressive Journey

The progression portion of the process also occurs while you are on the journey, as you make your way through each step and level that God has you placed on, learning dependence along the way. While you are making continuous and steady progress, God is a forward-moving God. But we must remember that we are still on one step or level. Thus, we have to complete all tasks and tests associated with that step before we can graduate to the next level.

69. Matt 11:12.
70. Prov 3:6.
71. Rom 12:1; 1 Cor 15:31; Gal 2:20.

Once we graduate, we must continue to remain mindful of the fact that we have to complete everything required of us. We have to overcome all obstacles, while keeping pace with God, in order to complete this level. Each step that we take, on each level, is designed for our good, and is designed to prepare us for the ultimate goal or prize of the higher calling.[72] This occurs after we have passed all tests on each level, including those on the final step or level.

Then, and only then, the children of Israel were fully prepared to enter the promised land.[73] When they were ready, the two and a half tribes who made their home on the east side of the Jordan were ready to go with the others to fight and conquer the entire promised land.[74] One might say that they were tested for forty years and prepared on multiple levels in their wilderness in order to be ready to fight for their promise, the promise that was originally given to their progenitor, Abraham.[75]

You can make the same argument, or have the same discussion, regarding our three primary characters relative to this discussion: Enoch, Joseph, and Job. They were trained on multiple levels to enter into their promised land. They were prepared by God on each level.

Each step had its own distinct and distinguishable tests, specifically unique to that level. God was the only one who could bring and work all things together for an overarching good purpose, such that when they were fully prepared by the time they passed the final step, they could help prepare those men to help "save many."[76]

They also learned obedience and complete dependence on God as they progressed through each step, heading toward the promise. They learned submission and to use each of the gifts given to them by God wisely. They were tried and tested, and gained an understanding of who they were in God.

---

72. Phil 3:14.
73. Josh 1–6.
74. Num 32:1–5, 11, 6–12, 19, 33.
75. Gen 12.
76. Rom 8:28.

God, What's My Calling?

Now I must say at this point that, quite often, so many people wonder, "God, what's my calling?" I have a short answer that will hopefully bring some peace.

Most likely, you are already doing it. You just haven't noticed. You didn't know that it was a calling nor did you know that this is what it was supposed to look like.

Joseph did that at each level: as an administrator and leader, a dream interpreter, and serving as the living interpretation of many executives' and kings' dreams. I was a Christian author long before I realized that a Christian guy who writes stuff, some of which gets published in various publications, is a Christian author. Who knew?

I also did not know that I could work with the only things that I was good at: people, more specifically college people. I just knew who kept showing up at my door. Subsequently, they kept leaving happy, blessed, and/or better for the encounter.

I often say to God, even today, "I do not want to know what I am doing right. As long as they keep coming back, I can reasonably assume that whatever it is that you are doing in and through me is working. So keep up the 'God-work' in and through me. And never let me know exactly what that work is because I do not want to mess it up."

You can rest assured that what you have in your house is likely already in use by God. His gifts and callings are not things that he ever takes back. We just have to learn to use them like he wants us to use them.[77]

Know this: if they keep coming back, whether or not you are transacting this activity in front of thousands of blessed people or in front of one, then that is likely associated with your area of gifting, calling, and purpose. However, you actually have many gifts and talents.

Progression

The final stage and thing that you have to trust and remember is that you are making progress. Keep pace with God. Do not give up.

Remember: each level and its tests are all vitally important. Also remember that when you graduate from a step, there is likely another

---

77. 2 Kgs 4:1–7; Rom 11:29.

step. Finally, God controls the clock and the tests; only he can bring all of this together. In this: your personal, stepwise-dependent progressive journey to "Was Not."

3

Step One: Faith

BELIEVING THAT HE IS

Now that we have the process down, we can begin to discuss the individual steps. The reason that step one is faith is because that's what the Bible says that Enoch began with.[1] Actually, we will begin with verse one of the book of Hebrews 11:1. It states, depending on the translation of the Bible that you are reading, that faith is the tangible evidence of the things that we hope for. We know that we hope for things that have been shown to or have been divinely revealed to us.

Those revelations come to us by developing a dependent and intimate relationship with God. However, Enoch did not begin walking with God until he was sixty-five years old. Thus, by implication, the initial stage of his relationship began in earnest around that time. At that point, Elohim, the creator God, could start to show him things that he may have read or heard about.[2]

Once Enoch developed his own relationship with God, he could begin to trust the one that he likely heard about in times past. Enoch likely heard about God from his father Jared.[3] He could then trust that what God was showing him was for him to become God's vision for his

---

1. Heb 11:5–6.
2. Gen 1:1.
3. Gen 5:18–24.

life. What Enoch had revealed to him at sixty-five years old was true, and he could anticipate that he would soon, likely very soon, come to experience and live out those things.

DEFINING FAITH

I have two primary verses that I, via creative and editorial license, rewrite as they were revealed to me. These serve as at least foundational definitions of faith. The first derives from an amended version of Hebrews 11:1. The second verse, as a matter of advancing the definition of the preceding, is best explained as faith begins with what God reveals to you by means of your intimate connection and relationship with him.

In the Gospel of John 15:4, 5, and 7, the Bible speaks of the true vine and the branches. Those vine and branches perfectly depict the unbreakable or inseverable relationship that we must have and pursue with God. He is the source, or sap running first through the vine, that breathes life into us as branches.

Without that life, we could never believe that he is, I am who I am, or "Ehyeh who Ehyeh."[4] Through the unbreakable bond that we must maintain with him, in order to have life in Jesus, he reveals himself to us through that sap. This sap is the ruach or breath of life. It is the breath of the life giving and the breath of the living God.[5] It is through him breathing life into and through us that we are able to believe and have faith in God.[6]

Thus, your faith could never have been what you could mentally conceive or what was born out of your human soul or ego. You could never "name it and claim it," in spite of what you may have heard—not with the included expectation of it ever being born, or of it ever coming to physical manifestation by the hand or breath of God.

The only things that you can name or itemize through faith, supported by prayer and supplication, is what is born in your Spirit and your intractable connection to the true vine.[7] You cannot even conceive of it, not if you want it to come from God, unless he, the Holy Spirit, gives birth to the idea inside of you through that relationship.

---

4. Exod 3:14; Heb 11:6.
5. Gen 1:2, 2:7; Job 27:3, 33:4; Isa 11:2; Matt 3:16; John 3:4–5; Eph 4:24.
6. Mark 11:21–23.
7. John 15:5, 7.

The initial version of the vision, dream, or divine revelation that you will see will not at all resemble the finished product. After you encounter the initial revelation, you will continue to walk with him and keep pace, ensuring that you never allow that constant connection to be severed; you will, by faith, have that initial photograph become both as real and as clear to you, in your spirit, as the final, manifested, tangible object that you receive in the end.

This physical manifestation will occur when God is ready to give you the tangible finished product, when you have traversed all of the requisite steps and passed all of the mandatory tests given on each level and phase of the walk.

In Hebrews 11:1, it is stated that faith is not only the reality that we have possession of what we cannot currently touch or experience, tangibly or intangibly, but faith is the equivalent and exact representation of what we have been promised. In other words, faith is the actual, tangible, or touchable evidence that we have full possession of what we cannot physically see, or intangibly experience and consume.

I have heard this portion of that verse explained as: faith becomes the chair that we sit on. In this metaphysical realm, there is no tangible chair there. Now, without faith, we fall on the floor every time. However, we can sit on our faith with full confidence that we have a chair right there behind us. Go ahead, fall backward.

Enoch's "Was Not" Faith

Now, in verse five of that same "Heroes of the Faith" chapter in the book of Hebrews 11:5, it begins a two verse discussion on Enoch as one of the patriarchs of the faith. This is one, the second, of only three mentions of Enoch in the Bible. It says that because of Enoch's Faith, he disappeared from the earthly realm and life.

In verse six, we continue the discussion on Enoch's faith, this time becoming more specific. The Bible says essentially that, if you want to have the kind of faith that Enoch had, a type of faith which was so pleasing to God that God was forced to take him from this life and earthly realm to be with Elohim, who we know to be a spirit.[8] Thus, if we want to have the "Was Not" type of faith, then we have to begin by believing, through faith, that God exists.

8. John 4:24.

This is the only way that we can begin our journey with God, and this is the thing that pleases God. This faith says that we believe God to be exactly who he reveals himself to be.

Additionally, we trust him to do what he promises that he will do and we trust him to complete what he has revealed to us. By faith, Enoch received all that God promised him. Although he had to progress through many steps while learning to trust and depend on God. Enoch received everything that God promised him because he started believing, possibly at age sixty-five, that God indeed exists. That is what I would call a foundational principle. We have to believe that God exists.

It seems simple, right? Well if it was that simple everyone would believe and receive all that God has for them. And right away. But we know that to be untrue in most circumstances regarding the experiences of most people, including many professing "Christian believers."

ENOCH BELIEVES

Enoch believed that God existed. He could not have started walking with God were this not the case. The tangible idea of receiving from God came much later. In Enoch's case, three hundred years later, when he passed the final tests, and was taken from earth to be with God.

From the time that Enoch was sixty-five, he began to live in close fellowship with God.[9] You cannot engage in a close fellowship with anyone whose existence you question.

There is a curious real-life example of a young man who developed a relationship with a person that he just spoke with via telephone, text, and social media. By the time he learned the truth, he concurrently learned that he was not involved in a relationship with the person that he thought he was talking to all along. He was a public figure and when word got out, he was publicly shamed.

The point is that Enoch engaged in a relationship with God because Enoch believed that the God who he could not see actually existed. Although he could not see God, he had evidence of his divine existence. Thus, he could enter into a long-lasting and intimate relationship with the God he could not see. How, you may ask? By faith.

Remember, I told you that Enoch's journey was discussed three times in the Bible. Well, the third instance occurs in the book of Jude 1.

---

9. Gen 5:24.

Jude was Jesus' biologically related brother. The book only has one chapter, but I believe that it discusses some of the other manifestations of the promises, as well as the divine purpose, which God destined Enoch to fulfill. These were purposes, promises, and a divine destiny that Enoch received by faith as he and Elohim progressed on their journey.[10]

However, God likely told Enoch something in the beginning, something so profound that it convinced Enoch that God was real. Enoch understood that he had better stick with Elohim. Such that, he could receive what God had promised that Enoch would do, see, and become.

ENOCH IN JUDE

In the book of Jude 1:14–15, we begin to see some of the revelations about Enoch's calling that God likely revealed to him at some point during their journey toward "Was Not." The same revelation which convinced him that God was real as well as faithful. God, along the journey, possibly at the outset, told Enoch that Enoch would essentially speak on his behalf to the wicked and perverse generation that existed during the time when Enoch lived. As the progress continued and the trust and dependence deepened, God told Enoch some version of, "I the Lord, your God, will one day, if you keep walking, transform you, and take you out of this earthly realm and into the kingdom of heaven."

I can state that with reasonable certainty because those are the things that Enoch did not see, but which he hoped for. He believed them as evidence until their reality had manifested. They also convinced Enoch to begin his walk with God, after sixty-five years of not walking in lockstep with God, particularly not in this way.

God Will Come

Jude says that Enoch prophesied to the people of his day. He was able to speak on God's behalf and tell them in no uncertain terms that God would come, and when he did, he would bring his angels with him. The Angels would execute judgement on the people. They would do this because of the behavior and lifestyles that were contrary to God and contrary to that which pleases God.

---

10. Gen 5:22–23.

Obviously, they were a faithless and perverse generation. However, if you refer to the verse in Hebrews 11:5, noting how Enoch pleased God by Faith, then you notice that this group was behaving in a manner that demonstrated their lack of faith and lack of relationship with God.

You have to know a lot about God to say these things to a bunch of perverse people. They may come after you with flaming torches for threatening them. If you threaten them on behalf of a God that they obviously do not know very much about, then you have to believe that exactly what you are saying to them is all true.

They were perverse. You can see Enoch's great-grandson Noah's story for evidence regarding how perverse they were beginning in Genesis 6. God most assuredly told him that they were perverse as they walked along on their journey, but God had to define for Enoch exactly what his standard for righteousness was.[11]

So, by the time Enoch was entering the last phase of his last Step, most likely, He knew God Intimately. He knew what Pleased God, i.e. a Walk of Faith. He also had come to know what displeased God, i.e. faithless and perverted living.

Enoch knew that the behavior of the people of his day was displeasing to a righteous God. He knew that God had an army of holy beings, angels, waiting to set things straight in God's created earth. Thus, God revealed both of Enoch's callings to him as they became more intimately acquainted on the journey.

Compare & Contrast

In other words, God revealed that Enoch would witness and be used as a prophet of God to warn the people of his day how displeasing their faithless, perverted lifestyles were to God. Enoch was to become a testimony for all time, an example of the rewards that God bestows upon those who walk by faith in an intimate fashion with God. Those people are the only ones who reach and enter into "Was Not." It all started because Enoch believed that God existed.

---

11. Jude 1:14–15.

The Journey That is Step One

Nothing happens for Enoch without the understanding and belief that God exists. Once we establish that fact we can begin progressing along the journey that is step one. God can begin to reveal exactly what his existence means.

He could show Enoch the difference between good and evil, and why good is so vitally important to God. He could also show Enoch what he would do for God in the future. God could, and did, show Enoch what pleases him as well as why pleasing God is the only thing.

Enoch's Twofold Purpose

God could show Enoch, his divine purpose for his life. Again, by my accounting, Enoch's purpose was twofold, wrapped up into one overarching theme. Enoch was to serve as a witness primarily to his generation. He was a witness relative to what a progressively developing dependent and intimate relationship with God will do for the people of his generation, as well as for those of us living in the here and now. Also, what that relationship will result in if you continue to walk in intimate and continuous fellowship with God. In short, Enoch would give all generations, for all time, something to shoot for and to aspire to become.

Enoch was a witness. He verbally witnessed, to the people of his generation, the power of God and the value in developing a relationship with God. Additionally, Enoch demonstrated, for everyone, the results of forming and maintaining an intimate relationship with God.

When Enoch's relationship with God became intimate and close, he could no longer live in this fallen fleshly state which we call human existence. Regarding historical context, Enoch was a man who was seven generations removed from his great-grandfather, Adam.[12] In essence, Enoch got so close to God that God had no choice but to take him to heaven. Thus, Enoch "Was Not."

He showed everyone what dying daily looks like, to such an extent that if you do dying daily correctly, you might not die physically. However, most do not have that same calling on their lives that Enoch bore on his. Enoch demonstrated the glorious results of dying daily to self on

---

12. Jude 1:14.

a consistent, pace-driven, submitted, and faithful basis.[13] Enoch became a living prophetic witness and then a translated one.

Moving to Cleveland

Everyone knew that Enoch lived at some point. And everyone knew that he did not just go and move to Cleveland in order to hide out for the rest of time. The Bible says that Enoch walked with God and he "Was Not" because God took him. Before God took him, God tested and tried Enoch at every level until he reached the last step. Then God let Enoch perform the earthly act, allowing him to prophesy to his generation a vital warning of things to come. As it turns out, they came to pass in the very near future during his grandson Noah's lifetime.

Enoch would not stay on earth long enough to see the manifestation of his prophetic witness. But he would state and declare God's word with confidence and boldness. Why? Because, Enoch had faith and believed that God existed. So much so, that he could no longer avoid being translated into heaven to be with God, in the spirit. The flesh nor fleshly realm could no longer contain him. So God took him. But Enoch's witness of faith was left for all to see and study, as a pattern of how to walk with God.

We should all aspire to become like Enoch and walk so closely with God that we have fully submitted our bodies and our free will to God, presenting ourselves as a living sacrifice. We should also know that this is how we begin our service to God and his plans for our lives,[14] the plans that he reveals to us are exciting for us because we were created by God and cannot wait to see them fulfilled and manifested in our lives. They are what we were born to fulfill. God places a strong, and overwhelming desire inside of us, one that compels us to see those plans manifested. It all starts with believing that God exists.

A Quick Story

I have one friend, one who through each vastly different confluence of circumstances, all orchestrated by the Good Master Teacher, I came to meet. These people will stumble into my life and I will end up serving

---

13. 1 Cor 15:31.
14. Rom 12:1.

in some sort of counseling and advising capacity. This friend ended up becoming, and is now, a true friend.

This particular friend, among a great many who share or shared this yearning, had a strong desire to be married. It was a desire that I knew was infused into her being by God, similar to what motivated Enoch to continue his journey with God, come what may.[15] Now she had one additional, confounding factor: a factor that many of us face, one which comes to get us off course.

Well, actually two: she had some recriminating self-doubt, and she was hooked up with, as well as hooked on, a horrible and callow human being, a human who served for years as the sole and exclusive target of her affection.

I told her, "Once you open your eyes and you begin to see this whole thing clearly, you will resent that man who has so taken advantage of your affection for him, as well as having taken advantage of your other gifts and talents." Those gifts included her giving, as well as caring, nature, desire to please, and the fact that she is a bit of a pastry chef.

Attempting to make a long story shorter, he basically ripped her heart out and announced that he had found some other woman: a woman with a perfect profile in writing. He found her through a closed-group, social media, date-a-mate, chat thing. He also informed my friend that he was going to marry the other woman. He did.

She fit the carnal man's perfect picture of beauty, brains, hobbies, and interests: a woman that each carnal and inexplicably insecure man would dream of, relative to their specific picture. He's a jerk, and as shallow as a kiddie pool.

He did not see what he had right in front of his face. He also loaded my friend up with most of that aforementioned recriminating self doubt (not to mention, a boatload of rejection). However, I do not believe that God intended him to ever truly see my friend for who God had created her to be, nor who she was allowing him to recreate her to become.

The Jones' Broke Heart Special

She had some desperate nights after that man ripped her heart out. She was devastated. I took her out for the "Jones' broke heart special." That is where we go over all of the horrible things that Jones told you about that

---

15. Ps 37:4.

lump-head. (None of which you believed.) Why not? Because, of course, no one listens to me—not at first anyway. But, even after the "broke heart special," she was still devastated.

We spoke on one desperate night, by phone. She began to question whether or not she was ever supposed to get married in the first place. She started citing the fact that Paul the apostle never got married. Paul said, by permission and his personal desire, that he wished none would marry. She said, "Some people are just not supposed to get married. And maybe I am one of them."[16] It was sad. Although, while helping her I was, as usual, emotionally detached.

The Orange MacGuffin

I have been at this for a very long time, long enough to know when people are just having a pity party and when they are completely serious, desperate, and questioning the validity of everything that God has shown them and infused into their lives. This infusion is that "carrot," which he places inside of you. Then he uses this Orange MacGuffin to get you to go and chase his vision, as a rabbit would chase a carrot tied to a string that keeps getting pulled away.

These are the callings and purposes of God that he uses to get us to begin the journey. He also uses those carrots to get us to stick with him until the end so that we completely see and realize that which we were burning inside to see throughout entire duration of the journey.

Big Swings for the Fences

I told her that this might have been an OK choice for Brother Paul, who said this stuff by permission from the Holy Spirit, but that I, for one, knew beyond a shadow of a doubt that she was destined to be married. At this point, I must mention that I have been at this for awhile. I can take "big swings for the fences" like this. I can step out on faith with divinely inspired certainty and state, almost unequivocally, that a certain thing will happen, or that God intended this or that, even to a woman wrought with despair.

I can do that because I know the signs and I have been on the walk with God for quite awhile. He uses me to bring some comfort by allowing

---

16. 1 Cor 7:1–40.

me to state that which can only be known by faith at this point in my life and life's work.[17] So, now, having been thoroughly vetted and tested by Paul's same Holy Spirit, I will launch right out there and make this sort of statement. You, most likely, should not.

However, I am accustomed to God's voice and leading in this area. Thus, if he is pushing me to say it and if he does not stop me from saying it, I will do so without hesitation.

Again, I have learned obedience through the things that I have suffered. Please do not just blithely do what I have just described. You can leave a lot of his people in a worse and more emotionally broken state than they were in prior to meeting or conversing with you.

So, I told her that I knew she was supposed to be married. She, through tears, asked how I knew. I told her, "God would not have placed that desire in you so strongly if he did not intend for you to be married."

I went on to explain, "We do not come up with all of these brilliant ideas regarding our future on our own."[18] We walk in blithe arrogance, if we presume to think that we, without God, have conceived these dreams and revelations from our own mind, flesh, soul, and ego.

It is God who places these things in our spirit. He reveals them to us through visions, dreams, and inherent desires.[19] That is, if we are walking with him in submission, obedience, and intimate fellowship.

These are all qualifications which this woman had met. The Spirit-infused carrots must *all* line up with the word of God. I told her that this desire to be married meets every aforementioned qualification. He obviously plans to use you and your marriage as a testimony, just like he did with Enoch's life, work, and "Was Not."

Fast-forward a few years. She, as I say, "hit a real hot streak." For awhile there, she could not throw a stone and not hit a man on the head. Prior to that "hot streak," she was walking through a barren desert place, one where she could not hit anything but sand on the ground with the stones she cast.

---

17. Matt 16:17.
18. 2 Tim 3:16.
19. Ps 20:4, 37:4.

Along Came Mr. Right, But . . .

Then along came Mr. Right—well, he was Mr. Almost Right who could have become Mr. God-Sent Right, provided that he take a few steps to be closer to God. As things progressed, some bombs were going off in my own life, so we were separated for a few months. During that separation, she up and got married.

I felt like we had just birthed a child—well as close as I'm gettin' anyway. I guess God had just birthed a dream or vision that I conceived and he revealed into "Was Not."

She was a testimony and a living witness, relative to doing it the right way. She waited on God and would not settle. Another friend and I told her, as pertained to Mr. Right, "Don't blow it." She didn't blow it.

The point is that she, just like Enoch, walked with God. She experienced some hard times. Some things were of her own doing, and a choice of her own free will.

However, even when her faith wavered, she allowed it to be buoyed. She and her story served as a testimony to me while I was on my last step before "Was Not." I also use it to help many others in this circumstance. God is a rewarder of those who diligently seek and trust him.[20]

JOSEPH BELIEVES

Joseph also believed that God existed. This was the beginning, some might say, of his troubles, but it was also the way that his journey with God, toward the fulfillment of purpose, began. Joseph is prominently mentioned throughout the Bible, including in the book of Hebrews. His entire story is chronicled in the book of Genesis 37–50.

The book of Hebrews speaks of his faith and some things he shared with his family that he would not live to see. They were things that God had shown him about their return to the land that God promised to Abraham, Isaac, and Jacob. He told his family that, although he would be buried in Egypt because of all he had done for Egypt, when they as the nation of Israel left Egypt many generations later, they should exhume

---

20. Heb 11:6.

his bones and take them to the promised land.[21] Moses did exactly that, approximately four hundred years later.[22]

Joseph, however, believed that God existed, at least from age seventeen. That is the first mention of Joseph with regard to the first dream that was given to him by God and how he shared it with his brothers. Apparently, dreams of the divine revelation sort, in particular, were very important to the people of Joseph's time and culture. The butler and the baker would share their dreams with Joseph, as would Pharaoh. But each of these dreams demonstrate some God consciousness—particularly, though not exclusively, on Joseph's part.[23]

By the time Joseph had his second dream, he again shared it with his brothers. However, this time he also shared it with his father. He would tell the family the meaning of these dreams, on the occasions of two. The dreams meant that they would bow down in deference and submission to Joseph.

A Dream About a Strong Wind?

He had to, as they all did, believe that dreams came from God. He had to believe that God could not only inspire them, but that God was powerful enough to bring them to manifestation. One innocent night, Joseph had a dream. In the dream, he and his ten older brothers were out in the field bundling wheat. All of a sudden Joseph's bundle stood up. Why he had only gotten through one bundle is not the point of this story. Joseph's bundle stood up, and the bundles of his ten older brothers, stood up and then fell down in deference to Joseph's bundle of wheat.[24]

Now for those who do not believe in a powerful God, one who is powerful enough to reveal himself and his plans to whoever he chooses, they simply see wheat standing up and then falling over—not much here other than a dream about a strong wind.

But not only did Joseph, as implied in the story, correctly translate the dream, the brothers also translated it. They said, "Are we supposed to bow down to you and your leadership?" So, they hated him. even more now than they did before. They already hated him, long before he shared

21. Heb 11:22.
22. Exod 13:19.
23. Gen 37–41.
24. Gen 37:7.

or interpreted his two dreams with them. Again, if this is a story about a strong wind, we do not get to see what happens to Joseph as he begins his walk with God in earnest.

I think it is safe to say that, since no one apparently translated this dream nor the one to follow (which was more obscure than the first to the naked eye), Joseph and his entire family believed that God existed. They believed that he spoke to people through dreams and other means. It is also safe to say that they were not just aware of the God of Abraham and Isaac, but they understood how powerful the God of Abraham and Isaac was.

The second dream stated that the sun, the moon, and the eleven stars would bow low in front of Joseph. This was all eleven brothers, the ten older and the one younger, as well as Mom, the moon, and Dad, the sun. The dream revealed that all were to bow before Joseph.[25]

Joseph Stepwise Journey Begins

The point is to simply demonstrate that Joseph, his father, who had multiple encounters with God by this point, and all of his brothers believed in God and his power. Armed with that knowledge, Joseph could begin the stepwise journey. Joseph is the best example of the stages and levels, as well as of the tests at each level, related to a stepwise journey.

I often say that Joseph must have translated the two dreams in similar context to the way that his father and brothers translated them. They all seemed to think that the scope was limited to the family bowing to Joseph. Since the first one began with them all working on their father's farm, they would seemingly have no reason to change the context to one outside of the farm.

Since the family was not filled with celestial bodies: stars, sun, and moon respectively, then there was no reason to relate the dreams to a galaxy far, far away. Finally, Joseph never protested when they asked, "Are we all to come to bow down before you?" He must have felt the tension in the room when they asked him about the meaning of his dreams.

Joseph was just beginning level one of his journey at age seventeen. Ultimately, the stepwise progression would take him far, far away from the farm and Dad's house. Well at least it would take him, via Midianite

---

25. Gen 37:5–11.

slave traders' caravan, down to Egypt. The experience would also have many steps and trials at each level.

God Tested Joseph

The Bible says in the book of Psalms 105:18-20 that Joseph's brothers bruised his feet by placing them in the irons of slavery, and placed his neck in a collar. Then it states that God tested Joseph many times and through many stages, until the time came for God to fulfill and manifest his dreams. Once the time of manifestation had arrived, the king of Egypt personally set him free to fulfill his purpose.

He experienced the murderous hatred of his brothers at level one. He was tested by surviving the fall into the pit and climbing back out of it, albeit with assistance, only to be sold into slavery. In Genesis 42:21-22, when the brothers unwittingly meet Joseph many years later in Egypt after he had been promoted to prime minister, they were in fear for their lives because of what Joseph was saying to them. Though, it was being said through a translator so as not to reveal Joseph's true identity.

Reuben said that we are obviously being punished for what we did to Joseph years ago. We heard him as he begged for mercy in anguish, yet we would not listen to him. Now we are in big trouble, and being punished by God for what we did to Joseph.

By this point, Joseph had passed his final stage in the preparation process and graduated into his promised land. At this point, the brothers had already bowed down to Joseph, in deference to his position and authority. They did this because Joseph was the only one in the region with food to sell. Their metaphorical—and actual—lack of bundles of wheat certainly bowed down to Joseph. Why? Basically because they had no wheat and Joseph had plenty.

By now, Joseph had passed all of the tests while still in the land of the Hebrews, i.e., Canaan. He then graduated to be sold as a slave in Potiphar's house where he would face challenges related to the administration, managing, and leading of Potiphar's household staff. He would also face tests of betrayal and lies coming from Lady Potiphar.

He graduated from there to jail, while averting death for the second time. He spent two plus years in jail and faced trials of patience and abandonment. However, he was again promoted to another, his third so far, position of leadership. He also had the opportunity to put his faith in

God to the test in a tangible way. This occurred when Joseph offered to translate dreams for his charges from Pharaoh's household staff: the baker and the butler.

Joseph's Final Semester & Comprehensive Exams

Once he finally graduated prison, he faced one final stage and one final set of tests. He had to put all of the knowledge, skills, and, most of all, faith into practice as he stood before Pharaoh. Joseph was the only man who could effectively handle "God's business" dream interpretation in this instance, for Pharaoh.

He would come to do this by translating Pharaoh's troubling dreams that were sent from a God who Pharaoh did not know. Joseph was the only one in the kingdom who could transact such a translation. This is because Joseph was the only one in the kingdom of Egypt who knew God and the only one who could translate God-given dreams.

He would also get to use the other skill sets that he developed as an administrator, manager, and leader at each previous step. Now he was fully dependent on God as he was promoted from prisoner to the penultimate leader of the entire kingdom of Egypt.

Only Pharaoh, who gave him the authority, recognized that he was gifted, graced, and anointed by God to lead and translate God-given dreams. Only Pharaoh outranked him in Egypt. Everyone else had to bow down to Joseph.

The larger point is that he was now ready for everything that God had actually called him to thirteen years prior, when Joseph had two dreams. This all occurred because Joseph, first, believed that the God of the dreams existed. It also occurred because that God, the God of the dreams, was faithful enough to make everything that he reveals to his chosen come to pass.

JOB BELIEVES

Job believed that God is, I *am*, and for that, he earned the respect and confidence of the God in whom he believed. Job was blameless and a man who feared God. Job's kids were a bunch of partiers, but Job was a man of faith and complete integrity. After these parties that were thrown by his children, Job would purify his children before God as a regular habit, lest they committed some sins, unwittingly.[26]

Then Job would face his first, ever-so-severe test on the first step. The enemy asked God for permission to test Job by stripping him of all earthly wealth. The enemy thought, and told God, "Surely if you remove your wall of protection from him and allow me to strip him of all of his earthly wealth, then he will curse your name." God said, "Do what you want, but do not touch his life, and he will never curse the one in whom he believes."

Recommended for Testing

God knew Job as a man of faith and integrity. God knew his heart so well that he knew that no matter what the enemy threw at him, Job would never curse his God. He recommended Job for testing at this first level.[27] Job's journey began long before the book of Job starts to chronicle the tests and persecutions inflicted on him by the enemy at the Lord's recommendation.

Job began to walk with God, learn of him, and to develop an unshakable dependence on God. We have discussed the fact that you cannot take the first step with God, on any journey, without having faith in God. Faith tells you that God will protect you, and it tells you that God will provide the manifestations of everything that he has promised to do for you.[28]

Job had walked a long way with God already. Job had developed his faith in God, which can only begin if you believe that God exists. Job had passed enough tests and graduated to enough advanced levels that he earned the respect and confidence of his God—so much so that God recommended Job for this test. This was a test, which included stripping

---

26. Job 1:1–5.
27. Job 1–2.
28. Rom 4:21; Phil 2:13.

Job of all that he knew God had provided for him. He simply said, "The Lord gives and the Lord—only—takes away." So I will bless that Lord for whatever he sees fit to allow to occur in my life,[29] even the loss of my wealth and children.

But the enemy was not finished testing Job in order to effectively try to strip him of the dependency which he had developed on God. He came to God again, sneaking in among the angels.[30] He informed God, "If you let me afflict him with all manner of illness, and if you allow me to strip him of his health, then he will definitely lose faith in you and curse you to your face."

God knew Job. He said, "Do what you will, short of killing Job. He will never curse or betray me." Job's wife and three best friends lost confidence in him. The enemy could obviously enlist allies, and he did so in these people. The wife told him, "Curse God and die already."[31] Job replied that he would not curse God. Then he said that she spoke as one of the foolish women—whoever they were.

Job Questions God's Logic

However, he would continue to question God's logic relative to why he would allow such calamity to befall his life. Job's querying of God's logic and intellect continued during Job's replies to his accusatory friends until God was ready to begin his retort to Job's questioning (Job 38:1). Throughout the previous chapters, beginning in chapter two, Job's friends said that he must have done something wrong. They accused him of the very thing that he used to cover his children for: a sin of omission. They accused Job of doing something against the God in whom Job so fervently believed.

At one point, Job said that even if it caused God to kill him, he would have his say. He would question God why he had allowed these horrific things to happen to him. He knew that he did not commit any sin.[32]

---

29. Job 1:21; Hab 3:17–19.
30. Job 2:1–10.
31. Job 2:9–10.
32. Job 13:15.

Send Him a Lady Boaz

Through it all, Job never lost faith. Job never forgot all that he had learned, in spite of the severe nature of this test on what must have been his final step toward the manifestation of God's promises and plan for Job's life.

See, Job's calling and purpose was not to get rich, nor was it to have God send him a spouse. I hear that one a lot, in churches, particularly from some of those aforementioned folks who want to get married. "God is going to send me my Boaz."[33] Now I know where those "foolish women" do their speaking.

This imaginary Boaz is probably driving the confused person's Cadillac. Brother Boaz is coming to pick her up and drive her to her mansion, this mansion, which is on the DC side of Warrenton, is filled with all of the requisite money to pay off all of her exorbitant credit card bills. That was not Job's calling—ain't likely theirs either.

The truth is that God had already blessed Job with a wife, kids, and wealth untold, all because Job, previously and consistently, walked with God. He had walked with God so closely, and with such integrity, for such a long time. He passed every test and graduated to each new level, such that God himself recommended Job for testing when Job reached the final step.

A Man of Complete Integrity

God stated, "This is a man of complete integrity,[34] one who is totally dedicated to me and not to his fleshly desires. Job is a man who would never curse me, no matter what you do to him or allow to occur in his life. Come what may, Job will stand strong in his faith."

God simply did not want to allow the enemy to take Job's life. Obviously, that would have ended the testing period. It would have also stopped the progress, journey, and ability for Job to demonstrate his faithful integrity.

At this final step, the testing was designed to take Job to a new, exemplary level for all who came after him to use as an example, relative to integrity and to the necessary elements for developing a faith walk. This faith walk demonstrates where a man can lose himself and his desires in

---

33. Ruth 2–4.
34. Job 1:8, 2:3.

God, where he can dedicate himself to the God in whom he believes and depends on for everything.

The Objective of the Pop Quiz

Graduation day for Job came after God gave him one really long pop quiz. It was an open book pop quiz where the answers were obvious.[35] God was not testing Job's knowledge base regarding the creation account rendered in Genesis (1–3).

The objective of the quiz was to show Job that he had, thus far, done very well to develop his faith in God. The quiz also demonstrated how far Job walked in lockstep with God, keeping pace throughout. However, he had not yet learned that Yahweh was sovereign.

If Yahweh decides to allow the enemy to test you, no matter how faithful you are, how well you think you know God, or how dependent on and dedicated to God you are, God does as he will. You must always humbly submit—that is, if you want to enter your true promised land of "Was Not."

If you believe that he is, or that he exists, then you must always live a life that is submitted to God, a life submitted to his time-frames, his plans and purposes, permitted tests and trials, steps and stages, and, finally, to his ultimate and overarching purpose for your life. You must submit, knowing that if this trial, in Job's case, is occurring, then God has a predominant and overarching plan and purpose.

You must realize that I am simply an actor in the play. He is the director, the choreographer, and the orchestra conductor. He can do as he pleases.[36]

Where Were You When?

God asked Job a chapter-long series of "Where were you when" questions, as a part of this pop quiz. "If the answer to each of my questions is you were not present, then I do not have to answer to you regarding any of my divine decisions, relative to why I allowed bad things to occur in your life when I had never permitted them prior to this testing season.

---

35. Job 38–42.
36. Ps 115:3.

You, Job, are not the boss of me. I AM the boss of you, and I do as I will, so do not question my ways and thoughts which are infinitely higher than your finite ways and thoughts."[37]

God's Purpose Revealed

Job, having had the mic dropped on him, for four plus chapters worth of God lecturing him, Father to son, could do nothing but acquiesce and repent. He submitted to God in one final act of humble contrition.

Then God restored him. God restored to Job twice as much of everything that God had allowed to be taken away. Now God's purpose had been revealed to Job. God is sovereign.[38]

Job believed in God. Job knew God very well. Job had developed a dependence on God. However, Job, though he was a man of complete integrity, needed to learn one last thing about God so he could serve as an example for all time.

---

37. Ps 103:11.
38. 1 Chr 29:11–12; Prov 16:9; Job 42:2; Isa 50:4; Rom 9:18–21; Eph 1:11–12.

4

Step Two: Pleasing God

THE MARKETING COMPONENT: A STEPWISE SETUP

As I mentioned in an earlier chapter of this book, when I finished my master's degree, Doc wanted me to go directly into a doctoral program. In a way, I wished things had gone the way he suggested. However, I learned that God had everything choreographed, orchestrated, and laid out exactly as it pleased him and his grand, overarching plan and purpose. In short, he set me up from the beginning.

I was not the best undergrad ever to hit a college campus. This wasn't because I was not fully capable of handling the work; I was more than capable. However, that was a time that I really needed to fully commit my life to the Lord. As it turns out, a few years before I "upslid," as my mother deemed my commitment process,[1] I was confused, fighting things in my heart and head and losing the battle. Thus, my work and focus suffered terribly.

That was one of my primary motivations for becoming an academic advisor, particularly for generally, as well as academically, at-risk college students. It drove me to the business that I have chosen, and that I was chosen for. It served as the impetus for the birth of the dream (more on that in step three).

---

1. Rom 10:9–10, 12:1.

I entered undergrad as a marketing major. Primarily because one of those career exploration tests told me that's what I was good at, or that was the major which my test results demonstrated most closely fit my personality. Much later, in grad school, I learned to give and score those tests while simultaneously becoming fascinated with some of them. I also learned that psychological personality typology and career exploration tests, without the proper corresponding, and godly counsel and advice, can be dangerous for the test-taker. I was definitely appointed to major in marketing, but I did not really like certain parts of it, nor did I assimilate and integrate into all of it as well as I should and could have with proper guidance.

Fast forward to learning that I could get an advanced degree in the only thing that I was good at ("college people") and then work in that field (college student development) for the next step of my career. When I found out that I could get a degree in this field, I was elated to pursue higher education.

By this point in my life, I had also dedicated my life to the Lord, so his purpose and calling began to come into focus for me. Albeit, the dream, vision or Chazown in Hebrew, remained in the distance for me.[2] Well, at least I had a dream, like Joseph. Though also like Joseph, I probably misinterpreted parts of the dream.

When my master's degree was completed, I continued the process of looking for my first job. I looked at universities that had the doctoral programs which I thought I would be interested in pursuing while also working there. Hopefully they would be within the field of at-risk student advising and developmental education.

The reason that I eventually finished my undergraduate program in marketing was primarily because I had gone too far in the program and did not want to turn to a new major. Also, I had no idea what else to pursue as a major and subsequent career path. I just knew that a direct route into marketing did not quite fit. But now I had a marketing undergrad degree and a higher ed advanced degree.

Marketing was cool, in parts. But I did not like the criminal side of it, even before I started pursuing a relationship with God in earnest. They kind of taught us how to go into competitors' stores and find out what they were selling, at what price, then come back and, shall we say, adjust our marketing strategies. Part of me loved the nefarious nature of the

---

2. Strong's Concordance, "Chazown." http://www.htmlbible.com/sacrednamebiblecom/kjvstrongs/STRHEB25.htm#S2585. Prov 29:18.

business. I like to fight and win. The other part of me was uncomfortable with something. There was something elusive about it that did not sit well with me.

Later, I learned what that was. It was a principle that has guided me through my career in higher ed and throughout my life. I learned two things, actually. The first one became one of my little sayings that I call, "Earlisms." That one states that, "I cannot sell it if I do not believe in the product." However, "if I believe in the product, I can easily sell it." I had the gifted ability for persuasion, after all. I was learning that God would, in a stepwise-progressive manner, bring together and use all of these things for his kingdom at a later time.

I CAN SELL ANYTHING . . . IF I BELIEVE IN THE PRODUCT

I had to believe that the product would be good for people and that it was good in an overall sense. I could not, for example, work for a tobacco company. I am not mad at you if you do, but it was not something that I could become passionate about selling to others. During my first professional position working in a certain college, I learned that some of my students, the ones who matriculated from certain demographic backgrounds, those students generally like to work with their hearts.

In other words, they needed to find a larger purpose in the work, a purpose that they could see and get behind to employ their acumen to the advancement of a good cause, which I believe will lead to the fulfillment of a defined, altruistic, and positive outcome. In short, those students, without knowing it, liked to live and work on purpose. So did I.

Thus, I could sell a university, particularly one where I was assigned to work. I would often do this for a university before God would be ready to move me on to my next step. When it was time to move me to the next step, God liked to use what I have come to call, "the scorched earth policy." He sanctifies the ground behind me in order to seal in me what I have learned before graduating. Then he burns the previous ground beyond recognition so that I never want to go or look back, like Lot's wife.[3]

---

3. Gen 19:26.

I Met My Match

Now, back to marketing and my next proposed step at a university with a doctoral program: one that had a job that would both capture my attention and help me to fulfill the dream, as I understood it. I largely remain in a state where I am perpetually attempting to fix the test before I take it. Another way of saying that is that I am always trying to beat the system. Sadly, I am usually successful. However, I met my match in God when he took me to this final step.

God created a series of tests, tests complete with concurrently occurring trials so confounding that none of my tricks, and all of my applied intellect, would allow me to wiggle, walk, or talk my way out of the situation. At least not until God declared that the time of testing was fully complete. Yet, in the end, I had finally found a job that included academic advising and teaching.

This university did not have a suitable doctoral program. However, it was in the region of the country where I wanted to live. It was located to the south of Pennsylvania, below the Mason Dixon Line. I was all in. Also, God began another habit as it relates to dreams.

Improved Hearing

As an aside, you can improve your ability to hear and understand the voice of God by spending more time reading his word. It familiarizes you with his voice, what he says, and how he says things. That's free of charge. The rest of this book costs money.

He told me, while I actually attended two interviews at two different universities, which were located about an hour's drive apart, God told me that the second interview and location was the job that I would end up taking.

Later, he would show me many other things of this sort. God would reveal many things relative to other parts of his overarching purpose for my life. I just knew in my spirit that this was the place.

Advising & Teaching

One other slight drawback, at least according to me, was that, although they wanted me to advise and teach courses, I would not end up teaching courses related to academic advising, as I had originally desired. Nor did they allow me to teach the course that I "thought" was most aptly suited for my perceived skills and abilities. This course involved those aforementioned personality tests.

When I accepted the job, I started working as the underling chief digi-brain at this university for the penultimate queen digi-brain of this particular fiefdom. However, when I arrived to work there, they told me that they wanted me to take over a new position for them. This position did not only include advising students, but it also included advising their academically at-risk student population. Can you hear the trumpets? Can you say dream? Can you say purpose and manifestation?

This additional responsibility was not in the job description, as such. I believe that I still have that original job description somewhere—probably where I used to keep my college degrees, in that backpack in my closet. Anyway, I did not learn of this additional, but welcomed, responsibility until I got there and had signed the contract. Can you say test, setup, and stepwise?

Because that's what it was. It was all a part of his orchestrated and unfolding plan. Needless to say, I did very well in that end of my job. However, the academically at-risk advising area of my job made me fight a good fight,[4] a fight that would allow God to invoke the "Scorched Earth Policy" for a second time. All of this was designed and perfectly choreographed to push me to the next step.

This job, as I mentioned, also came with teaching responsibilities, which is what I wanted. It was what Doc had groomed me for. So, again, I was all in.

However, they wanted me to teach two regular curriculum, three-credit, academic-based courses—not the one that I thought I was best suited for. They wanted me to teach marketing. What?

I did not like or love Marketing whatsoever. I liked parts, and it had been a few years since I studied it. Even then, it was only as an undergrad.

---

4. 1 Tim 6:12.

I Couldn't Teach Marketing, Could I?

Undergrad learning is very different from the more decidedly-focused coursework taken in graduate school. I could not teach marketing, could I? My advanced degree background is in higher ed, college people psych development, and administrative leadership, man. Clearly, I had been set up by the Good Master Teacher.

However, I had signed the contract. So I observed marketing classes during my first semester. It was teaching, which I had done precious little of in grad school. I definitely hadn't taught a full three-credit course or two, although teaching was my dream. I am not one to become intimidated nor do I experience recriminating self-doubt very often at all.

"No mistakes, no regrets." (That is another Earlism philosophy.) I have always been that way. However, this was tough and different. Also, I had to step into a spotlight—one that I did not and would not shine on myself. I like to control the spotlights that shine on me.

I Hated it

I hated that first semester. I was not perfect at it, and I liked to be and was usually capable of being perfect at things when I applied myself. I explained that in another book, including my mother's warning. Again, I am who I am. I know what I am good at and I fix the system. I cheat the test, so I can preset the outcome. Also, when given the choice, I "stick to the rivers and lakes" that I am used to.[5]

God is Testing and Preparing You

As I got older and developed a dependency on God for everything, I learned a lot about myself. I discovered what he called me to do, and how to proceed toward his light. Where in my cavalier past, I struggled to proceed toward that light in my own strength. Thus, all of my life, I had achieved varying and disparate measures of success. However, with age and dependence came wisdom and understanding.

My Aunt Bernie, my mother's youngest sister, was so proud. She was also a wonderful human being. She would talk to me and listen to me, and argue with me. Well, I did *all* of the arguing, fussing, and yelling. She

---

5. TLC, "Waterfalls," https://genius.com/Tlc-waterfalls-lyrics.

would just tell me, "God is making, testing, and preparing you." I would reply, "Making me what? Making me mad?"

Another friend always says to me, "I cannot believe that you talk to God like that." I have always asked questions of God. I guess there is a lot of Job in me.

I love and respect him, easily more than life itself. However, if he did not want me to say it or ask, he would stop me. Trust me. Yes, I have had to endure many arduously painful, "Were you there, when . . .?," sovereignty meetings with God, as did my friend Job.

I would ask God, "Why in the world do you have to test and prepare me like this? Does this stuff have to be this difficult? Why not just tell me how to do it, tell me what to do, and then let me go do what you have told me? What is the use or significance of the preparing and testing? How does that stuff help? Seems to slow things down, to me (in case he was wondering)." I enjoyed my comfort zones that related to and fit themselves nicely into my perfectionist nature.

But I suffered through it, learning obedience all along the way. I can't, to this day, believe that my aunt and godmother, though she rarely referred to herself as my godmother (she thought aunt was the higher calling), put up with me. And so patiently. I can be a handful—like King David going after Nabal.[6] It amazes me to this day. All she would say was, "God is making you, preparing you, and testing you."

I could not understand the purpose to a test and preparation. My question was always, "God, why in the world would this have to be this hard? Can't you just make me into 'that?' And then I will be good at 'that' too?"

Yep, I was questioning his logic just like Job. He is as patient with us, while we wander in the wilderness, as he was with the children of Israel. The forty years were all their fault. It was a forty-day trip, less than a triple fortnight.

I would later come to love teaching as a professor and teaching marketing. It definitely took a few years and a few—barely noticeable to anyone but me—stumbles. I attempted to use all of my tried and true tricks. Basically, this meant that I would completely memorize everything and then go from there. But, a call to teaching requires multiple skill sets all operating at the same time. I call it "symphonic listening."

---

6. 1 Sam 25.

Teaching requires skills far beyond rote memory, as well as an untested ability to relate to students in a classroom setting. I longed for the comfort of the advising side of my job during that first semester spent in the classroom. However, I had become a lot better at the job relatively quickly.

Yet, it was arduous for me. I had to do something that I was not perfect at doing, nor could I perfect this skill quickly. God was testing me and orchestrating things for the next step, all while eventually guiding, testing, and preparing me for the promised land of "Was Not."

Why, God?

My question was: why would God do that to me? What did I ever do to him to make him seemingly turn his back on me in that manner?[7] He threw me to the wolves and intentionally put me in a position where I had to endure suffering, in order to learn obedience. He made me perfect a skill set that I only passively or secondarily desired, yet it was a skill set that everyone else embraced.

Apple Grinders

I resented those who called me a professor, to the diminishment of my supposed true skill and calling: advising at-risk college people. They just passed right over that to focus on the "He's a Professor." That, secondary, title of mine made them feel proud. Then they started bringing me marketing ideas which I would later come to refer to as "apple grinders."

I would tell other people; "I will give them ten dollars to get that apple grinder off of my desk." I learned to use my marketing skill sets and acumen, though I obtained them and was gifted them by God, begrudgingly. In all, it was a part of the grand plan and purpose of the Good Master Teacher.[8]

---

7. Ps 22:1–2; Isa 55:3; Matt 27:46.
8. Matt 10:24; Luke 18:18.

Did It?

He allowed me to suffer through those things, as well as many others, so he could take all of the seemingly disparate pieces and bring all of them together at his appointed time. God did this such that when I had passed the final tests and graduated to the purposeful land of "Was Not," I would be fully prepared. I would have all of the necessary sharpened arrows available to me in my quiver. My issue was that it seemed like it pleased him to watch me suffer. Did it?[9]

DOES OUR SUFFERING PLEASE GOD?

All of the items will be discussed, in terms of how this symphonic principle relates to the succeeding steps. But, for now, we will focus on the last portion of that header statement and answer the question, "Does our suffering please God?"

Blind Faith & Submission to His Perfectly Unclear Will

We know that without faith it is impossible to please God. We learned that from one of our main characters, Enoch, as is stated in Hebrews 11:5–6. It is written that Enoch, before he was taken to the promised land of "Was Not," had earned the reputation as someone who pleased God. Thus, it is impossible to say that Enoch did not have great faith.

For three hundred years, while walking with God, Enoch must have suffered a great many things. Did he suffer these things while proceeding through every test, trial, tribulation, faced at every level and step? I believe that I can state those answers as fact, with reasonable certainty.

How so? Because the Bible says, in Isaiah 53:10–12, that it "pleased" the Lord to crush, bruise, test, try, and put through tribulation his only begotten son. His son was willing to make himself into a final sin offering for all of us. This was the ultimate and last test taken on the final step for Christ, just before he would ultimately die, be raised, and be seated at the right hand of the Father.[10]

That passage goes on to say that God saw the anguish that Christ, who is both God and man, experienced in his mortal soul. However, God

---

9. Isa 53:10; Col 1:19.
10. Rom 8:34; Eph 1:20–21.

also knew and orchestrated, even for his son, steps, tests, and graduations that were synchronously designed to "save many" through the earthly work and ministry of Christ.

God knew and orchestrated everything leading up to Christ's birth. He did the same relative to every occurrence that transpired throughout his son's earthly life. God knew that this was the only way that Christ could bear the iniquities of the whole world for all time.[11]

Verse twelve concludes the discussion about Christ's suffering that pleased God by stating that he will receive the honors accorded to the victorious general after winning a war. This, because he bore all mankind's sins, those who are friend, foe, and rebel alike.

It Pleases God to Try Our Faith

Thus, we can conclude that it pleases God to try our faith, in order for us to, eventually, be used by God to "save many." However, in order to get there, as did Christ, Enoch, and many others—and to pass the final steps to graduation—we have to endure suffering obediently until we reach the reward.

STEPHEN, THE DEACON, PLEASED GOD

Stephen, the deacon of the early church in Jerusalem, who is spoken of in the book of the Acts of the Apostles, is discussed briefly in Acts (6:1–8:2). He merits two chapters to tell his story. But at the end of his story, he was blessed to see the glory of God.

He also saw that God was very pleased with his heart, his faith, and with his submission to the Holy Spirit. The Holy Spirit enabled Stephen to preach God's word and to prophesy to the people of Israel, much as Enoch did centuries prior to Stephen's birth. At the very moment when Stephen saw God's glory, the people of Jerusalem would seize and stone him to death.

Yet, through Stephen's life and work, God demonstrated how pleased he was with those who obeyed his voice and walked with him on the journey to "Was Not": a journey that he has purposed and destined for each and every one of us. God showed all of us, through Stephen, that he was so pleased with Stephen's heart that he revealed to us that

---

11. Isa 53:11–12.

Christ gave Stephen a standing ovation, in appreciation and adulation, for his act of blind faith and submission to the complete purpose of God.[12] Stephen was even willing to submit to being stoned to death for the sake of Christ's good news.

Select Seven Deacons

The church in Jerusalem grew rapidly as the Bible reports that even many Jewish priests were converted to become believers and followers of Jesus Christ as the Messiah.[13] As the church grew, the demands to serve and manage the affairs of the parishioners began to mount.

The Apostles of Jesus Christ were the only ones in the church, commissioned at that time, to serve in a leadership capacity. So the people brought their issues and needs to the disciples. They however stated that they could not take time away from studying and preaching the word of God in order to serve and minister to the daily needs of the people.

They instructed the people to select from, among themselves, seven men who were full of faith and the Holy Spirit to serve as deacons. These men would become servant leaders among the people and be designated by the apostles to minister to the daily needs of the people.[14] Stephen was among the seven men chosen.

Based on the instructions given by the apostles to the people, these seven men, in particular, had demonstrated that their walk with Christ had begun in earnest. All of these men were "well-respected, full of wisdom, fully tested, and full of the Holy Spirit."[15] This suggestion pleased the people. Thus, they began the selection process from among those who met these qualifications. Obviously, all seven had already taken their first few steps walking with Jesus.

These deacons had all engaged their stepwise-dependent journey to "Was Not." They were also well-tested and had demonstrated godly wisdom, as well as a developed and dependent relationship with the Holy Spirit. They had all been tested by God, in addition to having graduated through a few steps. All of this occurred during the still foundational season of the church which began in Jerusalem.

12. Acts 7:54–60.
13. Acts 6:7.
14. Acts 6:1–7.
15. Acts 6:3.

Among the group of seven, Stephen drew specific and noteworthy attention for his faith, faithfulness, meritorious service, and walk with God. The Bible mentions Stephen first among those named as the first church deacons. It says that Stephen was a man who was full of faith and of the Holy Spirit.[16] It goes on to list the other men selected to become deacons, including Phillip, who would perform many miraculous acts under the power of the Holy Spirit.

A Standing Ovation

However, Stephen's acts would not only draw plaudits from among those in the church, but he would ultimately merit a standing ovation from Christ. Stephen and the other believers continued to attend synagogue as Jewish believers in Jerusalem. One day, Stephen was in the Synagogue of Freed Slaves, as it was called. He was discussing Jesus his Messiah with some of the others present on that day.

Stephen was well-known among his church brethren in Jerusalem, as well as among those in the Jerusalem synagogues, as a man who was full of God's grace and full of the power of God. Under this power and authority, Stephen performed many amazing miracles, other signs, and wonders in the name of Christ by the power of the Holy Spirit among the people.[17]

Similar to the stories of Joseph and Job, some of the people conspired against (and lied about) Stephen in order to get him arrested. This is another sign that demonstrates that Stephen was well on his way to "Was Not." The signs and wonders demonstrate the same authority and developed dependence that Joseph displayed in slavery and in prison, while translating dreams and leading men under the power of God.

In order to see the manifestation of the Spirit, you have to have walked with God and taken a few steps. You are also required to graduate from a few former steps while passing all required tests. The Holy Spirit, by intent, plans to work seamlessly in and through your life. The Bible discusses this phenomenon as having occurred within Stephen and Joseph, in particular.

---

16. Acts 6:5.
17. Acts 6:8.

Trumped Up Charges

The people in Jerusalem lied and got Stephen arrested for "blaspheming against Moses." They were trumped up charges, or "fake news," just as occurred with Joseph and Lady Potiphar. The misguided temple guards should have let Stephen go immediately instead of taking him before the Jewish High Council of the Sanhedrin. The Bible states that Stephen's face became as bright as an angel's face as the members of the Sanhedrin High Council stared at him.[18]

Does this scene sound similar to something that happened with Moses when he too encountered the very presence of God?[19] (Yes, the same Moses the lawgiver that they accused Stephen of blaspheming against.) Was it serendipity or an intentional plan and confirmation from God?

The high priest and the other members should have gotten off of the bus, right then and there. But, no, they pressed the issue. The high priest asked Stephen, with his face glowing like the face of an angel, if these accusations and lies were true. Stephen, with all due respect for his Jewish brethren and for his "fathers" on the High Council, went on to chronicle the long history of the patriarchs of the faith.

He started with Abraham. He went on to discuss Joseph, Jacob, Moses, David, and King Solomon as well as the promises that God had fulfilled for the Hebrew people. He also discussed how they treated these patriarchs of the faith.[20]

Then he cut loose on them. He told them that they were liars, murderers, betrayers, and blasphemous persecutors of the prophets who foretold of Christ's coming long ago.[21] He called them men of uncircumcised hearts who resist and reject the Holy Spirit. He finished by telling them that they received the law by the decree of the heavenly angels. However, they did not choose to obey it.

Does this part of Stephen's message to the High Council not sound like the same message that God used Enoch to give to the people of his day? Right down to the thousands of angels?[22] Sadly, these were the same disobedient grumblers who were present with Enoch. Same fleshly acts,

---

18. Acts 6:8–15.
19. Exod 33:11, 34:29–34.
20. Acts 7:1–53.
21. Acts 7:51–53.
22. Jude 1:14–1.

souls, and egos, anyway. But God had prepared and tested Enoch for his final step to "Was Not," just as he did Stephen.

God tests us at each stage and step along the journey. Such that, in the moment when you are before men who want to kill you, you are fully and unwaveringly prepared. You are divinely tested, tried, and truly full of faith. You are completely ready to deliver God's Word exactly as God puts it in your heart while you all are walking together in fellowship, just as God did with Adam, Enoch, Abraham, Isaac, Jacob/Israel, Joseph, Job, Moses, and, yes, Stephen the deacon of the church of Jesus Christ.[23]

Graduating with High Distinction

Stephen graduated from his final step. He had passed all of the requisite tests, and he had met all other requirements for graduation. I would dare say that Stephen graduated with high distinction.

That is a designation which they bestow upon a doctoral candidate, along with a medallion, when that candidate merits the highest grade point average attainable, such as a 4.0 cumulative GPA on that same grading scale. This occurs after they have completed all of their degree requirements and are "hooded" by their dissertation chair or some other representative.

I am bisemously saying that Stephen had passed his final test. He successfully defended his dissertation. He did this in front of his Sanhedrin Dissertation High Council & Dissertation Committee and graduated to "Was Not." This occurred while Jesus was standing in front of his Seat at the Right hand of the throne of the Father, looking down on Stephen as Stephen was given the manifestation of a vision or Chazown.

While Christ was standing in ovation, Stephen saw his Lord and Savior standing in deference to Stephen's dissertation defense. This was Stephen's finest hour and final act as he graduated into "Was Not."

Stephen was subsequently stoned to death, yet not before one more selfless act completed in the name of the Lord. He asked God to forgive those who stoned him and not lay their sinful act to their heavenly charge, just as Jesus did on the cross.[24] Wow.

---

23. Gen 3:8–10.
24. Luke 23:34; Acts 7:54–60.

God Takes Pleasure in Our Pain & Suffering

How could a loving and merciful God full of grace be pleased by, or even stand in ovation, as a result of our suffering? Unfortunately, pastors, Christian counselors, and other trained and skilled people helpers hear this question all of the time in reference to death. The truth, with respect to God being pleased when we suffer, is a result of his sovereignty and our free-willed, obedient submission. It also occurs in deference to our demonstration of blind faith when it comes to submitting to God's will, plans, testing, steps, and determination to actualize the plans, purposes, and callings that the Father has placed on our lives.

Thus, what he is actually taking pleasure in is our unwavering determination to keep pace with God. This is much easier said than done irrespective of the step or level that you are on in your walk. Walking by faith with God requires a person, many times, to walk toward the bullets like a soldier, while receiving, by faith, all that God has promised them.

Most times you have to walk headlong into the dangerous situation. Like Stephen, make your stand, knowing exactly the result will be derived from calling the High Council, effectively, a "brood of vipers."[25] Stephen knew exactly what calling the priests and scribes out on their lack of integrity would result in for him. But what would make a man face his accusers full of faith?

What would motivate Joseph to have such a profound faith in, and reliance upon, his God that when Lady Potiphar tried to tempt him into an adulterous relationship, he simply stated that he could not sleep with her because it would cause him to sin against his God? He knew that she was the deceitfully dangerous, manipulative scoundrel and wife of the commanding general over Pharaoh's personal bodyguard, as well as the chief executioner. She was capable of lying if he slept with her or even if he did not. But Joseph's integrity won the day, come what may.[26] Not sinning against his God was of paramount importance to him.[27]

The same thing can be said about Job, as his best friends accused him of being a liar, and his wife said to him the very thing that the enemy thought he could be tempted into doing, the thing that prompted the

---

25. Matt 23:33; Heb 11:1.
26. Ps 26.
27. Gen 39.

enemy to ask God for permission to take a blow torch to every aspect of Job's life, short of killing him.[28]

Job's wife said that he should go ahead, "Curse God and die." Again, Job's unwavering devotion to his God won the day. Job proved God right, as always. The same goes for Enoch. I am certain that he was tested and tempted many days during his three-hundred-year walk with God. He obviously passed every test and graduated every level, as did Stephen, Job, and Joseph.

They all, including Stephen the deacon of the church, entered into "Was Not." It pleases God to see us persevere. It pleases him to see us pass every test, take every step with him, and demonstrate our unwavering dedication while we also fully submit ourselves to his perfect will, plan, and purpose for our life. God shows us that will in an early glimpse or foreshadowing of things to come, and then he takes us on the journey to discover its surpassing meaning.

---

28. Job 1–2.

5

Step Three: The Dream

REVELATIONS AND TIMING

IN ACCORD WITH, OR as a part deemed necessary by Elohim, my personal journey with God revealed things to me. These are things, for the purposes of this discourse, that I call steps. God would reveal each step to me, typically before I made it to the next level of training.

However, he would never involve himself in any discussion regarding time spent at each step, when I would graduate and move to the next level, what I would learn or had left to learn at the current stage, and what radical changes would occur in my life at the next step. He would simply show me, as I came to learn, what was a very unclear: Chazown, dream, vision, or the impression in my spirit.

That sounds a bit like muddled nonsense to some people, but that is how it always happened for me. I continue to repeat the phrase, "for me," because I do not want anyone to assume that the parameters of their journey with God will mirror mine or anyone else's personal journey.

All we know is that not only will God take, via his divine providence, at his appointed time, all of the pieces of my journey, but God will mix those seemingly disparate pieces together with the journeys of countless others. The enmeshing results of that test will come together at just the right time, for all of those who walk in submission to his will. He will also do it for those who do not walk in submission to his will.

The result is that we will all arrive exactly where, when, and how he predetermined for us to arrive. We will all do, submitted to his will or not, that which we were destined to do.[1]

Not Quite Divine Providence

I do not often use the term divine providence in this book because I believe it to be too general a term to fit the stepwise-dependent journey. It provides an overarching view of the fact that God is in charge of the universe. However, it does not drill down into the specifics that God is an interpersonal and intimate God who desires fellowship with each person. He wants to take a journey with each one of us in the ways that I previously described in this book.

When you zoom the picture out to a macro level, you see that God will take all of the parts of your journey and bring them together with the parts of everyone else's journey or life, irrespective of their walk, with or without God. That is where you begin to be able to successfully employ the actual definition of divine providence.

I want to focus on Enoch's Walk as well as your individual walk with God to "Was Not." Acknowledging that your walk will then be jointly fit together for you, and it will be connected with the walks of everyone else, because He is the Sovereign Lord of all.

For example, God used Joseph's journey specifically related to the intimacy of that journey with God. This included taking all of the pieces that he obtained, as well as the lessons learned at each stage and level of the journey. The lessons included different tests, passed at each level, in order to show that when God was ready, and when Joseph was fully tested and proven, God would bring the steps and tests together in order to save the entire kingdom of Egypt, as well as all of the surrounding countries.

That meant the entire kingdom of Egypt area, including Canaan, the home of Joseph's mom, dad, and brothers. Thus, they would all have to bow down to, and become dependent on, Joseph for leadership and food, just as his dreams revealed. At the same time, God was working on something different with Pharaoh. Pharaoh was also on a different time schedule relative to that of Joseph.

---

1. Ps 37:23.

At the perfect time, someone accused a baker and butler of committing some act, possibly of treason. Or maybe not. But, they accused these two guys of committing some crime against the king of Egypt. This act so infuriated Pharaoh that he threw both of their butts in his personal dungeon. Possibly until he could have his other investigative people figure out who committed the supposed criminal act against the king.

Pharaoh threw those two guys in the dungeon, around the same time that Joseph was being attacked by Lady Potiphar and was subsequently thrown in the same dungeon. This, as opposed to Joseph being executed.

Joseph would be placed in a dungeon that he would be placed in charge of by the warden. So those two prisoners, the baker and the butler, would fall under the care and leadership of the dream interpreter of "God's Business": Joseph. However, God was not finished displaying his mastery of timing and confluence of puzzle pieces.

By the time Joseph was thrown into the dungeon, he had already served as a lead administrator over two houses, and he had attracted the eye and become the object of desire of the lust-filled Lady Potiphar. Yet, Joseph had earned enough trust with her husband that he was not killed for the adultery accusation, as was the custom of the day.

When Joseph was placed in a leadership position at each stop, I believe that the only one not shocked by these promotions, amid chaos and bombs going off all over his life, was Joseph. You see, he had already had two dreams, which were revelations from God. They were divinely inspired dreams about becoming a leader.

The manifestation of these dreams may not have transpired in the way that he thought they would. I am going to definitively state that for the record, based on my own personal, and very painful at times, experiences. These dreams, in their final manifested state, looked nothing like Joseph thought they would when he had them at age seventeen.[2] However, he knew that he had an anointing to lead people and manage things.

---

2. Gen 37.

STEP THREE: THE DREAM

WHEN I JUST *KNEW* THAT I "WAS NOT"

Previews of Coming Attractions

At times, and with some of us, God shows us some things in advance. Often, he desires to show us things. However, we are required to learn to listen and submit. Then he can reveal these desires through our developing intimacy with him in order to prepare us.

These revelations come to us via vision, dream, Chazown, or impression from God's word. We can read and listen to the Bible. We might get stuck on a specific spot or passage of scripture. In my case, one time, God had me reading Genesis (41) for what seemed an eternity. I did not find out until, actually just now, as I write this book, why I had to read that chapter so many times. God can also reveal things directly to us through the Holy Spirit. He can communicate directly with our spirit through visions, impressions, and dreams.

God would tell me things by impressions in my spirit, which is the best way to describe these revelations. He would show me a glimpse, or a blurry and out of focus snapshot, of things to come. Of course, I thought I had a twenty megapixel, 1080p full-length feature film of what was to come. So I thought.

In reality, this photo was quite lacking in focus and clarity, relative to the things soon coming in my life. Those things may have occurred on the next step, or possibly, as with Joseph, they may have been slated to happen on many succeeding steps. However, it was not until the final step, as a part of the final exam, that Joseph would clearly see and understand what the dreams actually revealed.[3]

These impressions, dreams, and visions must line up with the word of God. If they do not, they are, as my Pastor calls them, "pork chop dreams,"[4] meaning that they were based off of the fact that you ate something the previous day or night that you had no business eating.

So you had a dream that came from that culinary experience, an experience now requiring an antacid rather than a more in-depth explanation and clarification from God. However, if what you are experiencing is a divine revelation from God (Chazown), you will be able to find it in the word of God.

---

3. Gen 37:1–4, 5–11, 41, 42:6, 43:26, 44:14, 45:3–8, 47:11–12, 50:16–17, 18, 19–21.

4. Eccl 5:3.

Sowing in Tears

These impressions began very early in my walk with God. I remember God tricking me into saying or praying things that I would see manifested throughout my life, such as a gifting in an area of empathy.[5] The concept is derived from the Greek word used in the New Testament, paraclete.[6] It is also that which empowers the counseling and advising gift that operates in me.

I could feel the emotional distress that many people, whether in front of me, or if God decided to show me their face and pain. He would do this by impressing both their face and their pain in my spirit. I may be moved to cry deeply or sob heavily over these burdens and pains for these people.[7]

I had to learn, over time, what I was supposed to do with such experiences of empathy and burden. I had to learn when I could speak with the person, whose face I saw, about the impressions. I had to learn when I was supposed to simply pray, or when I should just cry and intercede for them in prayer, while never telling them what I knew. This all developed as I continued to walk with God.[8]

One of these times of painful intercession for a friend occurred during a Steelers playoff game. All I could say was, "Not now, God." However, not my will.[9] I was submitted, so I did my job. Thankfully, I was allowed to eventually return to the game, already in progress. And they won, but it was a close game. I missed like a quarter and a half.

Graduating Stepwise

I am discovering, while writing this book, that my steps seem to occur, change, elevate levels, and I graduate, during times spent at specific universities. I have been affiliated with many different universities, in various capacities, over the years. During each stop, generally speaking, I tend to graduate from step to step, concurrent with me changing professional positions.

5. John 14:16, 26, 15:26, 16:7, 13; 1 Cor 12:8; 1 John 2:1.
6. Wikipedia, "Paraclete," https://en.wikipedia.org/wiki/Paraclete#In_Christianity.
7. Ps 138:3; Isa 53:12; Jer 9:1, 18, 27:18; Rom 8:26–27, 34; 1 Tim 2:1; Heb 7:25; Rev 21:4.
8. 2 Kgs 4:27.
9. Luke 22:42.

Each level came with its distinctly corresponding tests. In his time, all of those steps and tests would come together to prepare me to take a new step. Usually, while I remained at the same university, and when I graduated to the next level, I would encounter new tests as I progressed on this stepwise journey.

Thus, I would not only graduate from college a few times on some of these steps, but I would graduate to the next step on the journey with God, headed toward "Was Not." These things would occur as I graduated from college degree program to college degree program. Additionally, these steps occurred as I changed work locations. At times, the degree programs overlapped with the jobs.

Thus, while I was on one step, in whatever capacity, God would show me a very specific kingdom, job, or academic degree program that I would ultimately obtain. As I mentioned, he would not show me any specific information that he was not yet ready to reveal. Some things I had to learn as we walked, just like Joseph and just like Elisha, in the book of 2 Kings (4:27).

God Shows Me What He Chooses & Only What He Chooses

Elisha was used many, many times to reveal things to other people. These were things that God first showed him. These were revelations fit for kings and common people alike.

One specific time, in 2 Kings 4:8–27, 28–37, God showed the prophet Elisha that a woman from Shunem would have a baby. Elisha, an itinerate prophet of God, used to stay with this family whenever he traveled through Shunem. She created a private room for him in her home.

This lady always wanted to have a baby. However, she could not have one. I will not blame the husband, as many of the errant ministers have done because ultimately, it was not his fault. When God was ready, apparently so was the hubby.

But the wife, the Shunamite woman as she was known, had her hopes dashed so many times, that she decided, on her own, to just forgo the dream of childbirth. She did this in an effort to avoid the experience of pain and disappointment over and over again. She let go of her faith.

Although, I believe that God had shown her, in the early stages when she began trying to become pregnant, that she was supposed to have a child. She just did not and would not have one until it was God's appointed time.

When Elisha initially informed her that she would have a child, she responded by requesting that he not get her hopes up. But sure enough, one year later, as the man of God said, she had conceived and given birth to a son.

A Few Years Later . . .

Fast forward a few years: the boy died on her lap after working the fields with dear old dad. Many suspect that he had a brain aneurysm, but no one knows for sure. Well, the woman from Shunem set out to find the man of God, Elisha. This was the man who had first overridden her wishes to remain unscathed in her emotions by not even considering the possibility of the manifestation of that Chazown, which God had first revealed to the woman from Shunem in the form of prophetic impression, dream, or vision.

She set out to find Elisha and tell him that he had to do something for her son. She felt that the fact that she never "asked" him for a son meant that God should not use Elisha to reveal his divine will to her. She was quite emotionally distressed, but she was also sadly mistaken. Job learned this little lesson, the hard way when Job was taught that God is sovereign.

She found Elisha at his home on Mt. Carmel, grabbed hold of his feet, and would not let go. She was in tears and obvious emotional pain. As I mentioned, when I feel those intercessory pains experienced by other people, they honestly feel like an elephant standing on my heart.

Elisha Had No Clue

This time, she was right there in front of Elisha, crying and holding his feet. However, Elisha had not received a revelation regarding this woman's pain. Thus, he had no idea why she was crying and in obvious emotional distress.

His servant Gehazi moved quickly to remove her from Elisha's feet. However, the prophet stopped his servant, mid action. He told Gehazi to "leave her alone, she is obviously in great pain. But God has not shown me what is troubling her so deeply."[10]

My Most Useful Verse of Scripture

I often use 2 Kings 4:27 to explain and demonstrate for people that God gives revelation when, where, how, and in what format he chooses. Our job is to ask him what to do with the revelation, and then wait for him to tell us.

The first thing out of the woman's mouth was, "Did I ask you to promise me a child? Didn't I tell you not to get my hopes up?" She did not need to finish. At that point, God showed Elisha exactly what happened.

Elisha gave Gehazi his staff and sent him to the Shunamite's house to lay that staff on the child. The woman had laid the dead child on Elisha's bed, at her home. She laid the child in the room that she and her husband kept for Elisha when he visited.

The Stick is Enough for God

Elisha knew the staff would resolve the issue, but the woman from Shunem was not satisfied with a stick. Even though she should have been.

She said I will not leave or let go of your feet until you come, personally, to my home and see about my dead child. Elisha went with her to the house. The staff did not work, primarily because the woman from Shunem did not believe that it would work. She unplugged from the power source. Elisha went into the room with the child, alone.

He raised the child from the dead and presented him back to his mother. The mother learned a valuable lesson about faith and sovereignty, one which she would later tell the king of Israel about. The experience also provided me with an often-used example about how and when God chooses to reveal information.[11]

---

10. 2 Kgs 4:27.
11. 2 Kgs 4:8–36, 8:1–6.

The Itinerant Man of God

God would go on, during our walk, to show me many other things. He would primarily, though not at all exclusively, reveal these things to me via impressions in my spirit. God shows me, as I transition from one step to the next, exactly what job he will give me, or whatever I may become involved with next.

However, he will not show me when a change will happen and how long a particular stay will last. I have had to learn to become an itinerant man of God, just like Elisha. That was to be my lot in life during these steps on the way to "Was Not."

The Three Moves Trick

Speaking of things that God "tricked" me into saying and praying: actually, in this case, an impression that He gave me long ago on step three or four. He told me the number of remaining moves that I would make, as a higher education professional lecturer and betimes chief of the digi-Brains. He told me, as I was leaving graduate school and prior to taking my first post-masters degree professional job that "you have three moves in you."

I knew, particularly by now, that this was God speaking to me, when He declared specifically that "you have three moves to make, before you are placed in one final location." That final location I would later come to know as "Was Not."

Go to Three Places That I Will Show You

Just as God told Abram to leave his family and go to a place that "I will show you,"[12] he also told Abram, after changing his name to Abraham, to go to a mountain in Moriah, that "I will show you. When you arrive, offer your son Isaac as a sacrifice."[13]

Prior to the first "I will show you" relocation, Abram moved to Haran with his father and his family. The journey would yet to begin, in earnest, until Abram actually obeyed every part of the revelation.

---

12. Gen 12.
13. Gen 22.

Abram then moved from Haran to the place where God showed him. Later, he also learned that he was headed to the promised land of "Was Not." Abram did not experience this immediately upon entering Canaan. But the point is that God told him to leave. I AM will show you where you are going. However, in order to get there, you have to obey I AM completely. Similarly, he told me that I was going to move to different locations. More specifically, there were three moves involved.

I Failed to Ask

He failed, or more accurately, I failed, to factor in, or request more information regarding, how long I would be at each location. He did not tell me, and I had also failed to ask under what circumstances I would leave and be transitioned from one step to the next. Additionally, I neglected to ask how many Lady Potiphars, queens, kings, as well as penultimate queens and kings of the digi-brain fiefdoms would wash up on my shores at each location. This digi-brained nobility, at times, found my shores out of the clear blue. In retrospect, he would not have cleared up the picture for me. Not even if I had asked.

He also did not tell me where I would attend church, or if I would be married—and if I would be married, would that occur after move number one, two, or three? He most certainly did not tell me that I would become the most happily divorced man that I know during one of the steps.

A Vastly Incomplete Revelation Via Impression & The Half-Move

So many other things that I failed to request as additional information upon receiving the simple, yet vastly incomplete, revelation. Relative to the specific revelation, which stated that I had "three moves in me," he also did not tell me that I would experience what I called, until corrected, a "half move."

However, he did correct me, following the half move, and let me know that the so-called half move was actually one of the pop quizzes that I was required to pass in order to advance on my journey. We, as Abram also learned, are all required to complete all graduation requirements on each step. These must be completed prior to "Was Not." So, in reality, I still have that third move as well as "Was Not" yet to experience.

However, there were some things that God did reveal to and clarify for me. He showed me, a few years ago, regarding geographical location, specifically where I would work. This is how I would know that I was actually entering the promised land of "Was Not."

God did not have to clearly reveal that to me. He chose to do so based on his sovereignty, and I believe that it was also based on the intimacy, relative to the dependent relationship that he and I have developed over the course of this journey.

God Showed me exactly where I would make my final approach and land this plane. Of course, He also did not tell me what constitutes landing this plane in "Was Not." Nor did He tell me if there was another place, on the final Step, as I was nearing "Was Not."

A place that I would be rerouted (by my accounting) through just before I got to the final destination. I.e.; was there a "Through Place," or a few "Through Places," before I arrived at "New Place?" "New Place" which is also known as, "Was Not."

You Never Wanted to Be Normal

I have often lamented to God, "Why can't I be normal? Why can't I live a normal life and go to one place? Why can't I just do one thing? Why can't I do the thing that you have created, purposed, and trained me to do? And do that one thing, in one place?"

He will not reply, like my name is Job or something. He gives me a passive response, in a still, small voice which says, "You are not called to be 'normal.' Nor have you ever desired to be 'normal.' And those 'abnormal' desires in your heart, they come from me."[14] Thus, often pensively, I have resigned myself to the quote that says, "This is the business that I have chosen."[15] I am a peripatetic man of God.

Faith is Gleefully Stepping into the Unknown

One specific day when I asked that question, Elohim replied, "Enoch 'Was Not' normal. Normal does not produce or write this book. Only as a

---

14. 1 Kgs 19:11–12.

15. IMBD, "The Godfather: Part II: Quotes," https://www.imdb.com/title/tt0071562/quotes.

result of all of the things that I AM has allowed Jones to obediently suffer because I willingly took a flying leap and a huge step out in faith."

Could I AM give me the words to write in this book, the one before it, and all that will likely come after it? I AM gave me this verse which he allowed me to adapt:

> Now faith is gleefully stepping into the unknown without regard for your personal safety or security, because God said . . .[16]

Wonderful Revelations

You see, when God gives you these wonderful revelations, via whatever the means of transmission,[17] he, in part, uses them in concert with the desires that he places in your heart in order to drive you toward the manifestation of the revelation. He will use the desires imputed into your very being, via Chazown, as fuel motivating you to relentlessly pursue and chase the carrot dropped into your spirit until you reach "Was Not."[18]

Jones, A Slave of Jesus Christ

How else would you explain your insatiable desire to serve as a slave in and for the kingdom? "Slave" is actually what the word "minister" (in and for the kingdom) means.[19] You will go anywhere and do anything. However, sometimes you will do things on your own, amid misinterpreted translations of the revelation, to get there.

The only way to actually get there is to stay on target and keep walking. I have often wondered to myself why I am so very driven. Why am I so driven that I pray daily, hourly at times, so that God opens very specific doors?

I am relentlessly pursuing him and chasing the dream's manifestation, which will inevitably result in more work than I have ever done in my life. However, when I arrive at "Was Not," I will finally find a new peace and satisfaction, one yet to be accessed inside of myself. All because I submitted to begin the journey with God.

16. Heb 11:1 (adaptation).
17. 2 Cor 12:7.
18. Ps 37:4.
19. Rom 1:1; Gal 1:10; Titus 1:1; Jas 1:1; Jude 1:1.

Then I decided to gladly receive all requisite and corresponding revelations, impressions, visions, and dreams. I have determined in my heart to keep pace with God. I have decided to be obedient to his will and way until "Was Not" is attained.

Why do I do this? Because he uses the initial and the subsequent revelations, like dangling a carrot in front of a rabbit, as a means of placing an internal drive inside of us. This passion, compulsion, and drive inside of us says, "We must press toward the mark in order to attain the prize of the high calling on our lives."[20] Another way of saying this is:

> If you delightedly embrace the revelations that God writes upon your heart, those which He makes so attractive that you are willing to pursue through all obstacles, even though they encompass what you have come to understand as an incomplete picture of those awesome revelations . . .
>
> . . . then God will, as you continue to walk with Him, give you all of those things which He has previously placed in your heart as desires. And they will exceed your fondest yearnings when you receive them as you arrive in the Promised Land of "Was Not."[21]

ABRAHAM'S VISIONS

God chose to reveal things to Joseph through dreams. In concert with that gift, God also gave Joseph the ability to interpret dreams. Both would become relevant and useful gifts after many steps and tests had passed. Particularly when the time came for Joseph to use them to help God "save many."[22] God chose to speak to Abraham using visions and personal encounters. During these interpersonal encounters, God would directly relay his word to Abraham.

We are going to take a look at all of the distinct occasions where Abraham encountered a revelation from God similar to Joseph's dreams, all of which told of the things to come in Abraham's life. The revelations came to provide direction for Abraham telling him where to go and what to do.

---

20. Phil 3:12–14, 15–16.
21. Ps 37:4; Eph 3:20; 2 Pet 1:4 (adaptation).
22. Gen 41–50.

The first time that God spoke to Abram, he spoke directly to him. In Genesis 12:1–3, God spoke to Abram. Abram responded by taking his first step. Prior to this conversation, in Genesis 11:31–32, the Bible speaks of Abram's father Terah as the one who initially had some impetus to go to Canaan.

When something impressed Terah to go to Canaan, he took Abram, Lot, his grandson, his deceased son, Haran, Abram's wife, Sarai, and Terah's daughter from another mother with him. This family group moved from Ur of the Chaldees to Haran.

As I mentioned, Terah was also headed for Canaan, although the Bible does not specify why he wanted to relocate the family. It may have been God, and likely was. It certainly was not the idols that Terah worshipped.[23]

However, we do not know exactly why Terah was motivated to relocate the family to Canaan. It is simply stated that Terah took his offspring, except for his son Nahor, and moved from Ur. However, they only got as far as Haran. It is said that Ur of the Chaldees was modern day Iraq and Haran was located in what is now known as Syria.

Whatever the reason, Terah was headed to Canaan via Haran, which was actually northwest of where some believe Ur of the Chaldeans was located. This was as opposed to going southwest to Canaan, which is where he was planning to ultimately relocate. He made a pitstop in Haran. And there, in Haran, he settled and eventually died.[24]

Abram was directly told by God to leave the native land of: your relatives, your extended family relatives, your father's offspring and go to a place that I will show you. As I mentioned, this was the first step in Abraham's journey. Abram left right away. If he and his father were both listening to the Lord, then by this account, Abram obeyed immediately, albeit partially. However, Terah took a permanent detour.

I state that Abram obeyed, partially, because the Bible says that Lot went with him. Last I checked, the son of your deceased brother still qualifies as family. This time the family reached the land of Canaan with one person more than was originally intended by God.[25]

The next time that the Lord had spoken directly with Abram, he finally came into full compliance with the Lord's directive—although it

---

23. Josh 24:2.
24. Gen 11:32.
25. Gen 12.

was passive compliance and not an active decision made by Abram. The family reached Canaan. However, the land and region were struck by famine.

So, Abram, his wife Sarai, and his nephew Lot, along with all of their herdsmen, went down to Egypt to ride out the famine. After a case of intentional mistaken identity involving the beautiful Sarai, a king, and a lie told by Abram, they returned to southern Canaan in the Negev.[26]

They were actually escorted out of Egypt by order of Pharaoh, because Abram asked Sarai to lie to the Egyptians with him and tell them that she was only his (half) sister. Thereby, obfuscating the fact that she was both his half-sister, as well as, his wife.[27]

I will not skip ahead. However, in Genesis 20, we find an example within Abraham's story where the Lord calls him a prophet and speaks to another king through dream.

Meanwhile, literally back at the ranch, Lot and his herdsmen had to be separated from Abram and his herdsmen because there was strife and contention between the two factions. As they traveled north from the Negev to Bethel and Ai, the tension between the two, now very wealthy shepherds, mounted. Abram, in an expression of generosity and family loyalty, told Lot that they should not fight. Although they had to split, there were more than enough resources available in Canaan for both of them to continue to prosper.

Abram gave Lot first choice. He told Lot, "If you go left, I will go right," and vice versa. Lot, of course was in the land promised by God to Abram and his descendants. However, since he was beyond the age of seventy-five, he was not likely, according to human convention, to have any children.

Lot looked out over the land and chose what seemed to be the best direction, where the ground seemed to be most fertile. In my opinion, Lot should have refused the choice offered by his uncle Abram, giving deference to Abram and his herds. Abram was the only one who God "invited" to go on the trip to Canaan. Lot "went with him."[28]

Abram allowed his nephew to join him and Sarai. However, Lot, at least, could have realized that the strife and contention between the two

---

26. Gen 13.
27. Gen 20:1–13.
28. Gen 12:4.

relatives' herdsmen only arose because the trip to the promised land had an extraneous passenger. In short, Lot, you were not invited.

However, Lot, the selfish nephew, took first choice and selected the direction with the most fertile plains. It also happened to be the direction that led to Sodom and Gomorrah. So, Abram was left with the choice of the other direction, which just so happened to be Canaan. This is where he was supposed to be without any extraneous family members tagging along from the outset.[29] Then, God spoke to Abram once again.

Once Lot left for the plains near Sodom and Gomorrah, God told Abram to look around in the land of Canaan, the land that God promised to Abram and his descendants. God told him to look to the north, south, east, and west as far as the eye could see. God told Abram that he was going to give all of that land to him.

Additionally, God told Abram that his children, of which he still had none, would number as many as the dust on the entire earth. You are probably thinking that you cannot even count the dust on that dresser of yours, which you have neglected for weeks. God's promises and vision were spoken regarding Abram's descendants who would be too numerous to count. Finally, God told him to look to the north, south, east, and west, as far as the eye could see. God told Abram that He was going to give all of that land to him.

He would reiterate this specific method of communicating. Such as when God spoke to Joshua when Abraham's descendants were finally ready to enter the promised land.[30]

Unclearly Speaking

God spoke promises, many of which were unclear, to Abram regarding their manifestation. Abram could not have known how God would give him that many descendants. Particularly not when he was old, as was his wife.

Both were well past child bearing age.[31] Abram was also promised by God that he and these yet-to-be-born descendants were to inherit the

---

29. Gen 13:1–12.
30. Gen 13:13–18; Josh 1:1–5.
31. Gen 21:1–7.

land of Canaan. However, by the end of Abraham's life, he owned little more in that land than a cave used for burial.[32]

Yet, Abram believed God, and for that, he was credited as righteous, by God.[33] That is why Abraham was called the friend of God.[34]

Promises Planted Deep Inside

This is also an example regarding how God will make a specific or a group of promises to you. During the initial stages, these promises are obscure. He will not clearly reveal all aspects immediately.

However, when God communicates his dreams and promises to you, he brands and burns them very deeply inside of you. Then God makes it the sole desire of your heart to fully see the manifestation of those promises. Such that you will do anything to actualize and to walk in the manifestation of those promises.

God created us so we could walk with him. The walk transforms us into someone who can fully possess the promises and do everything that we are called to do when we enter into the full manifestation of the promises. We just have to submit, obey, and keep walking. He dangles the carrot in front of us, and burns an unquenchable desire inside of us, one designed to compel us to see the walk toward his promises through to the end.

However, many do not make it all the way to the end. I would say that most do not make it to the end, primarily because they stop walking with God. In academic parlance, this is called being ABD: All But Dissertation, or in this case, ABWN: All But "Was Not."

When we stop walking, we do so because we did not keep the pace or the faith, or both.[35] In my experience, many do not reach the end as Paul and Abraham did. They do not do so because they do not choose to walk in lockstep with God along the journey for long enough to manifest the healing that was ordained and required by God.

---

32. Gen 23:1–17.
33. Gen 15:6; Rom 4:1–22; Gal 3:6–9; Heb 11:8–10; Heb 11:17–19.
34. Jas 2:23.
35. 2 Tim 4:7.

Allow God to Heal You on the Journey

A lack of healing will hinder progress on the overall journey to "Was Not." Ultimately, you will not enter into the full manifestation of your promise if you are, and remain, broken and damaged in your emotions. God has already afforded us divine healing.[36]

However, just as we do on our journey to the promised land, we must submit ourselves completely while allowing God to touch and heal us wherever it hurts. Even if those hurts occur, as they most often do, in the area of our emotions. We try to hide these damaged emotions from the outside world while still calling ourselves, "pursuing the promises of God." We have to allow God to become Lord of our entire life.[37] Trust me: he already knows.

God already knows and understands that it is difficult for us to allow anyone to see our scars and opened wounds. But, he has already provided the requisite healing. In order to complete the journey to the promised land, you have to trust God.

Abram had no idea where he was going. However, Abram trusted God. Similarly, we have to trust God on the way to the promise. We must learn to trust him enough to allow him to take control of every area and aspect of our lives, including, and dare I editorialize for a moment and specifically say, the area of inner emotional healing from scars and wounds, incurred as a result of living in a fallen world.

That "Was Not" At All What God Meant

Back to Abraham: ultimately, God had to reiterate, expand upon, and clarify the revelation given to him on a few more occasions. He also saw some clear manifestations, including the birth of his son Isaac, the son of laughter. He and my friend, Sarai (whose name was changed to Sarah by the time Isaac was born), tried to derail the conception and birth of Isaac with doubt and questioning.[38] However, to their credit, they kept walking. Somehow, they maintained the appropriate pace on their walk with God.

---

36. Isa 53:5.
37. Luke 6:46.
38. Gen 17:15, 18:12, 21:1–7.

As her contribution, Sarah offered her servant Hagar to Abram. This, in an effort to try to figure out what God meant by, "Abram would have a son and many descendants," on numerous occasions. For the record, God meant what he said.

In Genesis 15, God cut a contract for Abram in order to ensure that the promises that he made to Abram were consummated, sealed, and assured by no higher power than God himself. In Genesis 16, Sarai went for the quick fix. She doubted God and gave Abram her handmaiden, Hagar, to be his wife.

Sarah figured, "Since God has prevented me from having children (the child and offspring that he Promised Sarai), I will give you my handmaiden. Maybe, this way, God will give me children. Maybe, that is what God meant."[39] It "Was Not" at all what God meant. God meant what he said when he promised them a child.

In order to seal the deal, after the child Ishmael was born to Abram and Hagar, Sarah promptly kicked Hagar and the child out of the house, signifying that this "Was Not" a part of God's Plan. However, God knew what Abram and Sarai would do while on the journey. So God made provisions for Hagar and Ishmael, although this child "Was Not" a part of the promise. For the record, Abram was no better than Sarai because he agreed to the whole deal . . . you tell me why he agreed.

Abram to Abraham: Stepwise Progress

In Genesis 17, God confirms His covenant with Abram. El Shaddai, God Almighty, also changed Abram's name to Abraham. Thus confirming for Abraham that he would indeed become the father of many, which is the meaning of "Abraham." These name changes, as always with God, were a matter of God's perfect timing. And the changes were a sign to Abraham and Sarah that they were making progress on this journey, in spite of themselves at times. They kept the faith.[40]

God removed Sarai the Princess (the meaning of the spelling of her name) from the land that they left behind, Ur of the Chaldeans. God intentionally changed her name to Sarah. Sarah, which was reflective of the spelling of the same name, Princess. However, this new spelling was used

---

39. Gen 16.
40. Gen 17:1–5; 6–14.

in the promised land of Canaan.[41] God told Abraham of these changes, both of which signified that significant progress had occurred on their dependent journey.

Where is Your Past Located in the Present?

More notably, the name change signified the absolute importance of leaving your past behind as you progress on your journey toward "Was Not." God intentionally changed their names for all time, demonstrating that he plans to use everything. However, we have to let go of our past, in every way, to allow God to take control of all things in our lives, as well our emotions, and our past. Then we must move forward, steadily progressing toward and into the land promised.

We must not stop God from functioning as both Savior and Lord of our lives. If we stop him from taking complete control of our lives and over this journey and if we disallow El Shaddai from orchestrating the entire journey, then what may result is:

> What's past may indeed become prologue for you on your individual journey. If you are not careful, this path could lead you to a good, though not God-appointed, destination.

> The path could also lead you to an altogether bad destination, one which "Was Not" at all God's promised land and intended destination for you.

> This "Was Not" place where you may arrive, following your own vision, will depend entirely on where your past is currently located . . .

in the present.

Overaged

At this point, Abraham, now one hundred years old, and Sarah, ninety years old, introduce some levity into a situation that did not require laughter. Abraham considered the current circumstances, regarding how a ninety-year-old woman and a one-hundred-year-old man could ever

41. Gen 17:15.

make a baby. As he knelt in reverence to God, he behaved irreverently. He laughed at the promises of God as well as at the ability of God to keep his word.

Sound like Job to you? I will get to the time when I believe my boy Joseph also doubted a little, later in this book. But, the newly minted man named Abraham laughed. Thus, the meaning of Isaac's name, the son of laughter. Both Abraham and Sarah would stumble at the wisdom and ability of God to keep his word. Both would laugh regarding their pending pregnancy, during another conversation that they would have with the Lord. However, God is always true to his word.[42]

Final Exam

One last occasion where the Lord spoke to Abraham was after the birth of Isaac. The Lord decided to issue one more test. Honestly, it is difficult to know at which point in time during his journey, and on which step, this test occurred for Abraham. However, one can easily speculate why God decided to give a test like this to Abraham.

Isaac had been born. He was well into manhood when this occurred, according to the account of the Hebrew scholar of old Josephus.[43] This was a test for Abraham. Isaac was apparently just a willing and obedient actor in the play.

In Genesis 22:1–19, God spoke to Abraham once again. This time, God told Abraham to go to another place that he would show Abraham. God told Abraham to go to a mountain in the land of Moriah and sacrifice his only son to the Lord. Abraham, a man of quick obedience, set out early the next morning, just as he did when God sent him to Canaan.

He, apparently with permission this time, took two of his servants with him and Isaac. He would also bring the necessary items to make the sacrifice. Abraham, according to the account in Hebrews 11, figured that even if God allowed him to go through with the sacrifice, God would bring Isaac back from the dead.[44]

---

42. Gen 17:17–27, 18; 2 Pet 3:9.

43. Quora, "In the Old Testament, how old was Isaac when God asked Abraham to sacrifice him?," https://www.quora.com/In-the-Old-Testament-how-old-was-Isaac-when-God-asked-Abraham-to-sacrifice-him.

44. Gen 22:1–12; Heb 11:17–19; Jas 2:21–23; 1 Pet 1:3–4.

My point is that God "Was Not" testing Abraham's Faith. You know that many ministers believe that to be the case. God was not testing Isaac's Faith either. He might have been testing their patience, but neither of their faith or trust in God.

They both trusted God. Isaac trusted that Abraham would not, by this point, do anything that God had not commanded. That's how Isaac, Jacob, and, later, Joseph and his eleven brothers all began to develop a relationship and dependency on God. They all knew that God was trustworthy. They knew that anytime he communicated with a member of that family via dream, prophetic vision, impression, Chazown, or his word, they could trust him to manifestly fulfill his word.

God, in my opinion, was testing Abraham in order to confirm how much faith he had developed in God. He was testing his dependency on God, in and for all things.[45] God wanted Abraham to be absolutely certain in his spirit that God was a covenant or contract-keeping God. Like Enoch, God did it as a lesson from which future generations could learn.

God already knew that Abraham would go through with the sacrifice. Abraham, not being omnipresent or omniscient was the one who did not know, yet Abraham had made up in his heart and mind to go through with God's commandment. As a matter of fact, God had to almost physically restrain Abraham from killing Isaac by calling him by his (new) name, twice.[46]

While on the way up the mountain in Moriah, Isaac queried his father regarding the location of the sacrifice. Abraham said that Yahweh-Yireh the Lord would provide. The Lord would supply his own sacrifice.[47] That was enough for Isaac to submit to his father's wishes and his subsequent actions. Concurrently, that was enough for Abraham to submit to the command of God.

DREAMS ARE "GOD'S BUSINESS"

God reveals things to us through dreams, visions, Chazown, and impressions as well as through intimate contact. He always speaks to us through his word. The means of communication, as well as the method of transmission, involves God as the sender of the message and us as the receiver

---

45. 1 Pet 1:3–4
46. Gen 22:11.
47. Gen 22:7–14.

of the message. All of these elements in the communication process are absolutely dependent on God's providence.

Here, once again, we can appropriately use the words "divine providence" correctly. This simply means that God decides all necessary elements and parameters. Additionally, God's sovereignty means that God does what he wants, when he wants, and how he wants.

God speaks to us all of the time, actually. We have to learn to become sensitive enough to the sound of his, at times, "still, small voice" in order to comprehend what he is saying. However, during other times he chooses to speak in a big, loud voice.[48] He reveals many, many things to us in many ways.

At first, during the initial stages, within the context of the initial revelation, God reveals a photograph to us in a very obscure manner. However, in accordance with his perfect timing, he will allow the picture to become more and more clearly understood by us. Our responsibility is to keep walking, keep up the pace, and to remain submitted and obedient to him in every area of our lives as our journey continues.

God will burn those dreams inside of us to such an extent that we will be overwhelmingly compelled to follow him. Such that we will persist on the journey.

However, just like in doctoral programs everywhere, many people end up in the ABD (All But Dissertation) "graveyard", as they call it. Many people do not finish the journey with God, seeing it through to its designed and intentioned conclusion. Many discontinue the trip for various reasons. But if you want to see the manifestation of all of God's promises, those promises that you are so passionate about seeing fulfilled, then you must Keep Walking.

---

48. 1 Kgs 19:11–13.

6

Step Four: Obedience & Submission

WHY DO WE STRUGGLE SO WITH SUBMISSION?

The answer to that little life's question which occurs to me quite often is very simple: fear. The Holy Spirit, living inside of me and functioning in and through me, hates fear.[1] When we engage Christ's perfect love, that love is made manifest in and through us. This perfect love is simultaneously perfecting itself in our lives as we walk more closely with Christ on the journey.

While that perfect love is perfecting the godly love in all of us, it concurrently eradicates and casts out every particle of fear. Therefore, as is discussed in that passage in 1 John 4, we have no fear or dread of anything. Specifically, not of divine judgment.

We learn that God has not given us fear as a necessary emotion, or spiritual influence. This makes it unnecessary relative to our soul/ego because when he made us, he saw that we were very good.[2] He has not given us the "spirit" of fear relative to our mind, thoughts, memories, regrets, and human-based knowledge. Additionally, I choose never to live in regret.

Thus, God has not given us a "spirit" of fear in our soul or ego. Rather God gives us, by speaking to our spirit, a transfer or download

1. 1 John 4:18.
2. Gen 1:31; Jas 1:4

into our spirit of divine power, divine love, and of a sound mind, as well as self-control.³ That means a couple of things: if he gives us self control, then we get to choose whether or not we accept fear. It also implies that we choose whether or not we will live in, or accept, regret. I choose not.

Be Not Afraid

That is why I despise, resist, and begin to, if God lets me, psychologically and spiritually "poke at" the fear that I can sense or feel in many of the people that I encounter.⁴ In 2 Timothy 1:7–8, Paul instructs Timothy not to be afraid, so very eloquently, as he is preparing to face his Roman accusers.

Paul writes Timothy from jail in his final days. Paul tells Timothy that he should not be afraid of being associated with him, although Paul is on death row. Rather, Timothy should be prepared to suffer with Paul, for the sake of Jesus Christ.

All of this means that Paul was, at the end, fully obedient and submitted to Jesus Christ. He was totally prepared to step into whatever came next for him.

Paul was a Roman citizen. As such he, was readying himself to face the Emperor of Rome. He would face someone in governmental leadership, first in Judah and now in Rome, one last time, prior to what would inevitably result in his execution.

He would make his final impassioned plea before Caesar and then be prepared to accept any resulting consequences.⁵ In short, God had not given him a "spirit," or attitude, of fear or timidity. Therefore, he would not accept or embrace those things.

Paul had accepted the fact that he chosen to be obedient to Christ following his experience on the road to Damascus.⁶ He decided to submit to everything that Christ commanded him to do, and follow Christ all the way to and through "Was Not."⁷ Thus, there was no room for fear,

---

3. 2 Tim 1:7–8.
4. 2 Tim 1:7–8.
5. Acts 21–28.
6. Acts 9; Rom 12:1–2.
7. Phil 3:7, 8, 9–11.

timidity, regret, or concern about the consequences of his actions, nor as a result of his most willing decisions.[8]

So, when I say that the reason that we have such a difficult time with submission and obedience is fear, I mean that we know that we have a choice to fear or not fear, and most importantly we recognize that God is in charge. Thus, when we obey and submit, we are submitting to Jesus Christ, who is Lord and Savior. Then the act of submission, from finite being, to the Infinite, is, or should be, easy. Alas, it is not easy for most people. Why not?

MY MUSE

Speaking of going into a thing thinking one way, only to later learn that God is in control, I can say that about the academic advising portion of my career. I went into it with a strong desire to help students. Particularly, students who were academically or generally at-risk.

I wanted to help them overcome obstacles, including a less-than-adequate educational background, regarding the provision of sufficient college preparatory coursework taken during their K–12 experiences. Often, this background does not, at all, sufficiently prepare them for academic success in college.

Additionally, I wanted to dismantle all of the "worthless idols," issues, abuses, hurts, and pains that had piled up in the damaged souls of my future students. I knew that this background would negatively impact their ability to achieve academic and, therefore, life success. I desired, if they would allow me, to help them to eliminate all obstacles, as well as internal pain, that would inevitably hamper, impede, or entirely derail their prospects for academic success.[9]

I anticipated doing all of this at public universities, where I knew I was called to work. I wanted to try to "sneak some light into their lives."[10]

Put Your Flashlight Away

My former pastor once told us, "We are to let our Christ's light so shine before men . . . not run around shining our little light in everyone's eyes,"

---

8. 2 Cor 12:7–10.
9. Jonah 2:8–10.
10. Matt 5:14–16.

meaning that we have to trust and believe that Christ's light is constantly working on the inside of us as believers. We must have complete confidence in the fact that this light is sufficient to "draw all men unto him."[11]

Furthermore, we must believe primarily, if not at times exclusively, that through the "passive encounters" you will have with people (you being Christ's "living epistle."[12]), you must know that they will notice and be drawn to Christ's light. This occurs as they actively or passively begin to come to know Christ in the power of his resurrection because he constantly shines in and through your life as a believer.[13]

In other words, he was saying that you as a Christian did not have to run around saying to everyone, "Hey, I'm a Christian," and you need not go about daily uttering phrases like, "Praise the Lord," which some people use as their customary greeting to all mankind. This, instead of just saying "Hello." I avoid people like that, as he said he did, because I know that it is an insecurity, thus a fear, at work in the lives of these "Christians."

Why I Had No Desire to Become a "Christian Author"

I entered my professional life, post-master's, thinking that I would do exactly as I just explained. This is one of the reasons that I did not immediately embrace the idea of becoming a "Christian author." I like to simply let his light shine. I abhor the idea of telling people how to think.

I know that the light draws all humans to it. It does this by virtue of its nature, definition, presence, and operation. In this case, the light is working within me. Therefore, my work is no longer based on me, nor on my power or light. Rather, any ability to draw all men to Christ is based on the light of Christ radiating within me.[14] All I have to do is obey and submit.

My Sheep Know My Voice

I quickly learned that I would be in "my sheep know my voice" type of encounters with many of my students, or my "kids" as I called them.[15]

11. John 12:32.
12. 2 Cor 3:2; 1 Pet 2:9.
13. Phil 3:10.
14. Matt 5:14; John 8:12; Gal 2:20.
15. John 10:2–5, 27.

Now, many members of that flock are all grown up with lambs of their own. And nowadays they can afford to buy me lunch.

God had shown me, allowed me to connect with, and permitted me to feel many of my student's emotional scars, those scars which were typically accompanied by more observable academic difficulties.

In the end, many of the academic advising relationships that I would form would transcend strictly academic advising. They would enter into the realm of personal advising and counseling, as well as mentoring.[16] All of this was intentionally designed to help set them free, through the work of the light—academically, personally, and sometimes spiritually.[17]

Now I shy away from both of those words: (personal) advising and counseling though I function in those capacities almost every day, just as I shy away from the title, Christian author. Some people still insist on calling me those words as well as "Dr. I Shrink From Them All." The latter exception being my students in my classes and some good friends from my master's program. But, that was a nickname based on a movie, I think. As I have mentioned previously, I am actually a very humble extrovert.

However, so many, to the detriment of my humility in those areas, have foisted those titles upon me. Thus, it is beyond my ability to control their use. So I reluctantly accept, if not embrace, them. I am trying.

Anyway, I would develop these relationships with "my sheep" "who knew my voice," and I knew them.[18] I knew the ones who were supposed to be connected to me, while I would concurrently serve as a mentoring, counseling, and advising resource. Generally, because all of these students are seemingly "hermetically and biologically connected to their cell phones," I would usually get to know their parents as well. The parents would typically call during our formal and informal meetings.

I was able to distinctly recognize those who I would need to allow to have greater than the formalized and scheduled access provided through the traditional academic advising process. This entailed encouraging unscheduled and informal office visits, or university event encounters that extended well beyond the one or two formally scheduled academic advising appointments that we would typically engage in per semester.

Thus, I would regularly attend their campus events, extracurricular activities, football, basketball, and my new favorite, women's lacrosse

---

16. 1 John 3:18.
17. John 8:36.
18. 1 John 3:18.

games. "Showing my face," as I called it. Also, I was an official faculty advisor or faculty mentor for some of these officially recognized campus clubs, organizations, and activities.

Then, another strange thing began to occur. Those jokers would bring their friends around from other majors. Fascinating. But I still knew which ones were mine, and which ones that I was simply supposed to help as an advisor, administrative faculty/lecturer, underling or supreme chief digi-brain.

Ever My Muse

But oh, there was one. I still call her my "muse." She is the very reason that I still, and will always, wake up in the morning. I always say, "If I can get her . . ." Meaning, if I can be used of God to help alleviate all of those burdens she carries, and lift that internal countenance of hers, then I will have lived this God life to its fullest.[19] I will have run the race and have finished the course.[20]

Simply put, she is my "white whale." Though, in her present state, she is actually a rather, comparatively, gaunt child. Well, woman at this point.

> And upon this whale's white hump he piled, as well as, felt and experienced during each encounter. A sum of all of the rage and hate; as well as the pain and anguish, that she had felt inside, for generations and years.
>
> If his (my) chest had been a canon, he (I) would have launched his (my) heart upon it. And, upon all of her distresses."[21]

She was the reason that I was drawn to that quote. And she is the reason that I wake up every morning. My muse.

I would have launched my heart upon her aching and distress, though she would never admit to ever actually baring any of these sorrows. However, because I could so intensely feel them during every encounter, they were impressed upon and into my heart. Even now, as I write about them, I can feel the pains to the point of tears. I would

---

19. Ps 24:7–9; Matt 11:28–30; John 17:3.

20. 2 Tim 4:6, 7, 8.

21. IMDB, "Star Trek: First Contact: Quotes," https://www.imdb.com/title/tt0117731/quotes?ref_=ttgf_ql_4 (adaptation).

experience those same exact feelings every time I encountered her. It felt as if elephants were standing atop my heart.

None of my kids were quite as broken on the inside as her. Only one other person, though not one of my kids, nor my sheep, struck me in a similar manner. She was my "BFF#2 who-doesn't-talk-to-me-anymore." She was the only other person who bore such a profound and painful burden inside. But she is another story for another book. Yet she is not now, and has never been, my muse. There is only one who is, and will ever remain, my muse, in perpetuity.

The Muse and I had, and still have, kind of, as seldom as I see her anymore, a love/hate relationship. This is primarily because of the way we met, which was through my "wayward son." He spoke of her quite often, because he used to work for me as a student assistant during my Underling chief digi-brain, admin faculty/lecturer days. He also regularly told her, "You need to meet my boss."

Then, I finally met her, or should I say: when she finally, though mistakenly, decided to honor and grace me with the privilege of speaking with her. See, she never decided to take my "wayward son" up on his invitation, this for her own very complicated reasons. She was quite a complex creature, and she still is.

However, her internal distress shows in her eyes. At least it does for those, such as I, who can tell via, "The eye is the window to the soul."[22] Anyway, she had never actually come to the office to meet me at his invitation, nor had she ever seen me in person. I was simply a rumor.

"The fox," (my initial nickname for her) held my "wayward son's" heart right in the palm of her hand. Alas, that heart of his had many occupied chambers at one point. That was a part of her problem relative to trusting him. Though his occupied heart most likely did not encompass all of her concerns. She was complicated.

Are You Smiling?

So, after we met, and amid our love/hate relationship, I would most often see her at her work study job, which was in a student commons area. I would ask her upon each encounter: "Are you smiling?" Now she enjoyed

---

22. Matt 6:22; Luke 11:34. "Is That Really In The Bible?" *KeptByGrace.com*, www.keptbygrace.com/archive/is-that-really-in-the-bible/.

this antagonistic relationship that we shared as much as me. And of course, I played right along.

I was more than happy to oblige, if not pour my own gasoline on the fires. Remember folks, I am doing the Lord's work here, and attempting to sneak a new "healing light" past her complex maze of walls and filters, or so I had been "assigned."[23] (Yet always with my own personality and flair.)

I asked her this same question every time I saw her during the initial stages of our interaction. Whether I was in that building because I had a meeting in there (lots of meetings for the Digi-Brain Kingdom) or, if I was in the building for lunch, or, if I was just doing a drive-by, because God had laid her on my heart. Now that I had met the fox I made that building a more intentional and regular stop.

Again, the question that I would ask was, "Are you smiling?" She would, of course, reply defiantly each and every time. Simultaneously, she would roll her neck and eyes, and reply to my query, "I'm always smiling."

This was true, I must say. Sans when she was speaking with me. However, some people pack their masks, as readily as they pack their lunch.

However, one specific day, when she was likely also bothered by some other issues and concerns, as was often the case with my muse. What can I say? I knew her inside better than out. This particular day, my reply to her included an addendum because she had added a postscript to her customary refrain, "I'm always smiling."

It was time for me to up my game and insert an addendum of my own. However, this pending reply of mine made her face drop. Come to think of it, this was the second time, during our relatively brief encounters, that I had the fun-filled honor of making her face drop.

Our Initial Encounter

The first time that I made her face drop was during the occasion of our initial, face-to-face chance encounter. She came up to me, not knowing who I was, and introduced herself. She was networking after a panel discussion where I was a participating member.

As I recall, I think it was on careers for all majors. The discussion was held in a conference room within the same building where she worked. I

---

23. 2 Tim 1:1.

may have even received advanced reconnaissance via my "wayward son" who informed me that she was going to be there.

After the panel discussion, she came up to me and engaged her "elevator pitch networking introduction." I had seen pictures of her, so I recognized "the fox" immediately. But she had never had the occasion to see me because she declined to meet me. Thus, I knew this time I had her cornered, so to speak. I said to her, "I know who you are . . . you're 'the fox.'"

See, my "wayward son" had informed her of my little nickname for the ever-elusive vixen, who had, to date, refused to come and meet me, in spite of his persistent requests. Also, I knew, and was close to, a couple of her good friends. They may have been her roommates during that year. They were also my "majors." So, "the fox" was generally aware of me though we had never actually met. Thus, she would not recognize my face.

I am certain that she refused, in part, because he was so persistent, and because she knew that he had told me all about the primary target of his affection. She was, understandably, very guarded. Thus, I was kind of obliged to begin meddling. It's my kingdom job.[24]

She hated that nickname "the fox," but that day I so enjoyed watching her turn to frozen yogurt, and then scurry across the room. Away from my presence, to network with me no more. In retrospect, I guess I had sown the seeds for the resulting antagonistic relationship that we shared.

Are You Smiling? (Part 2)

Anyway, on to her now customary reply to my queries, "are you smiling?" Upon the second occasion, when I had the honor of making her face drop, she said, "When are you going to stop asking me that? I am always smiling." She rolled her neck and eyes, in a demonstration of defiant annoyance.

My reply, as I "upped my game," was one simple, insightful, and emphatic response. Looking over my glasses, a one-word response, "Inside?"

Eureka. Success. Once again, I had achieved stunned silence. And victory. With one word, I had drawn a blank, as well as a crestfallen look from "my muse, the fox."

---

24. 1 John 3:18.

I could concurrently feel, with the weight of a thousand elephants standing on my heart, what she almost assuredly felt inside after I supplied my rejoinder to her initial retort. "Smiling on the inside?" She had never looked at it from that perspective. She was too busy walling her heart off from the ever-intrusive and oft meddlesome, Jones.

I sincerely wanted that wall, transparent to me, to fall down. I so dearly wanted to get her to drop her mask. I had never met a person who had so deftly mastered the art of keeping all other digi-brains at arm's length, only allowing them to see what she wore on that mask, a different mask for each, I might add. I guess she liked to control her spotlights, too.

The antagonistic nature of our relationship's trajectory would not have appeared to be conducive to me getting her to drop her rock, her wall, or that mask. But I knew how this business, to which I was called and chosen, worked.

If I could get that mask dropped and the wall to come down, then the Light would take over from there. Following this, the Light and I might be able to help the afraid and hurting person, hiding behind the (transparent to me) wall, the wall that she so skillfully used to protect herself.

After that, we would likely, hopefully, and prayerfully get her to come out and talk.[25] That's why my "wayward son" tried to impress upon her to meet me.

He knew that she was in persistent emotional pain. He knew that I could help. However, he also knew that she was complex.

He wanted her to visit for help and because the multi-chambered heart of his in which the penthouse suite was reserved with her name on it! I had spoken with him quite often behind his walls, which were by no means as formidable as hers. Finally, from there "the fox" and I could work toward healing the broken person hiding behind the (transparent to me) wall. That's my job! And I love it![26]

He Is God

The point to this little story and how it relates to submission and obedience is that in order to engage and to be successful on this journey, you must believe and acknowledge that he is God. He is God, who is worthy

---

25. Song 2:14–15; 8:8–9.
26. 1 John 3:18.

of your complete submission and obedience. Then you must recognize that he is a rewarder of those who diligently seek him.[27]

To do that you have to relinquish those fears which precipitate masks, walls, and other impediments to allowing the light to enter into, as well as heal, all of our relative broken hearts and lives. God cannot come in uninvited.[28] As a wise pastor once said, "God won't take away your friends."

A SUCCESSFUL WALK

The Standards that Govern the Believer's Relationship

The only way to successfully walk with him is to acknowledge that he is the omnipotent, omnipresent, and omniscient Lord and Savior of all.[29] If you do not believe that in its entirety, then not only do I, as a believer, have no right to hold you to the standards that come along with that belief, but I cannot get frustrated with you because of what I perceive to be your life struggles.

John the apostle, particularly in the first epistle, spends the majority of the time speaking about Christ's love.[30] He states that your fears will not be eradicated unless you are, first, in a fully submitted and obedient relationship with Jesus. I find it fascinating when Christians expect non-believers to live up to their standards. Sad, but fascinating.

Non-believers would be required to accept that every word in the Bible is God-breathed and true.[31] Then they have to believe, as the book of Hebrews said about Enoch, that he is the "I AM." Only then can you believe that he is a rewarder. Following that, you can believe that he, as the omnipotent Lord and Savior, is the "I AM," where I, as the finite being in this relationship, must submit to and obey his every command.

I must completely surrender my free will, a free will that He gave me, along with my eternal spirit as well as my temporal body. But I cannot do any of this, nor can I begin the journey, much less, begin walking toward "Was Not" where I lose myself completely and where He has no

---

27. Heb 11:5–6.
28. Rev 3:20.
29. Gen 1:1; John 1:1–14.
30. 1 John 1–5.
31. 2 Tim 3:16.

choice but to take me in my Calling as He took Enoch. I cannot do any of this unless I completely surrender and obey.

That begins by submitting my fear. If a person does not believe in "I AM," then we have no right whatsoever to hold them accountable for the principles that govern our finite relationship with the omnipotent and infinite one.

Resisting Submission and Obedience

The reason that we do not believe and why we resist such things as submission and obedience is simple: fear. People fear "judgment" or a recurrence of oppression. In other words, they likely, as a result of living in this world, have encountered, in some form or another, abuse or bad treatment—treatment which has hurt and damaged them. Some, severely damaged.

It is hard to trust a God who is omnipotent, but who they concurrently view as, "having allowed that horrible thing to happen to me." So, they do what all humanoids with a free will do, they become self-protecting. Unfortunate, but true.

Becoming self-protective is as instinctively natural as snatching your hand from a hot stove and then avoiding all hot things. They may even develop an unobservable phobia toward the "hurtful thing." This, while incorrectly attributing the point of origin of that hurtful thing to the auspice and purview of the omniscient, eternal God who, in their opinion, should have protected them.

Sadly, this speaks to many of my broken-hearted children who inhabit this fallen world, a world that God designed to be populated by human beings, all of whom have free will. Life does not work that way.

Pain, abuse, and heartache of every kind will come as a result of the fallen nature of the people who inhabit the world, a world which he designed for us to have dominion over.[32] We have to submit all pains, heartaches, and abuses to him and to his plan for healing.[33]

Submission of our pain is easier to do when we have a scar on the outside. However, when we get near a source of pain, leading to the drastic conclusion of being burned by a hot and hurtful emotional mutilation, we develop an unobservable, internal scar and callous. Going forward,

---

32. Gen 1:28; 1 John 2:1, 4:4.
33. Ps 119:10; Jer 29:13; Jas 4:7.

we avoid those hurtful things, and the scar is unobservable to the naked eye.

Therefore, when someone else, someone who you expected to protect you from the hurtful thing but who didn't, in your incomplete opinion, the result is that you will avoid not only submitting to Him, and obeying Him, but you resist submitting to any and everyone else who looks like or reminds you of Him—your supposed failed Protector. For the record, we all look like Him.[34]

Submission—Not There

Another thing that I find fascinating is that we believers (we who comport to believe that he is "I AM," and we who have partially submitted to him in obedience, due to our baggage full of scars and callouses), stumble at the word "submission," when it comes to marriage.[35] I am not condemning us; this is my life's work and calling, so I get it. However, it still fascinates me.

Men are to submit to Christ as Lord of all. Wives, according to the Bible, are to submit themselves to Christ and to their husband.[36] Now, of course, maybe he or she has abused the position in the marriage that God has placed him or her in. In that instance, you, in my never-so-humble opinion, are required by God to get yourself to safety by whatever godly (but logical) means necessary. Never allow that to happen to you, ever.

Maybe you picked him or her out of a hat, or you selected them via a social media webpage and God had very little, if anything, to do with their particular selection. No matter, you have declared before God and mankind that this man or woman is "the one."

Thus, you are now in covenant. God does not want either party to abuse that covenant. Noting that both of you have free will to choose to be faithful and to treat your covenant spouse as Christ treated the Church.[37] You must treat the other covenant partner exactly as you would have them treat you.[38]

---

34. Gen 1:26–28.
35. Rom 12:1–2.
36. Eph 5:22–33; 1 Pet 3:1–7.
37. Eph 5:25–29.
38. Matt 7:12; Luke 6:31.

Now, in the instance that one party abuses the privilege that God has granted them by virtue of being in a covenant relationship with you and him, God provides legal- and kingdom-sanctioned remedies that will ensure safety and perfect peace for both parties who have submitted to him and live as believers. Some of you, please take advantage of those remedies and stop allowing yourselves to endure things that he never created you to endure.

Difficulty in Submitting Ourselves

However, for the rest of us, and getting back to the topic of submission and obedience, maybe someone else abused the privilege of being in some form of relationship with you and the God who lives within you. As a result, you now hold all others accountable for the wrongs that were done to you. You hold everyone accountable for the injustices, perpetrated by that husband or wife, mother or father, aunt, uncle, or cousin, friend or acquaintance—particularly those who look like or bare the same gender as the abuser of privilege. Even if it is God himself.

The thing that needs healing is in your emotions, heart, soul, and ego. Following that, submission and obedience to Christ, his plans, purposes, and his perfect will all become possible.[39] That goes for the husband to Christ, the wife to the husband and Christ, and submission and obedience, as is appropriate, in all other forms of human relationship. It's His world, and He set up the order. If you believe that He is I AM then He has the right to set the rules for the journey, and all other things as He sees fit. I know that is heavy, but it is true.

The Parable of the Head Coach, General Manager, & Team Owner

I believe that I have an easy-to-understand example which I will use to describe the order of things as they occur within the realm of obedience and submission. A professional sports team, though I will not name the sport, recently wanted to sign a controversial player to their team. The team had a definite need and this player was the best free agent player available, more than capable of fulfilling the team's need.

---

39. Eph 5:21–26.

STEP FOUR: OBEDIENCE & SUBMISSION

Also, the player was, relatively speaking, young enough to be in the prime of their career. The player was good, but they were a free agent because of the controversy swirling around them, not because of their past accomplishments in the sport.

The head coach (HC) of the team and the general manager (GM) of the team both wanted to sign this player to a contract. Both individuals had vast authority ascribed to them within the context of the organizational structure.

The GM managed their staff of administrators and personnel evaluators. The GM was also responsible for overall talent acquisition, particularly as it relates to players.

The HC managed the coaching staff as well as all tangentially associated personnel, such as the strength and nutrition personnel. The HC was also responsible for the in-sport player development regarding marshalling all collective talents and skill sets of the players. The HC had to ensure that each player, individually and collectively, was fully prepared to perform each season as a championship quality team.

The HC was also ultimately responsible for dismissing players, players who were not as valuable as contributors to the team's overall performance and production. Both had vast authority. However, their power bases also had limitations. They worked for the team owner.

The team owner had the final say on all things related to the team. After all, this person paid the full and substantive franchise fee required to purchase the team. They also paid all salaries, all operating expenditures, as well as most of the expenses associated with the facility where the team played and practiced. In short, they owned the team.

So the HC and GM both were in agreement: they wanted to sign the controversial player. But they could not just run right out and sign that controversial player. The team owner had the final say because they signed the paychecks.

The team owner agonized over the decision, attempting to balance the skill set of the player with the negative publicity versus, the positive benefits relative to including the skillsets of the controversial player on the team.

Alas, the team owner decided that the risk was not worth the reward. The owner decided, based on their authority and on the corporate hierarchical structure, that they would override, overrule, and go against the desires of the HC and GM. The team owner used the authority granted them; by virtue of title and organizational structure. They ultimately decided not to sign the controversial player.

The HC and GM could have been outraged. They could have gone to the press and made all sorts of slanderous and innuendo-laden statements to the media. They could have talked about the fears of the owner being placed above winning and doing the right thing for the team. "Right" is a very dangerous thing to have and be.

Both parties felt that they were right and that the risk *was* well worth the reward. They could have found a myriad of subversive activities to engage in, relative to undermining the authority of the team owner. I am a subversive, so I would have gotten a kick out of that reaction from the HC and GM.

They could have just fussed and pouted their way all the way to divorce court, making that CEO the most happily divorced person on the planet. I mean, they could have fussed and pouted to any and everyone who would listen, until they were both fired with pay, as a result of their binding contracts, by the team owner. You see, the rules say that the team owner has the final say. The team owner did not make the rules; that's just how things work.

The HC and GM did none of that. They submitted to the higher power, though they still wielded vast power and authority within the organization themselves. They obeyed the wishes of the CEO even though they likely still thought that they were right and the owner was completely wrong.

You never heard a cross word out of them. You, as a fan of that team, (which I am not) never saw cross looks in their press conferences or felt tension surrounding the team. They submitted and obeyed. Consequently, they yielded their vast power bases and authority to the ultimate governing authority in that organization, based solely on the organizational structure and rules that govern the transaction of business processes,within that sport.

You see, I would ask, why in the world would you accept the job as HC or GM if you do not want to follow all of the rules? You can go and purchase your own team. Except that you are comparably broke.

But you can get another job, or remain a free agent yourself, until you are afforded an opportunity to work for an owner who does not follow the rules as set forth by the league. You can hold out until you find a team that grants, ascribes, and seeds to you the authority to be: HC, GM, CEO, etc. of the organization.

Yes, without structure and order, you may get a lot done. However, the organization that you run will likely fail because it operates within a market environment that is concurrently governed by rules.[40] All of the teams within this league structure must submit to the overarching authority of the commissioner of that league.

Again, why would you accept the job if you have disdain for the rules? Or if you have hurts and pains that the Holy Spirit has been tugging on, attempting to heal you from? He has been trying to remove that horrific blight on our soul, so we can enjoy the life of freedom as well as submitted obedience that he has gifted to us. Yet we can only enjoy it if we would just receive it, and when we accept the fact that he makes the rules. As Doc says, "Don't nobody want that digi-brained job, anyway."

Think about it. What will you do? Submit and obey? Or just fuss until you get fired? Will you go and buy your own team? Or go and find others so that you can start your own league? You are still comparably broke, remember. Or will you wait on a CEO who will seed all power and authority over to you, so you can run the team in the "right" way? Don't forget about that commissioner. He has relative omnipotence.

Whoever has ears to hear, let them hear. Then go, do likewise, and sin no more.[41]

KING SAUL & SAMUEL THE PROPHET & JUDGE

The best way to advance this discussion on submission and obedience is to continue by discussing a man who eventually spiraled downward into vain defiance, disobedience, and rebellion against the Lord's commands: King Saul, a reluctant hero.

He was from the small tribe of Benjamin and never considered himself worthy of the crown. In short, he was fearful, fearful about a great many things. These were things packed in his bags that he never submitted to the Lord for unpacking, laundering, and healing.[42]

So when the children of Israel came to Samuel to request a king for the nation of Israel, they wanted to have a human king, just like the other nations. They engaged in their own act of willful defiance against their true King of kings, the omnipotent Lord.

---

40. Prov 29:18.
41. John 8:1–11.; Matt 13:43; Luke 10:37
42. 1 Sam 8–10.

They began with a curious, if true, insult. They told Samuel, "You are old and your sons, who you have appointed to be judges in your stead, are not like you. They are greedy criminals."[43] However, Samuel knew what their request meant. It was a real slap at the authority of their true King, Yahweh.

God told Samuel to give them what they are requesting. God set the rules, and they had free will. He told Samuel to warn them the consequences and negative ways that a human king, as opposed to the sovereign God continuing to function as King, would bring. They should know that a human king would rule them by taking taxes and whatever else a corrupt king might demand of his subjects.

But they did not care. They wanted their human king, irrespective of the potential consequences. That was the place where willfully defiant disrespect and a lack of submissive obedience to Yahweh will lead you.

Samuel took the entire ordeal personally. He was very submitted to God. He obeyed God quickly and at every turn.

Samuel learned what God's voice sounded like as their journey began.[44] God reiterated to Samuel that he was to go ahead and give them the king that they were requesting, as long as they were made aware of the consequences of replacing Yahweh, the King of kings, with a human, free-willed king. They insisted. Thus, Samuel was led to Saul. Subsequently, Samuel, at God's behest, anointed Saul king.[45]

Saul, the ever fearful one, while he operated as king in submission and obedience to God, did OK. Not great, but he had his victories, such as over the Ammonites.[46] Coincidentally, Saul was so reluctant and fearful of everything, including his deficiencies, that he ran out on his own coronation. He was found "hiding among (his own) baggage."[47]

As the wars with Philistia escalated, and as time passed, King Saul's fears caught up with him. His disrespect for God developed into a self-centered vanity and insecurity. This resulted in willful disobedience to the Lord. Fear of inadequacy, in this case, was at the root of all of the insecurities Saul held. They were also the primary impetus behind his devolving behavior toward God.

---

43. 1 Sam 8:1–9.
44. 1 Sam 3.
45. 1 Sam 9–10.
46. 1 Sam 11.
47. 1 Sam 10:20–22.

King Saul heard the Word from the Lord, spoken to him by Samuel the prophet.[48] God, Yahweh Tsebaoth, the Lord of heaven's armies, declared to King Saul that he was ready to settle all accounts with the kingdom of Amalek for opposing the children of Israel as he brought them out of Egypt and into the promised land.[49] God told Saul to sanctify, or completely eradicate, the entire kingdom of the Amalekites by killing all men, women, children, babies, as well as livestock, including camels and donkeys. Coincidentally, or not so, this eradication, was the same thing that perfect love does to fear.[50] King Saul was ready, until . . .

When God gives instructions, he expects us to follow them, completely and to the letter. Ask Abram and Lot. But when Saul heard an order, he decided, of his own free will, which parts of God's directives were most important, and which parts were say, negotiable. He told the Kenites to move out of the area, away from the Amalekites because they had helped the children of Israel as they left Egypt.

But when Saul went to fight against the Amalekites, he spared King Agag. He killed everyone else. However, he and his men allowed Agag to remain alive. They also kept the best of the livestock. As a matter of fact, they only killed the less desirable animals.

So God had another conversation with Samuel. If you remember me speaking about that elephant's foot standing on my heart, well God was grieved, and Samuel could feel all of the weight of the grief that God felt.[51] God regretted ever making Saul king.

I think that this next part is my favorite of all. The next morning, after crying all night long, Samuel went to find King Saul. Someone informed Samuel that Saul had gone to Carmel to set up a monument to . . . wait for it . . . himself.

That makes me happy. Nothing worse than disobedience with a side order of building a monument to that colossal failure—one with your face on it. Oh king, my king (though not for long), you have just enshrined your failure for all time. Or at least until the kingdom is stripped from you because of your disdain for the authority of God. Whichever comes first.

---

48. 1 Sam 15.
49. 1 Sam 15:2–3.
50. 1 John 4:18.
51. Eph 4:30.

Following the monument, the King went to Gilgal where Samuel caught up with him. So, at this point, does it dawn on King Saul what he has done wrong, how he has disobeyed the directives and commands of God in full view of the man that God used to anoint him as king?

No, King Saul shines his little light in Samuel's face and says, "God bless you," followed by, "I have obeyed and submitted to all of the Lord's commands." Best day ever.

Samuel replied, "If you indeed followed the Lord's commands to the letter, then why do I hear evidence to the contrary? Why can I hear the cows mooing and the sheep bleating?"

"Oh that," King Saul replied. "Yes, it's true," King Saul pulled a very subtle version of "it was that woman you gave me." "The Army kept the best animals.[52] But 'they' did it for God. They wanted to offer a wonderful sacrifice with all of the best livestock from Amalek to Yahweh Tsebaoth, the Lord of heaven's armies. But 'we' destroyed everything else."

Samuel, now furious, tired, in pain, and representing the more furious God that he served, told the king to listen to what God told him last night while he was crying all night long.

God said of King Saul, "While you may live in fear and think 'little of yourself,' you are the king of Israel, anointed by the Lord, the King of kings, to serve as such over my people."

God clearly identified King Saul's fears and insecurities. Then God highlighted them as the reason that he behaved in such a brazenly indifferent manner toward the commandments of the Lord. Samuel said, "God told you to completely eradicate Amalek."

Saul, at this point, chasing and skating backwards in defense of himself, told Samuel, "But I did do all the Lord commanded." Then Saul took a small amount of responsibility, although the Israeli soldiers were under orders and would have never done anything without King Saul's command. He said, "I brought back King Agag. However, the soldiers, 'my guys,' brought back the best livestock. However, they only did this in order to make a grand sacrifice to the Lord."[53]

I hate using block quotations when writing or grading papers. I consider them literarily lazy. However, that is the teacher in me trying to persuade my students to learn to paraphrase, and not cheat the game. But in this case, I cannot say this any better than Samuel the Prophet to sum

---

52. Gen 3:12.
53. 1 Sam 15:1–21.

up my point here regarding Step Four, specifically related to submission and obedience:

> But Samuel replied,
> "What is more pleasing to the Lord:
> your burnt offerings and sacrifices
> or your obedience to his voice?
> Listen: obedience is better than sacrifice
> and submission is better than offering the fat of rams.
> Rebellion is as sinful as witchcraft
> and stubbornness as bad as worshipping idols.
> Because you have rejected the command of the Lord,
> he has rejected you as king."[54]

God informed King Saul that he prefers obedience over any sacrifice that you would offer. The sacrifices were required for fellowship, before Christ came into the earth. When Jesus came as the Christ, he became the ultimate sacrifice, Savior, and Lord for all time.[55] So, yes, during King Saul and Samuel the prophet's time, they were necessary and required.

Yet God prefers and requires obedience and submission, because he longs to be your God. He yearns to have an intimate and interpersonal relationship with each and every one of us.

It is for that reason that Christ came and died for us. He did so, to allow all of us who would accept Jesus Christ's sacrifice, while simultaneously accepting God into our hearts, and allowing him, through his Holy Spirit, to become both Savior and Lord. Then you and he can begin the stepwise-dependent journey to "Was Not."

This can only occur if you begin the process of humbling yourself before the higher power, and recognize that he is the Lord and Savior of your life. You do this via a complete prostration and submission of your free will. You must walk in lockstep with Yahweh, in complete submission and obedience to his will.[56]

King Saul failed miserably at all of this. It grieved the Holy Spirit. Samuel, the prophet and judge in Israel, walked in such submission and obedience to God that he allowed Samuel to feel the entire weight of

---

54. 1 Sam 15:22–23.
55. Matt 27:50–53; John 2:19–21; 20:16–18.
56. Rom 12:1–2.

the pain. Because God made the disobedient, blithely disrespectful, and soon-to-be-deposed King Saul (likely an ISTP) the first king of Israel.

Samuel informed Saul that since he had ignored the Lord's command, he was no longer king of Israel. "God's spirit and his ordaining anointing has left you." Saul, now ready to admit his sin of disobedience, begged Samuel to go back with Saul, in order to worship and make sacrifice with him. He then grabbed hold of Samuel's robe and held on so tight that he ripped it.

Samuel informed Saul, the now former king of Israel, metaphorically speaking, "Just as you ripped my robe, God has ripped the kingdom right out of your hands. He has given it to someone better than you."

Already? Yes, already. God takes obedience and submission very seriously. Once we begin to walk with him, please do not look back.[57]

Samuel went on to say that the one who God has just given the kingdom to will not lie nor will he change his mind.[58] Once the newly-coronated and anointed king begins to walk with God, he will never turn back or lie. He will submit to and obey all of God's commands. However, Samuel, the ever merciful one, ultimately relented and went with Saul to worship. However, that act in no way squared things between Saul and God.

Saul was doomed. His fate was sealed by his own disobedient and self-aggrandizing decision-making process. He allowed fear to dominate and guide his decisions, as opposed to obedience and submission. Later, King Saul would grow to treat the newly ordained King David as an enemy.

Saul would try to murder King David, because he was insanely jealous of him. Saul would also betray David on countless occasions. Because the Spirit and anointing had completely left him, his fears and insecurities were now left unfettered.

After worshipping, Samuel, still judge in Israel, ordered that King Agag be brought to him. He spoke to him about his atrocities against God, Israel, as well as many others. Then Samuel chopped Agag to pieces.

Saul and Samuel never saw each other again, not after both left the place of worship and went to their respective homes.[59] Saul was still

---

57. Luke 9:62.
58. Num 23:19.
59. 1 Sam 15:24–35.

nominally the King of Israel, but God's anointing and authority had left him because of Saul's fear, lies, disrespect, and disobedience.

SUBMISSION & OBEDIENCE MADE EASY

Back to "My Muse, the Fox"

Eventually, a few years later, she came to understand more about me. Once, on the day of her graduation, I figuratively moved heaven and earth. I left my position at the graduation ceremonies where I was working. I was working in my digi-brain college. I had to travel all the way across campus in order to go to her graduation.

I did this, although many of "my kids" were graduating that same day. I was actually working at the graduation at the time, however, I snuck out to attend hers. Why? Because she needed a win.

She may have never felt it. She probably had no idea what I had done, nor all that I had to go through in order to be there. But I promised that I would be there. So I was.

At my graduation, I had the preferred faculty parking but I had to fight through campus traffic to attend her graduation on the other side of campus. I knew that she needed—actually, I think we both needed—me to esteem her, this one time, over her friends.

You Do Love Me

Then, yet awhile after graduation, we met up again at a celebration event for one of my other "kids," who was also her close friend. I first saw "my muse" at the graduation ceremony. This was at another university. The friend had earned an advanced degree from there. Coincidentally, I would come to work there, as chief digi-brain, a while after this auspicious occasion.

I made my normal grand spectacle out of the love-hate relationship that I shared with "the fox." I think I hugged her and got a picture of it. I told all of my former students in attendance how happy I was to see all of them. I named each of them, in the row, skipping her. Then I said, "Oh yeah, and you too, 'fox.'" I enjoyed pouring gasoline on that fire.

After the graduation ceremonies ended, we went to a restaurant on the other side of town. At the restaurant, I somehow learned that she could not afford to pay for her dinner. So, as prideful and guarded as ever, she decided not to order food or eat, although she had traveled a great distance to attend the graduation.

I offered to pay, while trying not to let her know that I knew why she was not eating. I may have asked the waiter to allow her to order and charge me. Earlier at the restaurant, we exchanged some of our typically antagonistic banter. However, I hugged her because I truly missed seeing her on a regular basis. She was, and ever will be, "my muse."

However, somehow she found out that I wanted to pay for her dinner (which is why I tried secretly to insist and imply that she go ahead and order dinner.) Yet, when she found out, she finally got it! I will never forget the moment of her epiphany! She said, "You do love me!" I replied; "I always have! And I always will. More than you will ever know or realize."[60]

Then she said, "But can we still act like we hate each other?" I said, "Sure, absolutely." I wouldn't have it any other way.

That was how she related to me, and how she maintained her safe space with me. She could not, and still cannot, drop those walls. She was damaged and hurting from a hurt that was broadly associative.

I am not always that easy to take! Particularly not when I already know where it hurts and have been released to try to help heal that spot, if you let me. I can be gentle; but at times not so much, depending on the person and the pain, if I'm relentless in my pursuit to find and aid "my sheep."[61]

Seeking Submission & Obedience Makes Everything Better

The aforementioned King David later demonstrated the importance of listening intently to God as well as seeking him. David also demonstrated how vital it was for the King of Israel to submit to and obey God with vigilance in all of their ways. The King of Israel and Judah had to allow God to direct all of the courses of his life and those of the entire kingdom.[62]

---

60. 1 John 3:18.
61. John 10:27, 17:11–12.
62. Prov 3:6.

STEP FOUR: OBEDIENCE & SUBMISSION

When David was a younger man, he was constantly on the run from the jealous and fearful King Saul who had betrayed David, his best general. He consistently tried to kill David.[63]

Before Saul died, though after God had anointed David as future King of Israel, King David sought the Lord in all things; before he went into any battle or made any decision, he consulted the Lord.

Subsequent to his ascension to the thrones of Judah and then all of Israel, the occasions regarding King David's continued seeking of the Lord, early and often, diminished to an almost nonexistent state.[64] Not so coincidentally, his troubles proportionally and commensurately increased.[65]

Submission and obedience are not easy. We have or have had bags packed full of hurtful items that we use as excuses not to submit to and obey God. I earnestly beg you to unpack those bags with the Lord.[66] Allow someone trained that God can use to help you unpack, wash out, and cast all of the contents contained in that old bag as far as the east is from the west.[67]

Once you allow the Lord to help you to empty the baggage, submission and obedience are made easy.[68] Then you can resume, or begin, your journey with God, unencumbered in your acts of full submission and complete obedience.

---

63. 1 Sam 16–31.
64. 1 Sam 23:2, 23:4, 23:12, 30:8; 2 Sam 2:1, 5:19, 5:23, 21:1.
65. Ps 63:1; Isa 55:6.
66. Heb 12:1–2.
67. Ps 103:12.
68. Matt 11:30; 1 Pet 5:7.

7

Step Five: Endurance, Perseverance, & Seeking Diligently

WORKING MY WAY BACK TO YOU

I BELIEVE THAT IS the title and refrain from an old Motown song. (I should know this.) Anyway, the common refrain is quite relevant, relative to this particular step in our journey. These steps, if you remember, are not stepwise in nature. Only God can organize the order.

He is the master teacher, orchestra conductor, and choreographer of the steps and requisite tests that we take on each level. Only he can bring all of them together, synchronizing them with everyone else's journey, at just the right time. Such that, when we enter "Was Not," we are not ahead of nor behind schedule.

However, this refrain works, irrespective of what you are working through and toward, on this specific step in the journey. *Some* of my formerly academically at-risk students come to mind. In all, I had academically at-risk, as well as academically good standing, students from multiple majors and minors in that college (not to mention all of those who "just showed up.")

All of the academically at-risk students "thought" that they were fully capable of "working their way back to" academic good standing. This, irrespective of the current state of their GPA. They all had "clear

STEP FIVE: ENDURANCE, PERSEVERANCE, & SEEKING 139

eyes and a full heart." Alas, many are called, yet few were, in this case, capable.

Each of my academically at-risk (AAR) students were capable of handling the work required to succeed at the university level. If they could not handle it, they would not have been admitted to the university. The combination of admissions tests and other requirements are there to separate those who need more academic preparation from those who, on a sliding scale, were prepared to succeed at the institution that admitted them.

I Was a Good Digi-Brain

Due to a combination of circumstances and reasons, too many to name, my AAR students had not, to date, achieved academic success at a level commensurate with their classmates nor with university minimum required standards. Yet, on another sliding scale, some could actually recover from academic jeopardy, while still others required an alternative course of action.

Based on the numbers when you combined their current GPA with the weight of their total number of credits, attempted and earned, including the number of repeat courses still available to them, we could easily calculate the number of semesters and at what target GPA, relative to each semester, they would be required to achieve, in order to attain academic good standing.

Some could make it in a semester or two. Particularly, if they had not attempted and completed comparatively as many total credit hours. This is called elasticity: GPA elasticity, in this case.

However, some had simply attempted too many credits in order to recover academically, particularly considering the constraints that the university handbook mandated as required progress for each student class: freshman, sophomore, junior, and senior. This included the corresponding attempted and earned credit hours, associated with each academic level.

Juniors and seniors had very inelastic GPAs. It was tough to help an overall GPA increase, even with a 4.0 semester or two achieved during the current and future semesters. They had simply attempted and earned too many credits. Therefore, we had to explore other options, including different majors and intended career paths.

However, freshman and sophomores had more elastic GPAs. They could recover from a bad semester or two with some diligent work and a change in their study habits, as well as making the necessary and required adjustments to the distracting condition of their psychological and emotional state. They could do this by removing any and all personal stumbling blocks from their path to academic success.[1]

If they did these things, they could turn their GPA around with reasonable and assiduous effort. However, all of my AAR students had every intention and plan to change. Now is the time. As small children say to their parents, "I can do it."

The saddest cases, for which a "Jones reality break" became imminently necessary, included those seniors who would try to convince me that "I can get a 4.0 GPA over the next two semesters and then I will graduate." Not so fast, my friend.

First, and most importantly, we are looking at the same exact transcript. You have never come close to earning a 4.0 semester GPA. (Nor a 3.0, for that matter.) That is why they sent you to see me. So, let us set more realistic goals.

Perfecting Each Gift

This is where I perfected my talent and gift in the area of being able to completely detach from my emotions, or from getting swept up in student's passions and emotions. This is a particularly useful skill to develop within the arena of academic as well as personal counseling and advising. Most do not realize that they are only listening to one side of a story, a story with many hidden elements. These elements are intended to bias and elicit sympathy and empathy from the listening skilled helper.

I became equally adept at demonstrating empathy and compassion for my students and "kids" who needed Jones the counseling advisor to help them overcome some of the more difficult-to-navigate affairs of the heart. We needed to eliminate the personal and psychological concerns such that they could begin to make academic, personal,

---

1. 1 Cor 1:23, 9:19–23.

professional, and sometimes spiritual, progress toward eliminating weights and distractions,[2] allowing them to get back on track.

I was just as good at telling students that I was signing off on dismissing them from school for a year or forever as I was at helping them through a myriad of academic (and otherwise) issues and concerns, such that they could begin to make progress toward getting back on track. It did not matter to me; either way they needed my help.

Besides, relative to those being expelled; they did it to themselves. As I always say, "No one listens to me." Not at first, anyway.

However, they all come back to me. When they do, I say, "Let's fix it from here," (relative to the options and remedies that may be available to them at the time of their return, and considering their present situation).

All of my AAR students were workin' their way back to academic good standing, babe, with a burning love inside. Temptations, maybe? The Spinners, actually. I finally looked it up. Before my time . . .

They all needed to keep the faith and remain steadfast, all while enduring hardships like a good soldier, persevering through each day like it was their last. They also would be required to change their habits, heart, and mind as well as remain realistically diligent about the best path, in order to pursue the actualization of their academic goals.[3]

THOSE WHO DILIGENTLY SEEK HIM

Enoch's Walk

In one way or another, this entire stepwise-dependent progressive journey "model" is derived from and based on the story of Enoch, including all five of the books in the Bible where he appears. Enoch walked with God. He did so for three hundred years before he "Was Not." During that time, while on that walk, we can definitively state a few things without question. Although the actual story of Enoch, as it appears in the Book of Genesis 5:18–24 presents the most comprehensive account, albeit only encompassing six verses relative to his life's story.

That may be the most comprehensive account. However, this particular step is derivative of the reference to Enoch and his faith walk as it appears in Hebrews 11:5–6. It states that Enoch walked with God.

---

2. Heb 12:1.
3. Isa 26:3; 2 Tim 2:3–7; 1 Cor 15:58; 1 Tim 6:12.

It then builds on the Genesis account of Enoch by telling the reader that Enoch was noted for possessing faith that pleased God. It goes on to explain the manner and process by which everyone might learn to please God. It says that it is impossible to please God. However, if you do want to please him, you must first believe not only that he exists, but that he is the "I AM" who rewards his diligent seekers.

"I AM"

God declared himself as "I AM" to Moses.[4] When God declared this, Moses was protesting or negotiating God's command that he return to Egypt to tell Pharaoh to let his people go. His dissent in this instance focused on asking God, "Who should I tell them sent me? No matter what, they will not believe me nor will they receive me." God replied, "Tell them 'I AM' sent you." God went on to refer to himself as the Lord God Almighty of their forefathers: Abraham, Isaac, and Jacob.

God concluded the discussion of his own name by providing a specific description of himself, relative to this instance. He told Moses to tell the children of Israel, upon his obedient return to Egypt, that Jehovah, the self-existent one, Yahweh Elohim, El Shaddai, the Lord God Almighty, "I AM who I AM," has sent you. (The actual name that God used, YHWH, actually cannot be translated correctly or appropriately into English.)

I feel safe in saying that God was conveying that he is the Lord God Almighty, the self-existent one, the "I AM." He is the one who *is* and who would be Savior for the children of Israel, both from Egypt and when Christ comes again.

The only way to please him, as we have discussed, is to believe that he is "I AM," as did Enoch. Then you must believe that he is a rewarder of those who diligently seek "I AM." Thus, I am safe in saying that since Enoch pleased God, Enoch Believed in "I AM."

He believed that "I AM" is a rewarder of those who diligently seek him. Enoch diligently sought "I AM." However, Enoch's story does not chronicle the explicit details as they relate to what that diligent-seeking process looks like. For that, we will have to use other examples from the Bible.

---

4. Exod 3:13–15.

CALEB'S ENDURANCE

The book of Hebrews 10:36 makes a statement that effectively undergirds and serves as the foundation for this book. It states that we all need endurance. Endurance supports the understanding that after we have done the complete will of the Father, then we will receive the blessings that he has promised, and enter into the promised land of "Was Not."

Caleb's life exemplified many elements of this scripture: the people who are justified in righteousness and those who are recognized as righteous by God. They shall, as long as these same people are those who live their lives by faith.[5] They shall be called God's people. In the end, their faith in God will be justified, because the promises of God will, in time, at his appointed time, manifest themselves.[6]

Caleb is not the typical biblical leader in the sense that he does not have a formal title, although he was one of the first judges in Israel, appointed by Moses.[7] Caleb is far more known for his belief in God, faith in God, and by his enduring lifestyle. Caleb was also one of the original group of twelve men who were selected by Moses to scout the promised land.

Caleb, the son of a Kenizzite man named Jephunneh, was appointed to be the scout as a leader in Judah.[8] Caleb and Hosea, who Moses called Joshua, were the only two of a group of twelve leaders, that Moses appointed to scout the promised land of Canaan. Their good report stated, "Although there are many giants in the land promised to us by God, we should leave right now. We should go and conquer this promised land, in the name of the Lord."[9]

These two men understood that verse in Hebrews which, simply put, says, "The just shall live by faith."[10] These two men were confident because they first believed that God is "I AM." They also believed that God provides what he promises, because God is a covenant-, contract-, and promise-keeping God.[11]

---

5. Heb 10:36–38.
6. Rom 5:1–5; Rom 8:28–30; Heb 10:26–39.
7. Exod 18:13–27; Num 13:1–3, 4–16.
8. Num 32:12.
9. Num 13:30.
10. Heb 10:38.
11. Eph 3:20.

Therefore, they believed God and they believed that it was the Almighty God who promised to give that land to their forefathers. Thus, it did not matter to Caleb and Joshua if there were giants who occupied the land, nor did they care that there was a wall around Jericho. They knew that, come what may, God promised, so let's go collect on that promise right now.

Caleb and Joshua's fellow spies, the other ten, were not in agreement. They told lies and stabbed their Hebrew brothers in the back, in order to get the other children of Israel to side with them. I have mentioned this same type of betrayal, relative to the people of God, who are on a stepwise journey to "Was Not" throughout this book.

These geniuses actually suggested that the whole nation of Israel plot a coup on Moses and return to slavery in Egypt.[12] The result of this entire fiasco was that God declared, through Moses, that they would spend another forty years in the wilderness, and that none other than Caleb and Joshua, men of faith, would enter the promised land. This, after Moses assuaged the anger of God, who was set to destroy all of the Israelites and make a new nation with Moses' children.

God would have still fulfilled his promises because Moses and all of them were the progeny of Abraham, Isaac, and Jacob. But I believe that God was testing Moses in order to get Moses to realize exactly how, "Ye and amen," or "Yes and so be it," are the promises of God.[13] Once Moses "convinced God" to allow his righteous anger and indignation toward the children of Israel to subsist, Moses informed the camp of their pending fate.

Faith That Endures

Moses told them that none of them, except for Caleb and Joshua, would survive to enter the promised land, relative to the nation taking possession of it.[14] By the way, this also seems to be a recurring theme throughout the book of Hebrews 11.

Those who live and want to remain in fear always want to stone to death, throw in a dungeon, attack, kill, lie on, etc., those who stand in faith. However, God keeps the faithful and righteous safe. He uses those

---

12. Num 13, 14.
13. 2 Cor 1:20–22.
14. Num 14.

STEP FIVE: ENDURANCE, PERSEVERANCE, & SEEKING

evil plans as tests and as stepping stones for the righteous on their way to "Was Not." For their part, the children of Israel wanted to stone Caleb and Joshua to death, in order to remain in and maintain their fears. Fear is the enemy of faith. Then they could return to Egypt and glorious slavery.

God is faithful and he gives grace to the humble.[15] Yet, that same God resists the proud. He can do nothing for those who choose the comfort of their familiar fears over faith.

God said of Caleb that he is a man of a different attitude and posture toward him. Caleb will survive this purging of the nation of Israel. God went on to say that everyone who was twenty years old and older was appointed to die. However, Caleb and Joshua would survive, living to enter and possess the promised land. Not only that, but Caleb, with the faith that endures, would live to inherit a full share of land.[16]

A Special Blessing for Enduring Faith

This meant that Caleb would inherit a special portion of the land that was dedicated to the people of Judah. This special allotment of land would be reserved exclusively for Caleb and his offspring. Caleb would live long enough to see these promises delivered to him and the nation of Israel by God. Those who survived anyway.

Caleb would also live to inform Joshua, as well as request, that allotment from him as the Leader of Israel, some forty years after they scouted the promised land. The original promise occurred back when Caleb was a forty-year-old man. Caleb, now an octogenarian, stated that he was ready himself to fight and to secure his special inheritance of land. He stated that he was just as strong, at eighty, as he was at forty. He would personally lead his clan to take possession of their special inheritance land, located within the land given to the children of Judah.[17]

Caleb would not only volunteer to lead and fight, but he would be assigned to the land where those very same giants resided.[18] It was those same giants who scared the other ten scouts, the ones who started all of this fear and treachery.

---

15. Jas 4:6.
16. Num 14:24.
17. Josh 14, 15.
18. Num 15:13–19.

The Heroes of Faith

The book of Hebrews 11:1–12 discusses enduring faith, such as that which Caleb possessed. In modern vernacular, we have come to refer to the entire group as the heroes of faith. Hebrews 12 discusses the fact that they and their faith serve as a great cloud of witnesses and testimony to the faithfulness of God. It discusses the manner in which these men and women walked by the faith which pleases God.

Those heroes of the faith should help us who read this book to prepare ourselves to vigorously run through the next forty plus years of our personal stepwise progressive journey, all the way to "Was Not." We should be fully energized to run with purpose and endurance, because we know that God has trained, taught, and tested us at every level. Thus, the next forty days or forty years, can be run with endurance until we reach and see manifested all of the promises made to us by God.

Caleb's "Was Not"

Caleb's "Was Not" occurred when he defeated that which defeated the children of Israel forty years prior. They were all afraid of the giants in the promised land which, save twelve, they had actually never seen.[19] Caleb possessed the same miraculous strength at age eighty as he had at age forty when he first scouted the promised land with Joshua and the other ten men appointed by Moses.

Caleb ran through his trial, one of which actually was the people fearing the unknown giants and other obstacles that lie ahead. This test was not the giants themselves. The test that Caleb, Joshua, and all of the children of Israel had taken, attaining varying levels of success, was overcoming fear.[20]

He also ran through his own kinsmen who desired to stone him and Joshua to death, followed by a desire to return to bondage in Egypt. All because Caleb and Joshua believed God.

It was definitely accounted to them as righteousness.[21] Caleb and Joshua were the only ones above twenty to run forty more years directly into their "Was Not." It was the "Was Not" for every one of the children

---

19. 1 Pet 5:8.
20. 1 John 4:18; Rev 12:11.
21. Rom 4:22.

of Israel, beginning with Abraham. Caleb was just as strong, on the back end, at eighty, as he was on the front end of his journey.

Caleb *ran* into the promised land and his "Was Not." He conquered every obstacle that would stop the children of Israel from possessing the promised land. Caleb, standing as a testimony for all time, ran to defeat the giants and possess his special promise. Finally, he helped to ensure that all of Israel would possess their promised land.

That is exactly how and when Caleb entered into "Was Not." He let the promises of God pull him through and into "Was Not," just like Jesus in Hebrews 12:2. Caleb's Faith endured. Like Job, he came out with much more than he entered the journey possessing.

PERSEVERING & STUMBLING THROUGH PLACE TO NEW PLACE

The concepts of perseverance and endurance are very similar. Yet, I believe that Joseph more closely exemplifies the true meaning of the word perseverance, particularly as it relates to the Bible and the manner in which I remember most scriptures (i.e., New King James Version, seventeenth century English).

I do not prefer that version for the purposes of reading and comprehension, because we are a few centuries beyond that era now. I guess, it's a result of the fact that the NKJV was the first Bible that I owned in hard copy, and that was the translation of choice for most people and churches when I was growing up. That's how I remember things.

That version has numerous New Testament examples where the translator employs the word "perseverance," within the context of the verses of scripture. The best example, relative to how I am using the word, in reference to this stepwise journey, is found in Romans 5. There, Paul is discussing all things as they pertain to faith.[22]

The Setup

Paul is discussing how faith helps us to find success amid trouble. Particularly when it is God-permitted trouble that we are encountering, like the two times that God set Job up. There really is no other fair way to describe what happened to Job, other than a setup.

22. Rom 5:1–5.

Of course, we know that God knows what is best for all of us. However, to my knowledge, there is not another instance in the Bible where God recommends one of us directly to the enemy, as he permit the enemy to attack Job in every conceivable manner, except that he could not kill him.[23] That's a setup.

Everyone, whether actively or passively, stumbles a bit through trouble. I can speak personally and acknowledge that it takes time for us to narrow our field of vision when we are going through a God-permitted, and probably encouraged, trial.

What I mean by that is, I am familiar with the process of hearing God speak. How to familiarize yourself with his voice is a matter for another book, one which he has not told me to write or even outline at this point in my mini-writing career. That last statement itself speaks of "hearing from God."

Hearing from God does not mean anything overly complicated. I know that many who, as I would say, don't trust it are probably making the process too complicated. I mentioned this earlier in the book. It is the only concrete way, other than just fellowship with God, walking as Adam and Enoch did, to familiarize yourself with the voice and speech patterns of God.

God walked with both Enoch and Adam. He walked with Adam, in the cool or relaxing, non-work-related portion of the day. But do not stop there. The best way to get close to God and become accustomed to hearing his voice is to live a life, walking with God, living in close fellowship with him for the rest of your life. Do this: before, during, and after "Was Not."[24]

What God Sounds Like

However, my earlier advice, beyond just learning to intimately fellowship with God, is to read and study his Word. I believe and can testify to the fact that, as you familiarize yourself with the scriptures, you will begin to learn what God sounds like. You will learn how he speaks because all scripture is theópneustos, a Greek word meaning God-breathed.[25]

---

23. Job 1–2.
24. Gen 3:8, 5:22.
25. 2 Tim 3:16.

STEP FIVE: ENDURANCE, PERSEVERANCE, & SEEKING 149

He has his own Ebonics-styled, heavenly, colloquial speech pattern and dialect." That was a humorous way of stating that each subculture within a larger society uses certain speech patterns and phrases. These patterns, phrases, and idioms are common and germane to, not only that particular subculture within a certain geographic region, but those things transcend geography and permeate the entire subculture located within a nation or country.

Yet they can be refined even further to make them germane to each household and familial clan, meaning that the Smiths do not sound exactly like the Jones'. And the Jones' do not sound very much like the Thomas'. And so on.

I am certain, during the days following the time when the children of Israel fully possessed the promised land, that the half tribe of Ephraim spoke differently than the tribe of Judah. For example, Samuel the prophet was from Ephraim, as was Joshua. King Saul was from Benjamin, and King David, as well as Caleb, were both from Judah. First Chronicles 12 discusses the people who joined the anointed King David at his stronghold in Ziklag, which was located in the southern portion of Judah.

First Chronicles 12:1–40 states while King David was hiding from King Saul, who wanted to kill him, men from all twelve tribes joined David out in Ziklag because he was the anointed king. It goes on to say that men from the tribe of Benjamin were great and ambidextrous warriors who could shoot arrows and sling stones. They joined King David's ever-growing army in the stronghold of Ziklag. That ability was attributable to no other tribe's soldiers.

Further, it says that some of the warriors from Gad, who were all commanders in King Saul's Army, defected and joined King David in Ziklag. The weakest of these commanders from the tribe of Gad could individually whip one hundred regular enemy troops. The strongest of the commanders from Gad could beat 1,000 enemy troops. Also, the men from Ephraim, almost 21,000 strong, were valiant warriors. Each of these men were highly respected within their own clan.[26]

After the Lord told David to move back to the mainland of Judah, the men from his tribe of Judah invited him to become their king.[27] Then, there were more defections away from the house of King Saul. While most of the men from the tribe of Benjamin, who were Saul's relatives,

---

26. 1 Chr 12:14.
27. 2 Sam 2.

remained loyal to Saul's house, 3,000 leaders from Benjamin joined King David in Hebron.

It is also said that the two hundred leaders, with their relatives from the tribe of Issachar, all joined King David in Hebron. These leaders, or chiefs, from Issachar "understood the signs of the times and knew the best course of action for Israel to take," relative to ensuring that King David not only became their king in Hebron, but that David would become king of all of Israel (which he soon would).[28]

The point of all of this is that David, who, at that time, was still asking God for direction, heard directly from God. God spoke to David and placed him where he would be even more widely received as king. Thus, many people from the twelve tribes of Israel joined David while he was still in Ziklag.

Also, and equally as important relative to this discussion, each of these tribes had their own special attributes, idioms, speech patterns, and mannerisms. These were exclusively germane to that specific tribe.

Thus, we all have certain subcultural speech patterns, and so does God. You have to learn to "hear God" so you "know what to do." Just like the sons of Issachar.[29] God, too, speaks in a certain way.

I believe that it is also dependent on his audience as well as the person that he is speaking through, the person that he is using as a prophet, preacher, or even as a writer. God breaths his word and his word is eternal.

I hope that I did not overcomplicate a subject that I was attempting to make a little easier for you. My desire is to make the idea of "hearing God speak" less intimidating and less complicated. My simple point is: read the Bible and I believe that it will help you to hear God speaking in his, at times, still and small voice which speaks inside of you, Spirit to spirit.[30]

PERSEVERANCE, A STEPWISE PROGRESSION, & FAITH

I started all of this by discussing the manner in which the NKJV Bible uses perseverance. In Romans 5, Paul is telling the Romans that we as believers in Christ have access to his grace or to his favor. He bestows his grace and favor upon us merely because he loves us, not because we have

---

28. 1 Chr 12:32.
29. Rom 10:17.
30. 1 Kgs 19:11–12.

STEP FIVE: ENDURANCE, PERSEVERANCE, & SEEKING

or could ever earn that love. Paul immediately shifts the conversation to discuss why we should glory, revel, and celebrate when we are amid tribulations and trying times.

Paul says that we should celebrate because if we are going through trials, tests, and other tumultuous periods in our lives with God as our guide, then that trial will produce some good fruit in our lives.

A trial will produce perseverance which is an internal drive to steadily make progress toward a goal, in spite of any incurred delays and/or difficulties encountered along the way. I am not citing a source here because I just made that one up. However, I believe that it is pretty representative of what Paul means.

Paul goes on to actually demonstrate for us what a successive, stepwise progression of incidents and/or occurrences looks like when written out. Paul states that perseverance produces integrity, spiritual maturity, and character in a person if they continue to endure and persevere, progressing steadily through the trial. That character produces an ever-developing confidence in God, which breeds a calming, blessed assurance and hope on the inside of us. This occurs with the progress that we continue to make on this journey through trouble. That assurance, as well as confident hope, will not leave us ashamed or disappointed in the end.[31]

It ends up producing a confidence in us which allows us to say that faith, for us (at this point following the trial) is the spiritual representation of the thing that we hoped for. Faith is the belief that we have what we cannot see, because we know that the one who promised will always make good on his promises.[32]

Set Up Inside of a Set Up

Through that stepwise progression, which Paul just laid out for us in Romans, we will, as a result of our humanity and being born into this world, inevitably stumble a bit on our way to "Was Not." As I briefly mentioned in this section, I believe that the process narrows your field of vision over time.

God begins by revealing to you what is actually a rather blurry, obscure, unclear, and obfuscated picture. That is, if he chooses to show you

---

31. Rom 5:1–5.
32. Heb 11:1 (adaptation).

anything at all. He chose not to do so with Abraham.³³ There, God just said "Go. And I will show you where you are going while you are on your way." Or maybe "I AM" will wait until you get there to show you. At that point, "I AM" will just say, "Stop! Hammertime! We're here."

If he shows you, as he has shown me, where you are headed, then, over time during the journey, you learn not to attach yourself to your preconceived outcome. However, even that concept is a learned skill. It is not something that is inherent or that comes naturally. It is, as Paul said to the Romans, a thing that the trial produced in you.

A Crucible Moment at a Comfortable Place

If you recall, the other times while I was in the classroom at some specific universities, I always had my digi-brained managerial responsibilities. Although I never actually left the classroom as a professor once I entered it, I simply may not have been teaching at and for the same college that I was serving as a digi-brain for. However, at one digi-brained-only stop, I became increasingly and totally exasperated—set up inside of a setup. Also at many university stops, God would reveal other places and the next place that He would inform me that I would "next" and "soon" work at.

So, by this point I knew his voice because I am his sheep. During this season God was also deftly, though slowly, dropping the cloak on other callings and areas of gifting. I knew about these areas, however I thought that I had successfully avoided them without repentance.³⁴ As I soon learned, I just *thought* I was avoiding those gifts and talents. He has an appointed time for those, too.

Fast-forward awhile at a new and comfortable place, or so I thought. He decided to bring me to a chief of the digi-brained, unruly people, crucible moment. He decided to invoke his Isaiah 53:7 "like a sheep before his shearers, so Jones, open not your mouth" clause.

Just like Christ in a fight, who could have called down legions of angels and won the fight, I, too, could have all too easily, won my fight.³⁵ Alas, it was a fight where this pugilist was forbidden from taking one swing and knocking the queens as well as the entire digi-brain fiefdom

---

33. Gen 12, 24.
34. Jonah 1; Jonah 2:8–10; John 10:27; Rom 11:29.
35. Matt 26:53.

and kingdom down for good. As it turned out, it fell very shortly thereafter on its own. But I wanted to do it.

The point is, he told me that I was going to a "new place." However, he did not tell me by what road, nor which obstacles would be placed in or permitted to enter the path. So, as I am headed to the "new place," he also never told me how long it would take me to get there. He just birthed a vision, or a blurry snapshot, inside of me, one so palpable that I would persevere through any and every trial to get there.

Funny thing: he also neglected to tell me that this "New Place" (I posted the entire discourse on my personal Facebook page), or what I thought was the "New Place" was, in fact, always intended to be a "through place."

Puzzling Reflections in a Mirror

That's the thing about perseverance: no matter the obstacle, you will fight on. You will be, what can only be described as Theópneustos-compelled on the inside to never quit. Further, you will never stop pursuing the prize.[36] You are compelled by the Holy Spirit and by the unquenchable desire to see the fulfillment of the vision. Even though in my story, the vision was clarified when I initially thought that it had changed.

I started out pressing toward what was in fact "through place," forgetting the declaration, which preceded the vision. Do you remember? I did not. "Once you get me back into the classroom, full-time, I will never come back out of it."

This is an example of the declaration and the promise birthed inside of you that makes you pursue and persevere to the end. As I went along, my vision, though not the vision itself, was clearing up.[37] I became more targeted and focused. I learned to move the weapon whenever he would shout out at a moment's notice, "There's the target. Hit it."

How Do You Hit a Target?

I used to ask my students, "How do you hit a target?" This is an Earlism, as I call these little phrases and teachable lessons. The correct answer,

---

36. Phil 3:14.
37. 1 Cor 13:9–12.

depending on how often you hang around with me and listen to me (no one listens to me, remember), is "Throw something at it."

In other words, you cannot achieve your goals without propelling a perfectly useful and appropriate projectile toward the goal or target. I will leave that one right there. You can decipher it for yourself.

Anyway, I learned to adapt and persevere. He could now take me anywhere. He could, and believe me, he did, throw anything at me. I would, fight on.

I was now battle tested. I could go through any "Through Place" now that I knew where "New Place" was located. I knew that I had to continue to trust, accept, obey, and continue to make progress, irrespective of the pain and discomfort, hospital visits, and a pugilistic sneak-attack. The latter was followed by a violent and torrential reaction, in and from me, one from which only the Holy Spirit could have restrained in me. Thank God, he did.

Now I could endure anything. I had to get there. I had to get to the "New Place."

However, I stumbled. I wondered, "God, where are you? Why didn't you come?"[38]

God did not come because Elohim never left. However, you will stumble. Just make it. Fight on. You will get better at making it. Perseverance and endurance will win the day. Why? Because you have diligently sought him all along throughout this journey.[39]

JOSEPH'S STUMBLES AND PERSEVERANCE

I believe that Joseph experienced one possible stumble on his walk. He would definitely merit high distinction on the faithful endurance, assiduous perseverance, and diligent-seeking graduate level rating scale. We will discuss his largely indiscernible stumble, then we will briefly mention the action of questionable origin at the end of this section.

At the age of seventeen Joseph endured a plot to kill him. The plot was hatched and concocted by his murderously jealous older brothers.[40] They literally planned to kill Joseph. They settled for listening to Reuben,

---

38. Gal 6:9.
39. Heb 11:6.
40. Ps 105:15; Acts 7:9–10.

and just throwing Joseph into a cistern. The plan was to allow him to die of natural causes in that pit.[41]

Reuben

If you want to talk about questionable motives inspired by reprehensible actions, then let's talk about Jacob's oldest boy, Reuben. Reuben actually tried to stop his younger siblings from killing Joseph.

Reuben had very selfish motives in mind relative to his desire to derail the planned murder of his younger brother. Joseph was their dad's favorite son because he was the son of his old age, and because he was the first born son of Jacob's preferred wife, Rachel.

Reuben slept with one of Jacob's handmaiden wives, Bilhah.[42] (So many people and ministers misinterpret that very straightforward, aforementioned verse of scripture.) Bilhah was the servant of Rachel. Rachel gave Bilhah to Jacob so she could bare children for her as a surrogate. Reuben wanted to bring Joey back home to dad in hope that dad would forgive his abominable transgression.

Back to Joseph: the brothers threw him in a pit as Reuben requested instead of outright committing murder. Now the Ishmaelite traders were the progeny of their Great Uncle Ishmael. He was the son of their Great-Grandfather Abraham's handmaiden wife, Hagar.[43] Thus, when they saw their distant relatives coming toward them, headed to sell goods, and likely other slaves in Egypt, they decided, why should we simply settle for letting a cistern kill Joseph?

We can fish him out of the pit and sell him to the Midianite traders for twenty pieces of silver.[44] By the way, Reuben also showed his true, duplicitous colors when he ripped his garments in grief as he returned to the pit. Reuben arrived, only to find that Judah had beat him to the silver punch.[45] That was Joseph's second trial, after God had birthed a vision of "Was Not" in his Spirit. The first trial written about was the jealousy he faced as a seventeen-year-old after describing "God's business" to his family.

41. Gen 37:1–22.
42. Heb 13:4.
43. Gen 16:1–16, 30:1–24, 35:22.
44. Gen 37:26–28.
45. Gen 37:29–36.

Joseph in Egypt

As Joseph graduated from a pit, the brothers' test, to Potiphar's house, he soon met Lady Potiphar, the lust-obsessed, controlling, lying, backstabbing wife.[46]

He gets through that, literally, with his skin still intact. Although he had been set up for death again (this time by execution as opposed to murder). All of this happened within the span of his comparatively brief young adult life. And, once again, he takes the next step . . . into prison.

However, Joey is progressing nicely in prison. He continues to take on leadership roles wherever he stops, managing to successfully lead homes and people, while dodging sex-crazed wives and murderously duplicitous, greedy, scheming brothers. Joseph then takes a slight stumble while using his gift to do God's business.[47]

An Imperceptible Stumble While Doing God's Business

If you are slightly to reasonably familiar with Joseph's story (which you are after reading the preceding chapters and corresponding scripture references in this book), you are also likely thinking to yourself, "What? He stumbles *after* surviving the two murder plots, and not before?" Yep, after. Joseph stumbles while in prison, translating the God-inspired dreams of two prisoners under his care.

The warden assigned Joseph to the penultimate leadership role in the prison, the position under the warden himself, just as Potiphar had done and just as Israel had done before Potiphar. The warden, too, recognized Joseph's extraordinary capacity for administrative leadership. Joseph's gifts and callings made room for him.[48]

God's vision, obscurely presented to Joseph in the beginning of the discussion on Joseph, compelled him along through each stage and its requisite trials, until he reached graduation and promotion to the next step. Joseph makes steady progress, always serving as every CEO's selected ranking vice president.

I refuse to call Joseph, or Daniel for that matter, digi-brains. They were not. They were anointed and extremely gifted administrative leaders,

---

46. Gen 39.
47. Gen 40:8.
48. Prov 18:16.

STEP FIVE: ENDURANCE, PERSEVERANCE, & SEEKING 157

men who operated in their areas of gifting, relative to dream interpretation and the aforementioned administrative leadership capacities under the grace and covering of the Spirit of God.

How Did Joseph Stumble?

Joseph, upon translating the dreams of his two beleaguered charges, while in Pharaoh's dungeon, asks one of those two gentlemen for help. This request is why I say that Joseph stumbled. The story is presented in Genesis 40.

The Bible states that Joseph noticed how troubled the baker and butler (both members of Pharaoh's personal household staff) looked one day. He asked them about their concerns and countenances. They told him that they both had a dream the previous night, and that they had no one to interpret their dreams.[49]

For the second time, the Bible makes an obscure reference to the fact that every dream, revelation, or vision that comes from God has a confirming, corresponding action. In this case, confirmation came in the form of a second dream.[50] Joseph responds to them by (correctly) telling them that interpreting dreams is God's business. "So, please, tell me your dreams."[51]

Joseph is acknowledging that he is gifted in the area of dream interpretation. He is capable, by the grace of God, of listening to God-breathed dreams. He is effectively telling the baker and the butler that he can understand God's initially obscure voice, and he is concurrently expedient in the area of translating that voice and vision.

The Living Embodiment of a Dream Interpretation

By virtue of his speedy promotions in any and every circumstance, Joseph is also gifted in the area of becoming the manifested translation of someone else's dream. These four men, Israel, Potiphar, the prison warden, and the Pharaoh of Egypt, all desired to run smooth business operations. They dreamed of achieving great success, relative to the organizations

---

49. Gen 40:8–23.
50. Deut 19:15; Eccl 4:9.
51. Gen 40:8.

or empire that each led, and they had a strong desire to see their dream come true.

When Joseph showed up on the scene, all of their dreams came true. This occurred because God used Joseph to make the crooked pathways straight, within any and every organization where he became affiliated.[52] All because Joseph received unmerited favor or grace, relative to the callings and gifts on his life (particularly in the areas of dream interpretation, leadership, and administration).[53] These gifts made room for Joseph, whether functioning as a beloved son yet despised brother, a slave, a prisoner, or as an ex-con.[54]

This gifted ability to become the living embodiment of a dream interpretation is an area of gifting that I believe we can all receive and walk in by grace. It is inherently placed on our lives as a part of God's overarching plan and purpose for our lives. However, we only will come to see it manifested with it most likely occurring at many stops along the journey (similar in fashion to how it transpired in Joseph's life).

The idea of "you are already doing it" previously mentioned in this book comes to mind. At every level and step, God employed, through his grace and Joseph's submission, the gifts and callings that he had placed on Joseph's life. All of this occurred in preparation for his big moment when he would go before Pharaoh. Again, we will only see this grace to become the living embodiment of many dream interpretations if we stay on the path with God, keeping pace, and vigilantly pursuing his will as we progress toward and enter "Was Not."

Renegotiating the Contract

Joseph, after translating the butler's dream, makes what I would tacitly call an error of conscience. He neglects or forgoes God's increasing blessed assurance, an assurance that comes and increases inside of us as we progress through the journey. This is an assurance that Paul would speak of in Romans 5. Joseph asks for help, but God never told him to ask for help.

---

52. Rom 11:29.
53. 1 Cor 15:10.
54. Prov 18:16.

Joseph Asks for Help

When you are on the journey with God, on the surface, at times, you will be embroiled within a "dilly of a test." Consequently, you need, or will soon need, help. Personally, I despised and still loathe that part. I hate asking for help or assistance—from anyone, with absolutely anything.

Joseph was accustomed to being the one providing the help. He probably preferred it that way too. However, this time, he asked the butler to remember him when he was released from prison in three days as per the translation of his dream. Joseph told the butler that he was effectively kidnapped from his father's home, the land of the Hebrews, in Canaan. He went on to say that he was locked in jail by a backstabbing, lying, Lady Potiphar. Though, of course, he did not use her name, in order to protect the ignorant.

I call it a slight, if even that, error of conscience and faith. Joseph, by this point, battle-tested, demonstrated some overt frustration. He had to have known by now that God was in charge, and El Shaddai, the Almighty God, was orchestrating *all* of the activities transpiring in his life.

Why Have You Forsaken Me?

However, with no apparent end in sight, and when faced with constant and recurring betrayals and horrors (which must have felt like recurring death every time they happened), it is a very true statement that your heart does not have a brain. ("I AM" made it so "I AM" knows.) But I will tell you from experience that at this point, your brain is at times on another mission!

You know that God has you in the palm of his hand.[55] But in that palm is an intense inferno, burning your flesh so badly that all you want to do is cry . . . or cry havoc, and simply get free for some relief. Why have you forsaken me? Why are you so far from my roaring and groaning voice?[56]

While, God, you seemingly and simultaneously ignore those who are torturing and backstabbing me, you (seemingly) allow them to lie, cheat, and mislead, without restraint and with impunity. It hurts worse

---

55. Isa 49:16.
56. Ps 22:1.

than anything that anyone could imagine. [57] That person feels abandoned by the only God that they have always known they could count on.[58] But, those on Enoch's stepwise dependent progressive journey also know, simultaneously, that God has actively orchestrated and permitted all of this—a completely, painfully confounding, enigmatic conundrum.

This is especially true for Job: right down to the boils on his skin that he scraped off with broken pottery; right down to his wife telling him to "Curse God and die"; and right down to his friends relentlessly accusing him of a crime that he never committed.

That stuff is not just a story in a book. Job, Joseph, and many others, depending on your calling and your "Was Not" may be required to live through some very painful, painstakingly arduous steps and tests. You might feel like no one cares, not that you trusted many from the outset. You really may not trust anyone now.

You have been left uncovered. Literally left for dead. This, by people who, at one time, you viewed as a parent, brother, or friend. They claimed that they viewed you in reciprocation.

So, you treat your children this way, huh? No, actually you do not. I know your children. However, *now*, I also know you.

Didn't You Realize I Was There?

Did my heart not go with you? Was I not there with you, in spirit, when you betrayed me?[59] God shows me a great many things. You, above most, already know that.

God has already shown me where it hurts. He sent me there to help you. It's not about me. He sent me there to guide you through his God-breathed process of healing.

He sent me there to help you overcome your many fears and control mechanisms. These fears have stopped you from becoming truly obedient, submissive, and intimately acquainted and walking in fellowship with his Holy Spirit. You thought that you had successfully hidden your dirty laundry, which you shoved in that packed suitcase for many years.

---

57. Jonah 4:1–4.
58. Hab 1:1–4, 12–17.
59. 2 Kgs 5:26, 6:8–23.

But your masks could not fool God. Through him, I saw right through them, too.[60]

But you refused. You refused his help, so vehemently, in fact, that you tried to do all you could to eliminate me, his representative. Blaming me for being the one who made you so completely uncomfortable inside, and then you set about, in true Lady Potiphar form and fashion, on the task of trying to turn all others against, not the Holy Spirit, but against me.[61]

Joseph Knew

Joseph knew. Joseph knew why Reuben did what he did. He knew exactly where Judah was hurting, and why he behaved as he did. No one, not even Potiphar, knew Lady Potiphar as well as Joseph the visionary, dream interpreter of God's business, knew her.

Remember, God only reveals to this select group of us what he wants us to know.[62] However, because he allows me, as well as Joseph, to endure so much, and because he so arduously and assiduously tests and tries us at every step, the Holy Spirit reveals a lot to Joseph and me, about many people, at his sovereign discretion.

The Father desires intimacy with each and every person, but he cannot have it with you if you have wounds that are not healed—wounds that you lie, cheat, steal, kill, and destroy in order to cover and protect.[63]

Joseph Wanted Out

Joseph wanted out, and he wanted out in the worst way.

He had just done a God-inspired favor for the butler. Joseph knew that the butler would be back in the King's palace in three days. Armed with this information, Joseph rendered his plea for assistance and mercy to someone who he thought could and would help him, not someone who God told him to ask. This is never permitted on the stepwise-dependent journey.

60. 2 Kgs 4:27.
61. 1 Sam 8:6–7.
62. 2 Kgs 4:27.
63. John 10:10.

I mean, really? Come on. Who do you think we are dependent on for help?[64] Who are we developing a dependence on via our perseverance? Jehovah God, the self-existent one.

A Mere Crisis of Conscience

That's why I say Joseph had a crisis of conscience, unless you consider being completely forgotten by a man who, just three days ago, had given you a blessed interpretation of God's business a horrible kingdom crime or sin (if you consider sin being forgotten by a man for whom, in all likelihood, this was the first time that he had ever encountered a God-breathed dream, and a subsequent God-inspired interpretation of said dream).

The interpretation involved him correctly predicting that you would get out of jail, and that you would get your old job back. That same man also successfully interpreted a dream that said that you would be completely restored to your former position as Pharaoh's advisor and butler, a position that likely landed you under suspicion of the crime which resulted in your incarceration in Pharaoh's dungeon.

If it is sin to ask for help from that guy, the one who, in three days (and maybe an hour), completely forgets about the man who interprets dreams and handles God's business, then it must also be a sin to ask for one human-inspired favor, a simple request stating, "Please remember me. Please. And mention me, as well as my plight (what you know of it, anyway). Mention me to Pharaoh, such that I might find mercy or favor from the king of Egypt, your boss. And 'get out of here.'"

If that is considered sin in your personal rule book, then Joseph sinned. However, if you consider that as less than a transgression of God's divine mandates to us believers, then you understand why I call what Joseph did, "a slight error of conscience."

A Forgotten Dreamer

The Bible states that the butler completely forgot about Joseph, never giving him, his request, or the dream another thought.[65] Two years later: you are still on the last step, awaiting your final exam.

---

64. Pss 121:1–4.
65. Gen 40:23–41:13.

If you call that punishment, then maybe he did suffer a consequence for his crisis of conscience.[66] I honestly do not know. However, I do know exactly how Joseph felt.

I have felt the same way at times. I am certain that you have also. Pain hurts. I do not blame him one bit for asking. Honestly, I am not even saying that Joseph was wrong.

But I am saying that God did not inspire that particular request. I feel certain in saying that. Doing things without first getting clearance for those who are called to make the journey to "Was Not," as was Joseph, is sadly not permissible.

However, in all, Joseph was OK. He just wanted out. You are supposed to want out. God wants you to want out. But he wants you to want him above everything, including wanting out.

Joseph turned out OK in the end. He graduated with the highest of high distinction honors. He received a big ole medallion. As Doc once said, "This is why we came."

Bottom Rail on Top

Later in Genesis 42, Reuben recalls how Joseph pleaded with the brothers not to hurt or kill him. Yet, of course, they would not hear the voice of his distress.[67] Joseph decided to play the first of a few games with them.

The boys, the same ten culprits, many years later, had come to Egypt. They came because famine ravaged the entire region. By now, Joseph was in charge. He was second in command, once again, only this time to Pharaoh himself. Thus, once again, Joey was placed in the administrative managerial leadership role that he was so anointed, and now thrice trained by God to perform.

PLAYING CLUE

Another way of discussing Joseph's slight crisis of conscience, as I have deemed it, is via another epiphany or revelation, one that God has recently provided me with on my journey. He showed me this one, just prior to reaching "Was Not."

---

66. Gen 41:1.
67. Gen 42.

Does anyone remember the old board game Clue? The object of the game was to figure out (seems so archaic now) which three cards were inside of a card-sized manila envelope. In there, the person not playing the game during that round would place three cards that were the solution to a murder mystery. Then the participants with their game board pieces, each comprised of differing colors, akin to the surnames of the characters, moved from room-to-room throughout the gameboard. Some random instrument was placed in each room that may or may not have been used as a weapon by some fictitious character in the old Victorian-style mansion where the murder mystery occurred.

I do not remember who the poor sucker was who served as the murdered one in the game. But the people in the house were all suspects. They were the only ones in the house when someone ended up becoming the victim of this crime. No one investigated motive in this game. However, in true crime-solving format, they did offer each participant means and opportunity. Two out of the three primary elements of a crime ain't bad.

You would roll the dice (either one or two, I forget which), and move through the hallways, proceeding from room-to-room around the board. Each number on the dice represents a step. In each room you receive a clue, the eponym of the game. All of the players would receive the same clue. When a player thought that they had collected enough evidence to attempt a formal guess relative to who committed the crime, with what weapon, and in which specific room in the house, they would hazard a guess.

I realized at an early age that I never lived in a house like this one. These people and others like them were living a completely different life than the one that this child had experienced. I knew what a bedroom was. I had a kitchen, as well as a living room and a basement—where to me, that would be the most logical place to commit such a crime. However, basement was not one of the options. I had never heard, until playing Clue, that there was a study and some of the other rooms in that huge mansion.

Anyway, if your guess was incorrect, you were somehow penalized for making an incorrect deduction, and everyone who heard the guess now knew and could summarily cross off one to all three items mentioned in the incorrect guess. We all had a card that represented a weapon, we were a character (and knew that we did not do it), and we all had a room card. I think that is how it went.

Maybe you were not penalized. I loved the game, but I do not remember all of the specifics. Many people thought it boring. However, even as a kid, I loved a challenge. I was able to use my intuitive, information-gathering and assessment skills, as any good ENTJ would. I loved the game—I think I will download the Clue app after I am finished writing.

The "Or" Game

What I have recently realized is, as I inch ever-closer to entering "Was Not," that God has had me playing Clue all along. Joseph was more than willing during the height of his minor "crisis of conscience" (when he asked the butler to remember and mention him to Pharaoh so Pharaoh could literally get him out of "the joint").[68]

In addition to playing Clue, Joseph was also playing the "or" game. He was willing to receive this "or" that on his way to "Was Not," as if God did not set out all of the parameters of the promised land before Joseph ever dreamed one dream.[69] Joseph was fully aware of what he was supposed to do. He realized that he was a natural born leader. He had that confirmed for him on multiple occasions.

These instances included working with his father's livestock, in Potiphar's house, and now in prison—the warden's house, if you will. So, he had definitive evidence that his dreams of leadership were certainly correct. The only problem was that he had no desire to live out those dreams as a slave, as a vilified brother, nor as a leader of the dungeon people.

This became his primary issue, which led to his minor "crisis of conscience." In effect, he said, "God, I get it. You have called, destined, and purposed me to be a leader as well as the living embodiment of dreams, proffered by many people of significant influence. However, based on my emotional, limited interpretation of the dreams about my brothers who sold me into slavery, after scrapping their murder plot, I never saw myself becoming a slave or indentured servant leader. Nor did I see myself as a prison leader, and definitely not as a leader of the murder people. I simply translated the dreams to mean that my brothers, and all members of my father's household, would come to bow down to me. As a result, I will take this 'or' that in order to get outta here and get back to the business of those murderers bowing down to me."

---

68. Gen 40:14–15.

69. Isa 46:10.

Clarification of the Vision

In Joseph's mind, the manifestation of the dream was way off track, even though it was actually manifesting every step of the way. He moved like someone playing Clue, from room-to-room. In each room, he would have another clue revealed to him, one that would help him solve the mystery and win the game.

We call this clarification of the vision. However, this was a clarification that he either totally missed or one that he did not want, because there is no way that God could possibly have meant "This, when he showed me that," right? Thus, he figured since the dream was already *way* off course, he would take the opportunity to get himself out of this circumstance, a circumstance which is actually a training crucible.

Or he would take it upon himself to get out of jail. Then maybe God would put the dream back on track. The most important thing to him right then was that he needed to get out of that jail, the "or" game. If not, his dreams, which were actually God's dreams, would never come true.

Joseph tried to settle. He was effectively stating, "God, you showed me leader. Thus, I need to get myself out of here so I can help you make your dreams come true."[70] This is always a no-no.

God never needs your help giving you what he promised you. Ask Abram about the covenant that God cut on his own. God signed, sealed, and delivered an unbreakable contract.[71] We tend to believe that God needs our help making his dreams come true in our lives.[72]

Navigation Help

We often play the "or" game with God when we are actually playing Clue. God shows us something via a dream. We do not see it manifesting swiftly enough for our taste. In accordance with our taste, it would happen the second after our dream. If you were Joseph, who after he had both dreams, he obediently told his brothers and father about them, you would expect that the guys would soon come to bow down to you and your colorful coat of leadership. You wouldn't think they'd dip your

---

70. Heb 10:23.
71. Gen 15.
72. Mark 11:22.

coat in goat's blood, rip it, and bring it to Dad, after selling you to the Ishmaelites.

Then we think, "God, there is absolutely no way that you could have meant that I was supposed to end up here, wait this long, travel this path, etc., as I progress toward the manifestation of your dream. You must need some navigation help. I will get this baby back on course. You can take it from there once I reroute this dream that you gave me."

We never realize, in our frustration and confusion, that God is doing all he can to give us that specific dream in his master plan. We, of course, think that it is all about us. It is never about us. It is always about saving many.

We never realize that all of the twists and turns in the journey are being used to prepare us to fulfill his purpose. Also, we never realize that we are seeing the manifestation of the dream being expressed in and through our lives at every step on the journey—all we have to do is continue to have faith in God, make sure that we are in step with God, and continue to make steady progress on the journey. We must remain in the moment and allow God to work out all of the details related to reaching "Was Not."

What Dreams May Come

The agony associated with some of the steps can cause us to hopefully temporarily get out of step with God. At times, we are also delusional enough to think that the finite being who was given the dream can help get the infinite one back on track.

Maybe we just lose hope and do not care what dreams may come, nor what may come of the dreams. We just want out of this current and most painful circumstance. What happens next will be a matter of what occurs once we get outta here.

Playing Stepwise Clue the Whole Time

It is very difficult to learn to be content.[73] I had been chasing the true meaning of that passage of scripture ever since God led me to it, shortly after I "upslid." At first, I thought it meant "this, then that." Yet, I never quite felt like I had completely solved the mystery, not until I learned that I had been playing Clue the whole time.

73. Phil 4:11–13.

First came the obscure dream, then I would step from room-to-room where a vital piece of information, seemingly unrelated to the dream, was revealed to me.[74] This piece would allow me to cross at least one obstructive item off of my list. However, the difficulty experienced while in each room made the ultimate goal, the dream, seem so far off that it no longer seemed that God and I were walking together.[75]

Thankfully, I never completely lost hope and said "God forget the Dream. I just need to get out of this roomroom! I will figure out where to go from here, once I get out." Sadly, many people fall into this trap.[76] They choose to lose sight of the vision,[77] possibly even supplanting it with their own answer, vision, or Ishmael.[78]

However, I never did. Nor did Joseph. God had firmly embedded that carrot, the Orange MacGuffin, the dream, in my heart. Such that I at least realized that each step, as disjointed as the journey seemed, was somehow related to the final outcome. Thus, each room in the mansion, as I traveled from chamber to chamber while encountering the other players, held a significant clue.

However, in this game, it was not a race, per se, to solve the mystery before everyone else. Rather in this game, I was playing with others. Actually, I was playing against myself or against my own desire—my desire to skip some steps and advance past the relevance of each clue found in each room, as I progressed toward the actual manifestation of his inspired dream.[79] At least Joseph and I maintained our hold on that part.

As I proceeded through each room, I realized that the dream was becoming clearer with each successive step. Joseph had two long years after he made his plea to the butler to gather and correctly process each room. This actually helped him to understand what the dreams truly meant. He had simply been playing Clue all along.

While playing Clue, Joseph and I realized that we were learning what it truly means to be content:

> Not that I was ever truly in need, for I have learned how to be content and how to get along happily, whether I have much or

---

74. 1 Cor 13:12–13.
75. Gen 3:8–9.
76. Prov 29:18.
77. Phil 3:14.
78. Gen 16.
79. 2 Tim 3:16–17.

little. I know how to live on almost nothing or with everything. I have learned the secret of contentment in every situation, whether it be on a full stomach or in hunger, with plenty or in want. What's the secret? I have learned that I can do everything God asks me to do, but *only* with the help of Christ who gives me the strength and power to finish the journey.[80]

That is when we solve the mystery and win the game.

JOSEPH'S "WAS NOT"

Joseph's "Was Not" began at the moment that he was called and sent for by Pharaoh. He was immediately brought from the dungeon in order to interpret the King's dream.[81] This went on until he not only became the living embodiment of Pharaoh's dream interpretation, but also as he became the personification of his own dream while his brothers bowed before him.

At the sight of his brothers, he recognized them right away. Even after all of these years, Joseph remembered his dreams, those he dreamed all those years ago.[82] He was overcome with many conflicting emotions.

So he locked his murderously duplicitous brothers in jail for three days. He accused them of being spies. In case you were wondering, I'm cool with this action.

Then he told them, "Go home and bring your (and my) baby brother Benjamin back to me in order to prove that you are who you say that you are." Now they did not recognize Joseph, who was likely nearing, if not forty plus years old by now. The last they saw him, he was the equivalent of a high school senior in modern parlance. But he recognized them. And he knew their language, as well as Arabic, as was spoken by the Egyptians.

So, he spoke to them through a Hebrew translator who worked for Joseph as a digi-brain. Sorry.

The Tell-Tale Heart

Consider this: if Joseph "Was Not" someone who did not know them from somewhere, then how would he know that he was looking at their

---

80. Phil 4:11–13 (adaptation).
81. Gen 41.
82. Gen 42:6–9.

baby brother when they brought him back to Egypt? They could have easily paid in grain for some random kid from one of the starving countries in the land of the Philistines which they had to pass through, going to and coming from Egypt. These guilt-ridden geniuses could have just paid some random kid, or Ishmaelite trader, a distant relative who looked a little like them, and said, "Come to Egypt with us and we will get you some grain too." They were, after all, the ten sons of Jacob the trickster.[83]

But not these idiots. These ten boys were haunted and petrified by "the tell-tale heart" that they buried under their floorboards so many years ago.[84] No, I have never read all of it. I do not read.

Anyway, they went all the way home, and told dear old Dad, Jacob, the whole story. Dad still reeling from the pain from losing his favorite son, Joseph. He said, "No way you guys are getting the other son of my wife, (of choice) Rachel." But hunger, "miss meal cramps" as some call them, got the best of everyone.

After Reuben's failed attempt to secure Benjamin by putting up his own kids as ransom, [85] Judah, the crooked murderer, who also slept with his sons' wife, vouched for Benjamin's safety.[86] They were all hungry. So they took their now honest, fearful (and appropriately so) selves back to Egypt to face the prime minister, Zaphenath-Paneah, whose name essentially means "the God speaks through this man and this God lives" in Arabic. Joseph's given name means "he will add" in Hebrew.

I say that Joseph probably played a cruel shell game with the brothers. Again, in spite of the preachers and ministers feigning as if they have any clue as to why Joseph engaged in his bit of subterfuge, other than for the heck of it, for grins, and for a small measure of revenge (also because he still struggles with holding a grudge. Wait . . . am I still talking about Joseph the ENTJ here? Or some other ENTJ?). He did this even though he was amid his "Was Not" season, and he was still functioning as Zaphenath-Paneah. No one actually knows why he did it because the Bible does not tell us.

Thus, we must speculate. However, it was not a very nice thing to do to the boys. But it does sound like *big* (largely harmless) fun.

---

83. Gen 25:26.

84. Gen 42:21–24; Edgar Allen Poe, "The Tell-Tale Heart," https://en.wikipedia.org/wiki/The_Tell-Tale_Heart.

85. Gen 42:37–38.

86. Gen 38.

Perseverance & a Slight Stumble

Joseph persevered through so much. He ran laps around Romans 5:1–5 about a million times, man. If anyone has earned some grace, at least from me, his fellow bondservant for Christ, Joseph earned it—times 1,000,000. However, I do not get to make that grace decision—not the ultimate one, anyway.

Joseph might have stumbled once or twice on his way to "Was Not." But Joseph persevered, endured, and diligently sought the Lord with his whole heart, far more often than he stumbled. The Bible does not directly tell us that he incurred any issue or judgment from God, relative to his interactions with his brothers, or otherwise, for that matter.

I, for one, am giving him the cleanest of slates and a complete pass. I mean this from the bottom of my heart: may we all do close to as well as Joseph while on our journey.

Please do your best to mimic Joseph's journey. You are being prepared to help all of those people, just as Joseph helped those people in Egypt. You, like Joseph, are being prepared on your journey to save many and they need you to get into position.[87]

---

87. Rom 8:18–23.

8

Step Six: The Reward & the Rewarder

THE REWARD THAT PULLS YOU THROUGH

I MENTIONED THIS EARLIER: as you endure and persevere, while continuing to diligently seek God on your way to "Was Not," your vision becomes clearer. You begin to understand, and can see in part, how the different tests and steps are beginning to fit together. This, while you continue the process of daily submitting to his perfect will and timing.

One of the other very interesting things that occurs while you are walking with God on the journey is that you begin to only desire the perfect version of his will, and you only desire the perfect manifestation of that obscure picture that he showed you when this all first began.

You do not want anything other than God's best, knowing that the version which has become the only desire in your heart now is also the only version that you will settle for. No matter how long it takes. You may be tired, as I believe Joseph was, when he asked the butler to remember him.[1] The more closely you walk with God, while diligently seeking him and keeping pace, the more your desires are transformed into his desires for you. I believe that is what is meant by "he will give you the desires of your heart."[2]

1. Gen 40.
2. Ps 37:4.

HE WILL GIVE & GIVE YOU THE DESIRES OF YOUR HEART

I believe that God imputes those desires into your spirit and soul. He brands them into your heart. I have seen people take a big needle, or really a syringe, and inject or infuse some flavor into a turkey prior to baking it for Thanksgiving. They want the flavor to bake through the turkey so every bite tastes like turkey with an infused flavor (as opposed to the regular turkey taste which some find dry).

Not me, I love turkey. However, only with turkey flavored stuffing or made from scratch. The point is that they impute or infuse flavor into the turkey.

I believe that God will give you the desires of your heart.

Then, like so many wives need to learn to do with their husbands, subversively trick them into thinking it was their idea. God is not a subversive like me. He just uses the reward as an extrinsic motivator.

However, he does not stop there. He will masterfully take you on a walk, using his power, to make the dream or vision a perfectly tailored fit for you.[3] This is based on your infused and inherently created personality type, as well as areas of gifting and callings. He will lead you to the best version of the dream or vision, which you have become increasingly so passionate about and relentlessly strive to attain.

Once these desires are infused into your spirit and soul, you become willing to do almost anything in order to remain in lockstep with God. You will endure all hardships to enter in to the place where you receive the reward, a place which only resides in "Was Not."

WHY ELSE WOULD YOU?

Why else would the children of Israel walk around a city with a giant wall around it in silence for six days? Then on the seventh day, do it a bunch of times and scream? Then blow a big ole horn called a shofar? And, to top all of this off, they all believed that God was going to, through the transaction of these seemingly innocuous activities, make that wall fall down. They were convinced that God was directing them, so they engaged in these actions with all of their might.[4]

---

3. Gen 2:18.
4. Josh 6.

How else would you explain why we keep going, why we continue to chase the dream? Another excellent example of this occurs in Hebrews 11:24–27. Why would Moses give up his cushy day job as a Prince of Egypt to go adopt onto himself the weight of the bondage of slavery? God will not ask you for the really "different" or to make the really "crazy" sacrifices until you walk along this journey with him for awhile.

A Stepwise Rewarder

God starts with the obscure picture, then he invites you on the walk with him by using the picture as motivation for you to take the first few steps. As you proceed, the tests, requests, commands, and challenges become increasingly more difficult. You simultaneously become more and more willing to face and pass all of them, simply because the picture, as well as your desire for it, becomes progressively clearer, thus serving as an impetus.

The last stage is where you realize that it is not, nor was it ever, about you. Rather you see that many are depending on your survival and on your arrival at "Was Not."

Hebrews 11:6 states that he is a rewarder of those who diligently seek him. The more progressively, consistently, and diligently you seek him, the more important the things that he shows you, as well as, the things related to the kingdom, become. During that last step, you begin to understand that the earth is enduring labor pains, waiting on you to get into position and to actualize the dream.[5]

All of this becomes an important motivator for you. In the beginning, it is sort of an extrinsic motivator. As you advance, it definitely becomes intrinsic for you. It becomes your passion and goal.

THE BALLAD OF "THROUGH PLACE" TO "NEW PLACE"

I continue to use the "place" allegory as an example because, in retrospect, there is a strangely transformative experience that I endured, relative to believing that this "place" showed me the initial version of the vision that God had already imprinted in my heart. This "place" was suddenly changed from being my desired final destination to a "place" that I would

---

5. Rom 8:18–23.

just pass through. Albeit, while passing through, I was assigned to do some significant work there.

However, the realization that I was not going to remain there, at this presupposed final destination had been changed, mid-dream, prior to my arrival. Mid-dream, I learned that it was just a truck stop on a highway. It was my Samaria on my way to the "new place," or to Jerusalem via Galilee.[6] That is actually quite an apt description of what I now call "through place." Thus, I need to go to "through place."

I Thought "Through Place" Was "New Place"

One significant thing that happened to me while I have been writing this book is that I realized what the real vision was. When I described the "Ballad of Through Place to New Place," both briefly in this book, as well as via social media awhile ago; I said that I thought, "through place was, in fact, new place."

I thought that Samaria was the final destination of the trip, i.e., Jerusalem. Alas, it was not "Was Not." The final destination was actually the location for the manifestation of the promise that God tricked me into making him. It was when I said, "God if you get me back into the classroom, I will never (of my free will) come back out."

Even now, I am tempted to want to settle in Samaria or in Haran as Terah, Abram's father did, while still on the last step of my journey. After all, I was a very good digi-brain. Like Joseph, it is difficult at times not to simply say, "I want out right now, and any place will do—even the kingdom of the digi-brained people place." Pain hurts. However, God was ready for a shift, a shift that followed my digi-brained preparation period.

Haven't You Figured This Out Yet?

Very recently, following the writing of the first draft of this book, I learned something completely new—something regarding the decision that God tricked me into making about getting back into the classroom. I had a Job-like epiphany moment. This occurred when God said to me, "Haven't you figured this out yet?"

What I had not realized or "figured out" was that once I got back into the classroom, both before, and most significantly at "through place,"

---

6. John 4:4–42.

I was never going to be capable of coming back out. Nor would I be permitted to come back out of the classroom once I had gotten back in there.

God would close all doors to any place that would not lead me directly and exclusively back into the classroom. I wondered for a long time on the final step in the journey, "Why won't these doors open?" I would apply for classroom only positions. However, I would also apply for hybrid digi-brain and classroom lecturer positions, such as the one mentioned at the beginning of this book.

During the most self-compelled, "desperate times," I would also apply for digi-brain only positions. Even though I hated the thought of taking one of those jobs, at this point in the journey, I was testing the theory—a theory for which I actually had only half of the information required to generate an appropriate hypothesis or research question.

I wanted to know, at this point, "Will God allow me to go back into the digi-brain chair while I complete all of the requirements associated with this final step on my journey to 'New Place?'" I knew that "New Place" would lead me exclusively back into the classroom.

But, what is the point to all of this? The skin boils and all of my children dying in an unusual windstorm? That is a metaphorical reference to Job's issues.[7] However, my difficulties were no less devastating for me.

The misinformed question was, "Why not just allow me to pass back through the kingdom of the digi-brains?" Either in part or in full while we await God's kairos (a Greek word meaning a propitious or favorable and opportune moment in time) timing, which will result in my arrival in "new place?"[8]

Geographically, and more specifically than that, I knew, at least in part, where both "New Place" and "Through Place" were located. So, (here I go negotiating again) "Let's do the digi-brain thing again while we work toward getting there." God "Was Not" working at anything. I AM already there.

---

7. Job 1–2.
8. Matt 8:29; Luke 19:44; Acts 24:25.

The Mount Moriah Test

This also reminds me of Abraham's last test when God told him to take Isaac, the son of promise, up on a mountain in the land of Moriah and kill him.[9]

What was the point, God? You know that he is going to do it in his heart, anyway. But Abraham needed to know something else.

That something else, as I mentioned earlier, was God wanted to ensure that Abraham was fully aware of how well he knew God as a covenant-keeping God, and how much faith and dependence on God Abraham had developed on the journey.

> Remember: a test is a measuring instrument that is used by teachers. It assesses the ability of a student to learn, memorize, and to apply knowledge acquired during a previous level, stage, or step. Teachers use tests in order to ensure that the students have not only acquired and retained the requisite knowledge from previous steps, but such that they can apply it to real life situations. All of this occurs prior to moving forward to the next step, grade, level, or portion of the semester.

Willing to Sacrifice the Reward?

Abraham learned and exemplified for all of us exactly what it means to sacrifice the reward. Abraham had finally caught the carrot. Actually, he caught his carrot, Isaac, awhile ago. However, God "Was Not" yet finished testing Abraham or revealing things to him.

Abraham knew that Isaac was the son of promise. However, Abraham's relationship with God and his allegiance to God were unparalleled. By this point in the journey; Abraham would let go of anything in order to gain Christ.[10] He was willing to let go of the son of promise, the very son that he had so desired to have with Sarah—most likely above anything else. And probably more than any other part of the promise.

God commanded Abraham to go to Moriah, to a mountain that I AM will show you, and sacrifice Isaac. At that moment of obedience, Abraham let go of his most valued promise. His vantage point and perspective changed, and he learned, as well as demonstrated for all of us,

9. Gen 22.
10. Phil 3:8.

that a closer relationship with the rewarder is of paramount importance.[11] It's even important enough to cause you to readily and willingly sacrifice the reward, if you must do so in order to gain the greater reward.

Abraham's "Was Not"

From the time that Abram was called to leave Haran and go to the unknown promised land, I believe that he entered "Was Not."[12] When he was called to take this test, Abraham needed to reaffirm his knowledge of God as a covenant-keeper, relative to both Isaac and the promised land. Everyone who came after Abraham needed to know that God would never let Abraham down. When God makes a promise, or tricks you into declaring the revelation of his promise and "Was Not," God is faithful.[13]

Thus, when I uttered that promise, it could effectively be restated to read as follows:

> This is the absolute end of my digi-brained career. I have taken you as far as I AM has desired to take you along this path. We will travel no further along this path. I have trained you here, to do, what I want you to do when you get there, i.e., "new place."

> So get out from among the digi-brain kingdom, and *go* to a place that I AM will show you.[14] There, you will inherit what your heart desires, which also happens to be what my heart desires for you. You will enter, as well as return, full-time into the classroom.[15] Do not ever look back to Haran, Ur, or to the digi-brained kingdom, not even in part. Because I AM has forever closed the doors to those places behind you. You will never again revisit Haran.

> I AM promised this specific land to Abraham, to Isaac, and to all future generations.[16] Just like Abraham, you will never go back. You are headed toward your promised land, "new place." As a result, you can never go back. You will never go back.

11. Rev 4:1.
12. Gen 12.
13. 2 Pet 3:9.
14. Gen 12, 22; 2 Cor 6:17.
15. Ps 37:4.
16. Gen 24; Gal 4:28.

Don't you understand, Jones? Haven't you figured this out yet? Don't you realize? I AM closed all of those doors that would in part, or in whole, lead you back to the digi-brained kingdom in Haran and Ur of the Chaldees.

You just need to keep moving forward. Understand that I AM will keep all of his promises. I AM will, at times, use you to declare them, or he may even trick you into declaring them, as you would say. However, make no mistake: this is my promise to you, my covenant with you.

I AM has sealed it: myself with myself by myself, while you were sleeping. Then I AM gave that covenant promise to you.[17] At exactly the right time, I AM will release the full manifestation of the promise.[18] But for now, we will go to "this place," "that place," "through place," "Samaria place," and "penultimate place"—as a matter of fact, we must need to go "through place."

There are some people that you need to meet there, some things that you need to do, things which I AM can only do, in and through you, at "Samaria place." Remember that, from here, until we arrive at "new place," and then going forward, while exclusively living out the promise of being in the classroom, we have officially left the kingdom of the digi-brains behind. Never to return again.

No matter how uncomfortable the rest of "Through Place" becomes, it's only temporary. It is one final testing place before "Was Not."

Negotiating to Reenter the Kingdom of the Digi-Brains

As previously mentioned, I always wondered, why can't I be normal? Why can't I just visit with the digi-brains until it is time to go to "New Place" and "Was Not?" All of my friends are normal, well . . . I mean . . . but still.

I was just like Joseph, negotiating to get out of jail early. He had a strong desire to get to "New Place" and "Was Not" earlier than scheduled. I too, wanted out, so many times.

17. Gen 15.
18. Job 14:14.

It takes attempting to renegotiate God's covenant dream and promise with a butler, a man with direct access, one who knows the King. Then, at this point, as frustrated as I am, and as devastated as I have been during this final step, I will take it. That's why God made my friend Joseph wait two more years.

Abraham knew. He knew that when God said, "Sacrifice the son of promise," God would still keep his promise, irrespective of the pain and difficulty that roiled in his soul on the way to the continuing manifestation and very life of the son of promise. God will always keep his promises.

Joseph and I had to learn to let God handle all of it. If he makes a promise, he will deliver at the perfect kairos time. Just do not look back. Those doors to past places are forever closed, and no man, not even you can open them.[19]

Haven't you figured this out yet? Alas, until just now, I had not. I kept trying to renegotiate and bargain. But no door would open. Just like Joseph's "please remember me" request fell on deaf ears, at least not until God had brought all parts of the stepwise-dependent journey into perfect alignment. Then the butler would remember and Joseph would move forward into "Was Not."

The Vision of "Through Place"

The vision that I had regarding going to "Through Place" was just a motivator, the carrot that God used for me. He did this by imprinting the vision in and upon my heart so strongly that getting there became essential to me, come what may. However, I was the one who looked around at my circumstances and the other tests that God was throwing at me, left and right, with increasing rapidity and velocity. I was the one who extrapolated from the vision that "Through Place" is definitely my "New Place" and final destination.

I lost focus, while trying to focus. Yes, the vision was definitely for an appointed time.[20] However, I would come to realize that it "Was Not" as much a destination, as it was a "place" revealed to me, in order to serve as a course-altering, graduation type epiphany. God wanted to change my mind-set.

---

19. Isa 22:22; Rev 3:8, 4:1.
20. Hab 2:3.

He wanted to show me and then motivate me to change the course of my professional career and desires. He wanted me to focus so intently on that change that I would not allow anything such as location and things that I had resisted about that profession (strangely enough like writing) to stop my progress. He had to get me to leave my comfort zone or "comfortable place."

He wanted me to overcome all obstacles. Later, he revealed to me exactly how critical for the kingdom, which I was already passionate about, it was for me to make a shift, a shift from the digi-brained kingdom. Although, some parts of it still felt like a "comfortable place."

God Orchestrates & Uses it All

God did this by using the job long ago, post-master's, to introduce me professionally to the field of higher ed. Actually, it was pre-master's when I realized that I was only good at college people. Then he used my master's jobs, internships, and practicums to spur my interest in both higher ed and, more importantly, teaching.

Next, he took me to the succeeding step of purpose. This was within that same digi-brained field. However, I would be in a higher position, as full chief of the digi-brains, doing a slightly different job. Subsequently, he used all other positions in higher ed on the stepwise progression to continue to stoke the fire. All of these steps became my primary rip current of motivation, designed to carry me to the next step, "New Place," which was the new professional field.

Make no mistake: the final destination location was and would be of paramount importance to me, but the impetus to pursue, through all things, was the rip current at this point. Albeit, it was also the thing that I was most easily willing to compromise on as the difficulty of the tests increased.

I was willing to take another split digi-brain and teaching faculty job on my way to "new place," whether that was staying for a longer period of time at "through place," or if that meant going to the geographic location of "New Place" only to work at "Almost Place," which was not far from, yet not at all, "New Place." I would have done almost anything to get myself out of the dungeons that I had encountered.

I was more than willing to compromise, justifying it to myself by saying, "I will do this in order to get in, and God is allowing me to apply for this position in order to get me in the door. Once in, I will then be able to move over and get into the classroom, ultimately full-time. At that point, I will never come back out." Now I sound like Sarai trying to find a Hagar, so I could help God out.[21]

I also, of course, looked to go directly past go and collect my two hundred dollars, while I was actually on a course, headed directly into the classroom. Now, relative to becoming a full-time professor, I still resisted what I called "bighead writing." How do I come up with these terms? I don't know. They are simply an expression of my personality portrait.

Bighead Writing

I resisted the heck out of writing for academic journals. I hate admitting that preceding fact here. This, in spite of the fact that I already had a sole author article published in a journal. However, I essentially submitted that article to that journal on a "personal dare" of sorts, just to see if I could get it through. When it did, I just laughed to myself with a wry grin or smirk on my face and added it to my list of accomplishments.

See, I never wanted to be a writer or an author. Honestly, I still do not. I do not like to read. Actually, the things that I do or will read, I read in short stints and segments. I read for informational purposes only, in order to understand concepts, or while looking for the specific bits of knowledge that I desire to obtain, with the larger purpose in mind, of supporting one of my intuitive ideas.

That is why I can quote Cicero, Shakespeare, Melville, Robert Frost, or Edgar Allen Poe so readily.[22] It is the idea of a thing. The quote or phrase that speaks of a larger concept fascinates me, not the experience of reading a comprehensive novel and taking the journey with the author.

However, I knew that if I were going to write, it was going to be a book that everyone could enjoy and benefit from. It would not be one that bigheads, or academics like me, as I also later accepted about myself, would write or exclusively understand and enjoy.

I was a kid from a housing project in Pittsburgh. I had a rep and "street cred" to protect (or so I still idealized in my head). Truthfully,

---

21. Gen 16.

22. Cicero, "Ut imago est animi voltus sic indices oculi"; ("The face is a picture of the mind as the eyes are its interpreter"), https://www.phrases.org.uk/bulletin_board/41/messages/1097.html. https://en.wikiquote.org/wiki/Cicero.

I had lost all of that, eons ago. At one time, I actually did have a little, until the hand of God plucked me out of there because he had a higher purpose for me.

Someone once said of Muhammed Ali, "*He* is the heavyweight champion of the world? Heck, he's not even the toughest person on his old block in Louisville." The remnants of the mentality, sadly, never left me, even years after I "upslid" and had walked, many a mile, with God.

Anyway, I wanted to write something interesting and worth reading to everyone, not something exclusively for academics, those who I had no desire to impress in mass. Nor it wouldn't be something that I could tell them that I had written. I am too humble for that behavior or mind-set. I never care what people think of me anyway, save Doc and the Liberian ninja.

Writing was one of the many obstacles that prevented me from desiring to enter the classroom full-time. You have to write for Journals as a tenure line professor. It was also my desire to hang on to the types of student relationships that I had formed via academic advising, in addition to those formed with my students as a professor. I immensely enjoy and cherish both.

Taught to be Made New in Your Thinking

There is a certain initial reverence that is attributed to a college professor. Although it is like a sink with a stopper in it: if you are not a good teacher, the water will run out of that sink really quickly, and vice versa.

However, I could be more interpersonally connected with my advising students and get to know as well as help them in many areas of their lives. In class, I was the subject matter expert (SME) relative to one specific topic. A marketing professor should know nothing about human psychology, nor about the things that are hurting inside of one of the kids. However, these things affect the student's performance in my or other classrooms. I was the rare combination who knew both, and I loved to interact with the kids on both levels.

The Obvious Yet Anonymous Christian Advisor, Professor, and Author

I could just as easily relate to my students who were not Christians as I could to the relatively few who were. I never wore a big cross medallion on a chain around my neck. The only medallion that I wanted, I got. It was for high distinction honors in my doctoral program.

That's just because I am an obsessively nuts, love-a-challenge perfectionist, which is what that medallion signifies. Upon receipt of the medallion, I had finally achieved a symbol of my nuttiness, and I could actually prove something to the entire world of academia. Only if I was forced to. Otherwise, anonymity and winning the nutty, self-imposed fight in order to obtain a measure of perfection was enough for me.

Other than that, I loved to hide those parts of myself, and welcome in my students who were not believers, just as much as those who were.

But remember, I am nuts, and a perfectionist trained and tested by God to win the fights. So, writing was, unfortunately to me, going to be large-scaled, if I would ever do it. Thus, I did not want to be an author and definitely not a Christian author. If I became that, I would lose my anonymity.

The Truth

My colleagues always knew that I was some sort of a believer, both because of the university that I attended relative to receiving my doctorate, and because I was not shy, bashful, or ashamed of being a Christian. I simply never shined "this little light of mine" in anyone's eye. I never will. But I do, proudly so, allow it to "shine" in and through me.

However, due to the fact that my colleagues knew a different side of me, they could observe, and largely only observe, how differently I carried myself. As I always say about myself to myself, "You do not want to have that conversation with me." I generally believe that my colleagues also knew that about me.

I know my Bible better than you know your little argument against it, and I will dismantle that fallacious argument against believing in Elohim in a New York minute. However, there is no reason for me to do that if you oblige and simply don't go there with me.

See, I genuinely believe this and I have mentioned it in this book. If you do not believe that the entire Bible is the God-breathed, Word of life, manifested in Christ, from the beginning,[23] then I have no desire to have a theological discussion with you. Particularly not one based on the Bible serving as the ultimate truth.

You do not believe that. Thus, we actually have no basis from which to operate nor to have this proposed theological discussion. We are at polar opposite ends of the spectrum, relative to the Bible and theology. So, if we avoid that conversation because you do not ask me, I will not tell you.

I will embrace the relationship that we can form based on our mutual compatibility and places of agreement. Let's just avoid that topic, because if you ask, I will tell you the truth. Believing it or not is up to you.

However, that truth is only based on the fact that I know that the Bible is the only immutable truth. However, you have every right not to believe that truth. I also recognize and embrace, as a person with free will, (given to us by the God of the Bible), that you can choose to do whatever you want. I will never try to stop you. I will embrace the person that you are and have become, while never, ever, ever compromising my knowledge of the truth.

I will not arbitrarily hold you to my standard. I chose to accept my standard of truth and fully embrace all that comes with that, i.e., the journey. You have every right to choose a different one. No further discussion about my truth, or your truth, is necessary. Yet, I am fully capable of doing this. However, in my experience, many (also in my opinion) insecure Christians cannot do this, same thing goes for the insecure non-believers.

Remember, as I have mentioned, "I never sit around wondering if I am wrong." Insecurity breeds that questioning relative to the faith. It also breeds recriminating self-doubt. It bemuses the idea that the other person, and what they choose to believe, just might be correct. So the insecure person begins to question their personal beliefs. I do not experience any of that. It is just another expression of my personality and of my relationship with God.

He made me secure. He did this by allowing me the privilege of permitting me to learn how to die daily,[24] while he allows me to walk with him all day, every day. Thus, in summary, I did not desire to do any of this, including becoming a Christian author.

---

23. Gen 1:1; Luke 16:17; John 1:1, 14; 2 Tim 3:16.
24. 1 Cor 15:31.

The True Vine Vision Works the Same in the Classroom

As I continued to walk, though much later, I realized what the real vision was, the vision that God had, without my full knowledge or comprehension, imputed into me. While walking on the journey, I started to encounter tests and steps that showed me that "Through Place" was not "New Place." Rather, it was a place that I had to go through like "Samaria place," such that I could meet a bunch of university women and men at the well, as did Jesus in Samaria.[25]

There were so many significant encounters that I had at "through place," encounters that confirmed for me what the true vision was. This vision was becoming increasingly clear to me, particularly while I was at, as well as subsequent to leaving, "through place." It was the vision that was revealed to me, now long ago, via my branch relationship with the true vine.[26]

I used that intuitive gift, actually spiritual discernment, that God gave me in order to identify a student who, while leaving a test very early in the semester, I could feel how heavy the burden was that this student had been carrying.[27] I had done this same thing many times, at many steps and locations, both in my advising setting, relative to higher ed and in many other venues and locations. I asked the student about it as they dropped the test off. They offered me what I knew was an excuse. They feigned that they would be "OK." God compelled me to follow-up, as I did via email. Lo and behold, the student actually allowed me to help.

From that I learned that I am expressly who he has called, created, and trained me to be. If I am in the classroom, I still carry the same gifts, talents, callings, and can still do his work. But now I can be more effective because I am positionally in the right, graduated, next-level arena, i.e., in the classroom.

I could do the same things in the classroom that I had done in the advising session, but in the classroom, I could do more of them, and do them better than ever before.

This helped clarify the picture. Many other things, similar to this incident, occurred, all while I was at "through place." I was beginning to

---

25. John 4:4–42.
26. John 15:5.
27. 1 Cor 12:7–9, 10.

STEP SIX: THE REWARD & THE REWARDER

more clearly understand why God was calling me higher.[28] He was calling me to a new level or step, one that could only occur in the classroom.

If I had not yet fully submitted to and learned to depend on God, him being the stepwise orchestra conductor for my very life, I would not have arrived at that place in my walk. I would have totally missed the fact that "Through Place" was just that: "Samaria place," a place that I must go through, a necessary encounter place.

This is a place where I had to meet some people, where I had to experience some things, both for their sakes and for mine.[29] However, it was not to be "New Place" or "Was Not," as I had originally imagined. That was just fine with me. Although I still wanted out of the dungeon. The place that I had prayed so fervently to get to was "Through Place," a place where I was so happy to finally arrive. It was also a place where I had to force myself to let go.

Ultimately, I was, with difficulty, able to let go of my attachment to "through place," at least as the vision for "New Place" came more clearly into focus. I was attached to, but had subsequently let go of, the location, area, and all of the life that I thought I wanted, a life which surrounded "through place." This was a life that kingdom business, as well as many friends, beckoned me to remain a part of.

That same life had influenced me, incorrectly, to chase that "Through Place" as the "New Place" vision, as opposed to focusing on the true vision and the vine. However, if I am honest, I also had a difficult time, for the first time in my "upslid" life, fully letting go of a "Through Place."

I definitely desired to go to "New Place," like a deer panting for the water brook.[30] But, for awhile there, I had planned my entire remaining life around "through place," thinking that it was "New Place." Everything made sense at the time.

Thus, even Jones, the one who attaches himself to almost nothing, save Doc and the Liberian Ninja (although that Liberian Ninja was in the vicinity of "Through Place"!). Thus making it, at times, a little more difficult and confusing for me, one who wanted out, not to try to negotiate and turn "Through Place" into "Placeholder Place."

However, God the rewarder used the reward, both the "I must need go through Samaria" reward, and the true reward of "New Place," as well

---

28. Rev 4:1.
29. John 4:4–52.
30. Ps 42:1.

as my unquenchable desire to get there, all working together, to motivate me to keep walking and pressing through every trial that comes with each step.

PRESS TO POSSESS

God left the children of Israel out in a wilderness for forty years, filled with difficult trials, in order to rid them of the reproach of slavery, sans Joshua and Caleb. Once that occurred, they were finally prepared to enter the promised land.[31] Two and a half tribes were already settled on the east side of the Jordan River. However, they were still obligated to fight with the others, until all of Israel possessed the entirety of the inheritance: the land that God had promised to Abraham.[32]

Joshua led them to their first location, a "Through Place" if you will, but they knew that Jericho was not the full reward. Rather it was just part of the inheritance.

They had bigger fish to fry. They had their eyes on the entire prize. They were sufficiently motivated to continue to press to possess the entire promised land.[33] But to get to the complete portion of "new place," their first stop was Jericho, the walled city.

Jericho was one of the first places that the scouts, forty years prior, had entered, including Joshua and Caleb. Ultimately, Jericho would be conscripted to be inherited by the clans of Benjamin.[34] However, to get there, and everywhere in the promised land, they would have to fight through this huge test and obstacle. But they were ready, and the attainment of the full reward was in sight.

The question is: was that sufficient motivation for them to obey God this time? From a human perspective, absolutely not. Joshua had secretly sent two spies into Jericho, in order to reconnoiter the place, before they were to engage in this initial battle.[35] Once there, the men were protected by a prostitute named Rahab who would, for her efforts in this instance, earn herself a place among the heroes of faith. That is what some call the biblical hall of fame, located in the book of Hebrews 11:30–31.

---

31. Num 34:15.
32. Gen 12.
33. Phil 3:14.
34. Josh 18:21.
35. Josh 2.

Then the Lord spoke to Joshua, because it was time to make the battle plan to enter Jericho by overcoming the wall that surrounded the city of Jericho. They then were to conquer its warriors who resided inside of the wall, men who were ready to defend their home against all unprepared attackers.[36] Just as God had revealed his vision by speaking directly to Moses, he would now directly address Joshua.

Battle Plans: a Dialogue

God gave Joshua the battle plan. The battle plan stated that they should gather as many qualified archers from each of the twelve tribes as could be found. Then they should have the archers stand on the highest bluffs, opposing Jericho, preparing to pick off anyone foolish enough to go to the top of the formidable Jericho wall. After all, the tribe of Benjamin could shoot arrows with either hand.[37]

Next . . . wait, none of that happened.

The Battle is the Lord's

The battle plans that God laid out for Joshua were quite simple:[38] gather up every one of the children of Israel, and tell the priests to get out in front of the congregation of Israel. Make sure that they are carrying the Ark of the Covenant, which we will get to next, out in front of Israel.

"Now, listen closely Hosea: I want you guys to walk."

"Oh, OK, YHWH, walk with the ark, thus the presence of God out front, and weaken the wall so we can shoot grappling hooks into it with ropes attached. Then we all climb up the ropes, surrounding the city with our swords, bows, and arrows strapped to our backs, then God, you will give us the victory over our enemies."[39]

"No. Walk in complete silence, one circuit around the wall. Do this for six consecutive days. Got it?"

36. Josh 6:1–5.
37. 1 Chr 12:1–2.
38. 2 Chr 20:15.
39. Ps 18:47.

"Ok, with you so far."

"Now, on the seventh day, Joshua, this is what you must do: you walk around that same wall seven times. But this time, on the seventh day. Continue to leave your grappling hooks, ropes, bows, and arrows back in the camp."

"Only this time, Josh, you will need to carry some weaponry."

"OK, God. Now we are cooking with hot grease."

"Now pay attention, Joshua. Tell the priests to bring their shofars, the ram's horns."

"OK, ram's horns, huh? Wait . . . one question, Lord. Just the hollowed out horns? With no rams attached to them horns?"

"Nope, just the hollowed out horns.

"Then I want you guys to tell the priests to blow those horns with all of their might."

"Oh, OK, blow them at the wall and you will supernaturally empower them with the Ruach, breath of God, and this will weaken the wall. Then I can send Othniel back to Shittim where we sat 'em to get the swords, bows, and . . . "

"Just blow the ram's horns, man. Follow me. This is not complicated. Don't lose the pace; you know how important that is to I AM. Now, this next part is critical. After all of the priests blow their shofars, I want you guys to scream at the top of your lungs."

"Scream?"

"Yep, scream."

"Ok, Elohim, now I get it. We scream, so you can disorient the citizens of Jericho. And then you will get Rahab to come open the door, and then we will . . . "

"Nope, just scream.

"Now Joshua, here's the big pay off. Are you ready for this? The big kicker, le pièce de résistance . . . wait for it . . . the walls will all fall down."

Selah

Insert selah, a long pause, here.

The Lord of Heaven's Armies

"OK, Yahweh Tsebaoth, the Lord of heaven's armies, let me get this straight, so I can tell *your* people. . . . for the first six days, . . . priests out front . . . total silence . . . walk around wall . . . one time.

"Seventh day . . . walk around seven times . . . priests bring your horns . . . blow them . . . everybody scream . . . walls fall down?"

"Yep, you've got it. Any questions?"

"No, sir, El Shaddai, God Almighty, the self-existent one, Yahweh Elohim. None, sir . . . wait . . . one question.

"Are you sure?"

"Absolutely. I do not sit around heaven wondering if I am wrong."

Battle Plans: Part 2

Joshua returns to the children of Israel and relays the message. Everybody prepares their walking shoes. Now Joshua, I am certain, via the Lord's direction, had the unarmed fighting men for the six days walk out in front of the Ark of the Covenant.[40] Of course, because of their submissive obedience, everything went according to God's plans, in order to fulfill his purpose. At the end of this experience, Joshua's reputation spread throughout Canaan.

40. Josh 6:6–12, 13, 14–27.

How Did This Happen? Follow the Rewarder, Receive Their Reward

How did this happen? Why did everyone believe without question? Forty years prior, when the scouts returned from the promised land, everyone questioned everything. They questioned to such an extent that some of the children of Israel, the ones over twenty years old, I assume, wanted to go back to Egypt.

Some wanted to stone Joshua and Caleb, and run a coop on Moses.[41] That was all a part of the stepwise, learned dependence, progressive journey to the promised land of "Was Not." God used the reward of the promised land to motivate.

God used every step and test, discipline and purging, as well as times when they thought that one thing was the vision, only to stick with God long enough to learn that walking around a wall, thirteen total times, over seven days, most days in complete silence, while blowing horns and screaming at walls, will cause all of the walls in your life to utterly collapse. Such that, you can run in and reap the full benefit of your true reward. Obedience is much better than sacrifice.[42]

God demonstrates how we become more obedient through the things that we suffer and persevere through.[43] Through persistence and passing all tests, at each level, we come to better understand God's voice and vision.

It all becomes clearer, such that when it is time to enter "Was Not," we do not question anything that he tells us to do. You are worn down by the tests, but by concurrently learning to trust and depend on God, those fleshly desires are worn away.

When you reach the walls to your promised land, you are so well-prepared, having passed all tests, that if God says bring grappling hooks and archers, then that is what you do. If he simply wants you to walk around in silence then, on the seventh day, blow a hollowed-out horn, you are willing and obedient, knowing that this is the only way to eat the good of the land.[44]

Why did they choose to accept everything that God said to them, at the very moment of contact and crisis? Because they were fully submitted

---

41. Num 14–15
42. 1 Sam 15:22–23.
43. Heb 5:8.
44. Isa 1:19.

to God's leading, testing, and training. They followed the rewarder, seeking him diligently.

They endured all hardships like good soldiers. He eliminated all of those who were not ready to trust and depend on Elohim completely, and with all of their hearts.[45] Yes, the children of Israel, post-forty years in the wilderness version, submitted to, obeyed, and followed the rewarder. For that, they received their promised reward, one that they did not have enough room to receive.[46]

WHEN THE REWARDER MAKES A PROMISE, HE MAKES AN UNBREAKABLE CONTRACT

In Genesis, after God had already spoken to Abram regarding a land promised to his descendants, God decided to make it more official. He cut a contract between himself and Abram. This was the third conversation that the Lord would have with Abram. First, he told Abram to leave his father's home and second his homeland to go to a place that God would show him.

Abram left. Although God told him to leave all of his family behind, Lot, his nephew, went with him. God spoke to Abram again, once he arrived in the land promised, following the inevitable split between him and Lot.[47]

The third instance occurred here in chapter 15. God started by telling Abraham that he is I AM, "The God who pays in full on his contracts."[48] To date, Abram and God made a verbal agreement.

God told Abram to leave and go to a place where God would show Abram. Abram left. He did not ponder. Abram just left and found out on the way where he was going. This speaks to and demonstrates the heart of Abram.

---

45. 2 Tim 2:3; Prov 3:5.
46. Mal 3:10.
47. Gen 12, 13:14–18, 15.
48. Gen 15:1.

Abram's Covenant Reward

God told Abram that he would reward him in great abundance. The word reward in Hebrew, sakar, means to pay a salary or to pay out a contract.[49] One problem: they had not yet cut a physical contract.

God planned to make a covenant with Abram, right then and there. God wanted to seal the promise with Abram, because there was an issue that Abram had regarding the wording of the verbal contract.

Considering the Circumstances

God told Abram that his heir would inherit all of his wealth. This son would also inherit the land that God had, on the two previous occasions, verbally promised to Abram and his descendants. Abram was an old man at this point.[50] He and his wife were well past child bearing years.

Abram had no heir. Thus, all of his wealth and any land left for inheritance would pass down to the oldest servant born into Abram's house. Abram was not sure that God knew what he was contractually obligated to do for Abram.

However, God had just announced, reiterating for the third time, that he is the rewarder and that he will give Abram the reward. Abram, understandably, particularly when you consider where he was at this stage in his stepwise journey with the Lord, asked the Lord, "How can this be, considering the circumstances?" But God had promised Abram, each time, that he would give the promised land to Abram and to his heirs.

God told Abram that your servant will not be your heir, but that you will have a son who will be your heir. I find Abram's doubt to be understandable.

I am sure some would read this and project forward about 3,000 years relative to applying their own sensibilities to the situation. Albeit, erroneously so, in my opinion. They would arrive at the conclusion that Abram should have just believed God.

I understand the speciously derived thought. It is based on all logical and observable information available to Abram, including his faith.

---

49. The definition of "sakar" can be found on "King James Bible: Strong's Hebrew Dictionary," http://www.htmlbible.com/sacrednamebiblecom/kjvstrongs/STRHEB79.htm#S7939.

50. Gen 15.

Abram's faith was strong enough for him to leave the home of his family and just go. Also, God was faithful and Abram believed that. But, logic would dictate, "How in the world will an old man like me and an old lady like Sarai have a son?"

God told him that it would not be his servant who would be his heir. God became very specific and told Abram that his heir would be his biological son. This is the point at which God must have injected Abram, via a Holy spiritual syringe, infusing Abram with additional and requisite faith in the rewarder.[51] The Bible says that this is all that it took for Abram to be convinced that God had his back, and that he would deliver on his promises.

Then Abram asked for a confirmation that what God was saying to him was true, and definitely going to happen. God became more specific with Abram this time. He told him what would happen to his biological heirs and descendants up to and through the fourth generation of Abram's natural birth family.

God Makes Covenant by & with Himself

Then God simply told Abram to prepare some animals for sacrifice. After Abram chased the buzzards and the filthy ravens away, as all good people are supposed to do, he fell asleep and had a nightmarish dream.

God decided to pass through the middle of the sacrificial animals with fire and a smoking fire pot. This is how God cut the formal and binding contract, or covenant, between himself and Abram. God preceded this event by providing Abram with more specific, confirming details about the pending covenant.

God will cut his own contract. It can be said that God can find no one with any more integrity than himself. Thus, God put Abram to sleep, and then God, himself, signed, sealed, and delivered the contract to Abram. It was not about Abram. It was all about God.

Also in chapter 15, you can see that Abram's faith was buoyed by God as he provided Abram with additional details. God may not always provide us with more details. However, when he does, God sends the details as a confirming word, sort of a down payment, on which we can proceed.

---

51. Gen 15:2–21; Heb 11:6.

Abram/Abraham was a man of Great Faith, but Abram showed us all something else. He demonstrated that prayer and persistence pays off. God created a formalized covenant between himself and Abram.

God notes Abram's faith in Genesis 15:6. God also provided Abram with information that would serve to help Abram through difficult times, tests, steps, and stages, all leading up to the time when a one-hundred-year-old man would have a son with a ninety-year-old woman.[52] God rewards people who please him because of their faith, people like Enoch and Abraham. God also rewards those who diligently seek him.[53]

PREPARED TO MOVE FORWARD

By the time I had finally arrived on campus to teach at the university that I have dubbed "through place," I was already prepared to ultimately, maybe even shortly, move on to "new place," my promised land. By now, I knew that this "Through Place" was not my final destination.

At one time, I thought and just knew that this was where I would be for a long time, likely for the remainder of my career. But God had other plans for me, once he clarified the vision, and he was very specific with me regarding where I was to go next. Similar to Abram, I believed him.

I did not continue to hold on to the idea of "through place." Although betimes, I was tempted to stay on a little while longer, while God ironed out all of the details. I guess, in a sense, I, like Joseph, asked my own butler to remember me. However, same as Joseph, my butler forgot all about me too.

Alas, I was to remain in a dungeon for many days. This, prior to moving to a different jail. Though the new jail was far, in every way from my previous dungeon, I recently learned that the dungeon may have been located under the jail and surrounded by walls.[54] However, the dungeon for Joseph and me was much worse. Thus, in the jail, I still was not free, nor was I yet able to go to "new place."

For Joseph, the Bible says that it was "two years later," and Joseph was still in prison, in spite of all of the facts. Then God pulled him out.

---

52. Gen 17:17.
53. Heb 11:6.
54. Gen 40:5,15.

STEP SIX: THE REWARD & THE REWARDER

God helped Abram's faith after Abram, once again, demonstrated his, now elevated, faith in God.[55]

Joseph, Abram, and the children of Israel had walked a few steps with God and they had passed some tests. They also demonstrated an increasing level of faith while they were on their journey with God. Thus, when God was ready to announce himself as the rewarder, in each of these lives and incidents, God noted the participant's faith prior to allowing them to move forward.

Then he decided that now was the appointed time to reveal himself as the rewarder. Each had pleased him with their faith,[56] and each, though all three operating on different time schedules, had demonstrated that they would diligently seek God.[57] Thus, the rewarder could, at his chosen time, reward each of them.

---

55. Mark 11:22.
56. Heb 11:5.
57. Job 14:13–16.

9

Step Seven: "Was Not"

THE DISSERTATION PROCESS

SOMETHING HAS BECOME ABUNDANTLY clear to me as I complete this book: this book, for me, is sort of another dissertation and defense in partial fulfillment of my requirements for "Was Not." What that means is that, as a doctoral candidate, we are required to complete all coursework prescribed for students in the program. Then, we finish comprehensive exams, relative to the content covered in the coursework. Finally, we enter the long and laborious dissertation phase of our program, provided we have successfully completed all previous stepwise progression requirements.

For most doctoral candidates, at most traditional universities, the dissertation process consists of three stages: prospectus, proposal (followed by completion of the writing and prep for the defense phase which occurs post-proposal), and finally, the dissertation defense. I am explaining this primarily because the stepwise progression, relative to the dissertation process, is like a stepwise progression inside of a stepwise progression at the final stage of one's doctoral program.

Sounds like muddled nonsense, but stick with me. Also, many of my former adult students ask me about what those terms mean, so I will explain them, for the sake of those who do not know. More importantly, the entire process lends itself metaphorically to the manner in which we progress through with God on our stepwise dependent progressive journey to "Was Not."

Mini Steps

During the final stage of your doctoral candidacy, you progress through three "mini steps," if you will. You have to pass each step in order to move forward, and with good reason. You are conducting an actual research study which will contribute to the "well of research knowledge" in your particular field of doctoral study. I have always found that last quote to be one of the most ostentatious and hyperbole-filled loads of nonsense that the bigheads have ever uttered. Sorry, guys.

The fact is that initially elevating doctoral research to a level where, upon completion, you generally do not respect that which is completed due to the fact that a doctoral candidate completed it. This, as opposed to a "professional researcher" with a doctorate degree and research position in hand.

You all effectively diminish that research in value upon completion and subsequent publication. Dissertations are published when completed at traditional Research Universities. Then, my fellow bigheads summarily dismiss it as "novice research." But, they just said that it contributes to the "well of, . . . " sort of like an innocuous drop of water contributes to the ocean, right?

But, I love my bighead brethren. We are who we are. However, I am also a highly trained observer of the human condition. Additionally, I love humans.

Personally, my dissertation has been downloaded over seven hundred times around the world, at the time I am writing this book, likely many more by the time of publication. There is a link and map which I can use to show me exactly where and when it was downloaded. Most recently in Surbiton, England, UK.

My dissertation has been downloaded so often only because of the subject matter: academically at-risk academic advising. It is a very useful research study, relative to that specific "well of knowledge."

The study is reliable and valid (an issue that I had with a publisher, coincidentally), and the results significantly contribute to a specific area of knowledge within the field of proactive or academically at-risk college student advising. Most dissertations are not required to rise to that level of rigor and usefulness. You can finish your doctoral program, with a successfully defended dissertation that makes the contribution to that well using a much smaller portion of water than my dissertation did.

Prospectus

Now back to the topic: the summary of this book serving as my metaphorical dissertation phase, relative to the completion of this final step in my personal journey to "Was Not." This allegory seems appropriate.

As a part of an actual dissertation phase, first, you progress through the prospectus phase. There, as I remember, you write the first two or three chapters of your dissertation.

The prospectus serves as your template. The primary focus being your review of related literature portion, chapter 2. It lets your committee know that you have a credible topic, one worth studying. However, it also has to be a study that has not yet been completed in your field, thus breaking new ground.

Hopefully, you successfully get this prospectus past your dissertation chair and committee, which is no cakewalk. If your study is poorly constructed, if there is no actual use for your study within that "well of knowledge," or if it simply will not add up when you complete the preliminary research, your chair and committee are required to send you back to the drawing board. However, if you pass this phase, you move on to the proposal phase of the process.

Proposal

During the proposal phase, you formally complete the first three chapters of your dissertation. You complete everything from the title page through the references, of which there shall be a great many—like the sands on the seashores and stars in the skies.[1]

First, you complete the abstract, table of contents, chapter 1 which is the introduction and discussion of the relevance, as well as linear order of the study. This chapter also includes your hypothesis and research questions. Next, chapter 2, which is your review of related literature chapter. Then, chapter 3, which is effectively your methodology chapter.

---

1. Gen 15:5.

Here, you discuss the stepwise progressive plan and mathematical model, which you propose to use to analyze the data output results produced from your study. Finally, you complete the references section (see above), and appendices. Depending on the nature of the study, quantitative research or qualitative research (look them up), your study will either encompass five total chapters, or six, respectively.

This proposal constitutes the first three formal chapters of your study, including the stepwise study plan. This is not an outline, template, or a draft. You either plug this cord into the light socket and "let there be light" or enlightenment. Or perhaps, darkness will hover over the face of the deep.[2] You present the proposal to your chair and two other committee members. I cannot resist seeing the "Father, Son, and Holy Spirit" saying, "Let us make man."[3]

The Serpent Who Walked Upright

The traditional, private research university, as opposed to my undergrad and grad university (which used to be called a "medium public university" by the bigheads in their infinite wisdom) added a research consultant position. This, atypical position at most universities, is a quality assurance type who works for the academic department—not me. This person specialized, in my case, in quantitative research.

The research consultant was sent into the garden of Eden to ensure that Adam was completing research that would enhance the quality of research produced by my department and not place a blight on it. Most schools do not include such a person. Mine did. I like to call this person, in my case, "the serpent who walked upright."[4]

This person was a tempter and an impediment, which was their job. I say this laughingly, if not also seriously. As you may recall, I like to fight. Thus, this was a marvelous stage designed for me to whip three people who were for me, and one tempter who uttered some hindering phrases like "Did God say," "Surely you will not truly die," and "If you truly are the Son of God . . . might as well jump."[5]

---

2. Gen 1:1–5.
3. Gen 1:26–30.
4. Gen 3.
5. Gen 3:1–5, Matt 4:1–11.

We had to step on the head of that serpent and make sure that they crawled on their belly throughout eternity.[6] The research consultant added some challenges, stiff ones in fact. However, quality control, in the long run, was a good thing. That person served as a good tempter during my final stage.[7]

Proposal Defense

Defending your dissertation proposal is a very formal process. To defend the proposal, you have to set up a conference call with your committee. I am not sure if the "serpent who stood upright" was on the line for this or not. I don't think so.

Anyway, this is the "pretrial" of the actual dissertation defense. You create a PowerPoint and defend your first three formal chapters, including your methodology. Then they put you on hold and they talk about you. If you pass muster, you can move on and conduct your study.

Relative to this final stage in my stepwise dependent Journey to "Was Not," I have learned that writing this book will serve as a final component for me. I have been defending it all the way through this final step.

However, I have been developing the life that led to this manuscript, through this final stage, since I was born, or born again. Following the completion of the proposal stage, you gain approval from the university's institutional review board (IRB), if you are using human (or other living) subjects. As a "highly trained observer of the human condition," I would have it no other way.

Research Study

After that, you conduct the actual research study. My study was quantitative research which I prefer because of the objective, numerical-based, statistical analysis. Choosing this model, I had two more chapters to complete.

After conducting your study, you chronicle your findings derived from the completed research study in chapter 4. Then you discuss your findings in chapter 5 (of a quantitative research dissertation study). Next stop, the formal dissertation defense.

6. Gen 3:14–15.
7. 2 Cor 12:7.

Dissertation Defense Day

Luke Skywalker versus Darth Vader, his emperor, a few random stormtroopers, and those red-clad personal guard dudes is how I framed it, anyway.

You and your chair schedule a formal defense. This one is not via teleconference. You have to go back to campus for this one.

You go into a room, with Lord Vader, the emperor, the serpent in my case, as well as the stormtroopers and red guard guys. Actually, anyone who decides to wander past the dissertation defense room can walk in, pick up a copy of your dissertation, and sit in for the defense. Well, anyone at the university, who serves as faculty and has a doctorate, can wander into your defense. Normally the announcement is only sent to your entire college or school. Most people are too busy to show up.

On the day of your scheduled defense, you walk in, and conduct your defense via PowerPoint presentation. Then you fend off all of the lightsaber-wielding members of the dark side, and repel all phaser blasts from the stormtroopers. After shooting and swinging at you, the committee (and the serpent who walks upright) kicks you out and talks about you.

At this point, you either, pass, fail, or have to go back and redo some parts of the dissertation. The latter is most common. You fix some of the things that were in question, although your committee has reviewed your manuscript prior to scheduling the defense. Why didn't they just ask about that stuff then? That part is associated with, as I call it, the Guardians of the Profession or "Was Not." Essentially, the room full of loyal soldiers of the empire are what I call Guardians of the Profession and doctoral ranks.

They effectively play defense against you getting in to the Dr. club. If you remember: the name Enoch means "to be initiated or inducted into "the God Club." They do the early review to ensure that the dissertation manuscript is in proper order, post-proposal and study. However, when they review their preview copy of the actual study, they may notice some things that need to be improved, things that they, and "the serpent" in my case, will ask questions about during your defense. This is where they begin wielding their lightsabers and firing phaser blasts at you in order to prevent you from traveling in the E-ZPass lane into "Was Not."

They will not allow just anyone to enter "Was Not." You have to earn it. Although, essentially, they all want you to come in, to be knighted or hooded and become Dr. (insert-surname-here). They want you to come in because the whole earth groans with the travail of the pains of childbirth, awaiting the time when you get into position and enter "Was Not."[8] In this case they are awaiting your contribution to "the well of research knowledge." They also desire the future contributions that you will make. But, to get there, they want only those who the guardians deem worthy of ascension into their austere ranks.

THIS "WAS NOT" IS DIFFERENT FOR EVERYONE

All of this means that I was inspired and released to write this book, a book that I never thought I would write because I do not favor revealing practically anything about the real me. I prefer that you get to know me aside from the titles and degrees. That process allows me to know if you are genuinely interested in knowing the real me; if you need my assistance, which is also more than fine as that is my job; or if you are the serpent looking to disrupt the process for me, as well as that of those who are groaning in travail.

Yes, I have, by permission, become quite adept at keeping the "real Jones" far removed from public scrutiny. Many people know me and call me a friend. I cherish each and every one of them.

But few, save the Liberian ninja and Doc, know the real me. However, I have had to learn to open up certain things about myself to people for the purposes of counseling and advising to encourage reciprocity. But even that occurs only as is relevant and necessary, all the while, still maintaining appropriately comfortable anonymity.

All Stepwise Journeys are Different

Thus, the writing process relative to this book has been more open for me, though still limited in specifics, than I would ever prefer or engage in, unless required to do so. That is also because every person's entire stepwise journey looks different. I do not desire for my personal journey to bias the sample by comparison. Some will suffer mightily. Some will suffer comparatively less. However, to them, and everyone, their personal journey is as arduous as anything or anyone's in the world.

---

8. Rom 8:19–23.

So, I was chosen to write and provide a scant template of one modern day person's journey. While I was also directed to write about the lives of biblical leaders, about fifteen or so received extensive and detailed attention in this book, each who engaged a distinctive and distinguishable journey to "Was Not" relative to their own. Each pathway was different. However, the destination was the same in all instances: "Was Not."

The pathway was different, because the body has many parts,[9] and each body part has a different purpose and function. However, all parts are of equal importance. All contain the same aforementioned "sap" or blood cells, which all derive from the true vine.[10] Most importantly, the creator jointly fits them all together. He uses them as he wills, in order to accomplish his overarching purpose and plan.

WHAT DOES "JUST BEFORE" LOOK LIKE?

Your "Just Before Was Not" at journey's end will look different than anyone else's. As I previously outlined, everyone's journey is different. Thus everyone's "Was Not" and individual purpose is different. However, the final step that I metaphorically described at the beginning of this chapter may look somewhat similar for each of us. It may look something like that doctoral dissertation process that I used to represent the penultimate or "Just Before" dissertation defense. This occurs prior to ascending into "Was Not."

You will likely encounter one final test, a final exam of sorts, as did the two biblical leaders that I will primarily discuss in this chapter: Paul the Apostle and Queen Esther.

"Just Before": Joseph

However, your final test may resemble, in form and function, the process endured by my friend Joseph. His final exam was less of a dissertation defense, per se. Joseph's final exam was comprised of a test of endurance, perseverance, and diligence.

Joseph wanted to get out of jail. He was more focused, at that specific frustrated point in his journey, on, "Get me outta here," as opposed to the manifestation of his dreams from long ago and their "Was Not"

9. 1 Cor 12:12–27.
10. John 15: 1–4, 5, 6–8.

manifestation. At that point, it did not much matter what the end of this journey looked like, in reference to his dreams.

When he happened upon the butler and his dreams, he saw and availed himself of an opportunity to just "get out," irrespective of how "getting out" would play into the overall manifestation of the dreams. To him, right now, "These dreams are God's business."[11] Joey just wanted out.

Even though this was hardly a Get Out of Jail Free card to be provided by Pharaoh's butler.[12] Thus, in reality, Joseph's final exam was a test of his ability to wait and trust God that the end and the beginning were coming at God's appointed time.[13] His test was to endure.

Specifically, Joseph's "Just Before Was Not" occurred during the subsequent full two years that followed his personally driven attempt to secure his own release from prison, lasting until the time that God and Pharaoh needed him. All of this transpired when that butler forgot all about the gifted interpreter of dreams, who he and the baker met in Pharaoh's prison.

Pharaoh's butler and advisor completely forgot about that same guy, Joey—most likely due to his elation over being released from jail and not beheaded like his comrade, the baker. "Just Before Was Not," for Joseph, happened when he learned that God will use that, as yet to be conferred doctorate, exactly when I AM needs it.[14]

"Just Before": Paul

For Paul, "Was Not" occurred after his stepwise progression training and testing had occurred. Paul's "Just Before" included his Pharisaical training, the stoning of Stephen, the Road to Damascus experience, as well as the three year retraining period that followed. Then, Paul completed his dissertation defense "Just Before" he was sent up to Jerusalem as a changed man. Now he was ready for the big stage and "Was Not."

You may wonder, or at least contemplate as I did, when did "Was Not" occur for Paul the Apostle? Was it at the time he wrote 2 Timothy? This, as he sat in a Roman jail, awaiting his last opportunity to defend his actions and his born again life's work in front of the Roman emperor.

---

11. Gen 40:8.
12. Gen 40:5–41:1.
13. Gen 18:14.
14. Gen 40:8; Phil 4:11–13.

Paul held dual citizenship as Judean/Israelite and as a man with Roman citizenship based on the fact that he was born a Hebrew, in Tarsus of Cilicia, a Roman province.[15]

This meeting with the Roman emperor occurred after Paul had been prepared to serve Christ with the same zeal that he employed to serve as a Pharisee, one who persecuted Christians on behalf of the Jewish leaders of their Sanhedrin high council.

I believe that Paul's "Was Not" occurred well prior to the meeting with the emperor of Rome. In contrast to Joseph's "Was Not," which occurred after he met with Pharaoh, the ruler of Egypt, Paul's "Was Not" occurred as he was released to the uttermost parts of the world. This, after being sent to Jerusalem for the first time (prior to his missionary journeys and subsequent incarceration).

"Just Before" for Paul encompassed his retraining period. For Joseph, "Just Before" occurred as a test of his endurance, including the butler and the two years of being forgotten.

"Just Before": Enoch

We never got to see what Enoch looked like after, or even during, his three-hundred-year journey toward "Was Not." His prophetic actions, spoken of in the book of Jude, were not a part of "Was Not." This act preceded "Was Not."

That event may have been Enoch's comparative "Just Before" dissertation defense or final exam. However, we are not sure when that event occurred. It could have happened at some earlier point during his journey to "Was Not." We will never know because the bible does not provide specifics.

"Just Before": Queen Esther

Queen Esther's "Just Before" time entering into her "Was Not" was clearly defined by the writer of her eponymous book. The Bible tells us that her cousin Mordecai asked her to speak to her husband, the king, on behalf of her kinsmen, the Jews. Mordecai told her, "You were called, prepared, and tested in order to be used for such a time as this."[16] Once she accepted

---

15. Acts 21:39-40, 22:22-29.
16. Esth 4:14.

his words as true, she prepared herself spiritually, as well as in her heart and mind, to be used by God. "Just Before Was Not" for Queen Esther occurred over a two day period as she went before the King.

Those are just a few examples. They speak of the fact that everyone's journey as well as what occurs individually "Just Before" and after we enter into "Was Not" will occur very differently for each of us. This will depend on the person and the calling. However, the testing and steps leading to "Was Not" will be comparable for each of us.

WHEN IS "WAS NOT"?

This really tempted me for a minute while I thought about including Paul's journey in this book. At first, I focused on the period of Paul's life when he was about to die. However, Enoch, the progenitor of "Was Not," did not die. That's the point. Enoch was taken from earth to be in the presence of God, never to be seen again.[17]

"Was Not" is the place and appointed time that occurs post-preparation, steps, and graduations (which is the end result), as well as the beginning of what God has promised to you, via obscure dreams and visions. It is where God uses you to fulfill the dream that he placed inside of you long ago. It is where you actualize your purpose. Thus, for each of us, it will look as different as the purpose for which we were born.

For the Apostle Paul, it did not occur at the end of his life and earthly existence, as I originally brushed over. It occurred when he was changed into a usable format: a man of God, fit for his work and for the fulfillment of the purpose for which he was actually created, destined, and called.

"Was Not" is not the old hymn, "Nearer my God to Thee." That's the stepwise-dependent progression. It is (the song) "In Your Presence."

Saul the Young Pharisee

When Saul, who would later become Paul, entered Christ's presence, he began entering into his "Was Not." Our introduction to Saul, the young Pharisee and persecutor of the Christian church, occurs at the triumphant demise of the aforementioned Stephen, one of the initial seven deacons in the early church in Jerusalem.[18]

17. Gen 5:18–24; Heb 11:5–6.
18. Acts 7:58.

Saul watched over the coats, as the members of the Sanhedrin high council and other Jews stood and watched Stephen defend his dissertation. He preached the good news to them. This occurred just prior to them stoning Stephen to death. Stephen's "Was Not" also occurred beyond the view of recorded biblical history.

Then we are provided with a more in-depth introduction to Saul of Tarsus in the succeeding chapter.[19] It is said that Paul was in full agreement with the execution of Stephen. It goes on to say that the stoning of Stephen was sort of a next step in Saul's progression—although he had learned absolutely no dependency on Christ during this phase.

However, the groundwork for this dependency was laid through the expression of his fervency. It was all a part of the imputed personality type given to Paul by God. God was able to bring all of these pieces together, including consent to execution and persecuting his countrymen. All of this led to Paul's ultimate purpose.

Saul Persecutes the Church

A new and devastating wave of persecution was initiated by the high council, including the eager young rabbi, Saul of Tarsus, against the early Christian church on that day. Many Christians, save the apostles in Jerusalem, were scattered from Jerusalem throughout Judea and Samaria.[20] Saul was personally responsible for dragging men and women out of their homes, and going everywhere to persecute the early church.

However, another one of the original seven deacons furthered the process of fulfilling the mandate of the great commission.[21] As Stephen's death was used as the impetus to scatter the believers far and wide, and as persecution from the Jewish high council was raining down relentlessly against the early church, the Gospel began to spread from Jerusalem to Judea to Samaria, the former capital of the old northern kingdom of Ephraim/Israel, and ultimately to the uttermost parts of the world. This was all a part of God's, the master teacher and orchestra conductor's, plan and purpose to spread the Gospel.

Phillip, who was ordained with Stephen, went to Samaria and interacted with Simon the sorcerer. Then Phillip preached to, and baptized,

---

19. Acts 9:11.

20. Acts 1:8, 8:1–3, 4–40.

21. Matt 28:16–20; Mark 16:14–18; Luke 24:44–49; John 20:19–23; Acts 1:8.

the eunuch, who served under Kandake, the queen of Ethiopia, on the road south of Jerusalem that led to Gaza. When Phillip had finished, he was caught away, like Enoch.

However, he ended up in Azotus and preached the good news all the way to Caesarea. Saul had started a movement while he was trying to do, what he understood to be, the right thing. He was snuffing out any remnant of the early Christian church that spread throughout Israel and to the uttermost parts of the world.

A Pharisee Among Pharisees

Later, Paul tells everyone that he was a Pharisee among Pharisees, circumcised on the eighth day, but that he considered all of his work persecuting the church and all of his former rabbinical credentials as rubbish (he used another word), with respect to what he gained when Christ found him.[22]

Saul the persecutor was unwittingly used by Christ to spread the good news throughout the world. Then in a strange, though actually not at all strange, stepwise plot twist, Saul, as he would also unwittingly do, entered into the service of Christ as an apostle, and began to knowingly spread the gospel, beyond Samaria, to the uttermost parts of the world.

Paul's Dissertation Process

Acts 9 then speaks of Saul's conversion process. I would call this his dissertation process, metaphorically speaking. He had completed his coursework while becoming a "Hebrew among Hebrews, born of the tribe of Benjamin." (I just enjoy the eloquence of his thesis, as recorded in Philippians 3.) He also completed his comprehensive examinations by persecuting the church and simultaneously spreading the Gospel throughout Judea and Samaria.

But the uttermost parts, which would primarily be done by him, would require that he take a few last tests. Then he had to defend what he had researched and learned. Finally, he could enter "Was Not," fully prepared to handle any subsequent challenge. Paul, like Joseph—like us—was destined to be used to "save many."[23]

---

22. Gen 17:12; Phil 3:3–11.
23. Gen 45:1–8, 50:20.

Like Joseph, we are permitted to see what Saul's, who was by now called Paul's, "Was Not" looked like. Also, we are permitted to see some of the results, as per recorded biblical history.

Acts 9:1 says, "Meanwhile, Saul was uttering threats with every breath and was eager to kill the Lord's followers." They could have just said, "Man, Saul was running around threatening everybody." No one could or would escape Saul's wrath.

He went to the high priest to request letters addressed to the synagogues in Damascus, which would permit him to continue his campaign of dragging men and women out of their homes, corralling them, and taking them back to Jerusalem, in chains. That is, if they were found to be in the way. Meaning, Jewish believers in Jesus Christ as Messiah.[24]

Blinded by the Light

Saul was blinded and fell down to the ground (knocked off of his high horse). Then Jesus, surrounding him with light, asked him why he was persecuting Christ. Saul, who did not recognize the voice or speech patterns, asked who was speaking to him. The voice said, "It is Jesus, who you are and have been persecuting."[25]

His companions heard a voice or something. However, they did not understand the words and saw nothing. Jesus told Saul, like Abram, "Get up, go to the city of Damascus, and I will tell you what to do from there." This was all a part of the graduation process for Paul.

When a Roman . . . What Do You Do?

Paul was trained and educated, as he later states, as a Pharisee under the tutelage of Gamaliel the high priest in Jerusalem.[26] This occurred, although he was born in Cilicia, in the city of Tarsus, which is how he gained his dual citizenship. Saul was performing as he had been trained, prior to the Road to Damascus. He was persecuting people who had spoken against Hebrew custom and the law of Moses. On the road to Damascus, Saul received a new revelation, and a new assignment.

---

24. Acts 9:2–31; Gal 1:11–2:10.
25. Acts 9:1–19.
26. Acts 22:1–30.

Jesus ultimately sent Saul to a Christian man in Damascus named Ananias. He was appropriately afraid of Saul, let alone at the suggestion from Jesus that he would be the one who was needed to lay hands on Saul and pray for him that Jesus might restore his sight.

But Jesus told Ananias, through a vision, that he had selected Saul to be the one to take the Gospel past Samaria (even though he was actually responsible for the dispersal and spreading of the Gospel to Judea and Samaria, albeit indirectly and unwittingly).[27] Saul was set aside or sanctified by God to take the Gospel and preach it to gentiles and kings in the uttermost parts of the world.

Paul's Three Years of Doctoral Studies

Paul, as he would later be addressed, explained this experience of training for "Was Not" in the book of Galatians. He said that he did not rush right out and begin to preach the Gospel, although he had received his revelation of Christ person-to-person as did the other apostles.[28] He says that he went to Arabia from Damascus and later returned to Damascus.

He had studied Hebrew law under Gamaliel but he went to Arabia, then returned to Damascus, before going to Jerusalem in order to consult with human beings. He learned of Christ by consulting with Christ and the Holy Spirit. This occurred during his dissertation phase which preceded his dissertation defense.

Paul went to Jerusalem, in total, three years later. This, before he spent time with the apostle, Peter. He stated that the only other apostle who was in Jerusalem, three years after his Road to Damascus conversion, was James the brother of John, the beloved apostle. He went to Jerusalem in order to spend fifteen days with Peter.

Pork Doors

I mention this because the book of Acts, written by Luke, progresses through this time line by proceeding to James' death. This occurs after Peter meets with Cornelius and has a dream of a pig in a blanket. That event began the process of spreading the Gospel to the gentiles. In my

27. Acts 9:10–15.
28. Gal 1:11–2:10.

opinion, throwing the pork doors opened for everyone to consume, if you so choose.

Christ was writing a new law, if you will: the dispensation and era of grace.[29] He confirmed Peter's vision, three times (see previous mentions of confirmation via two or three witnesses), instructing him to rise, kill, and eat. Peter objected to eating pork, as any good Hebrew man during that time would.

However, Christ told Peter not to call unclean, according to Hebrew law, the same Hebrew law that Christ breathed. He told Peter not to call anything that he, I AM, Emmanuel, God, Jesus, the Christ and Messiah, the Lord and Savior, calls and makes clean. This meant both pork and the gentiles, who were about to receive the word of God. By the way, I eat very little pork—too much grease for me, as I get older and further away from such. However, I could if I wanted to. Why? Because Christ, God-breathed, ruach of God, called it clean, and so it is.

Paul's Dissertation Defense

Paul, as I was saying, completed his dissertation defense process during these three years of studying in Arabia and Damascus. Then he went up to Jerusalem and met with Peter for fifteen days. He was Dr. Paul of Tarsus, if you will, by the time he went to Jerusalem. This occurred prior to him engaging his first professorial teaching assignment in Antioch with his fellow assistant professor, Barnabas.

Some fourteen years later, Paul would return to Jerusalem with Barnabas and Titus, now all tenured full professors in the church. He returned in order to ensure that all of the research and teaching that he and his fellow professors had completed by taking the Gospel to the gentile world on his first missionary journey was not undone.

The leaders of the church in Jerusalem had attempted to impose the tenants of Hebrew law, specifically that of circumcision, which was instituted prior to the inception of Hebrew law upon the early Christian church. Circumcision was first given to Father Abraham.[30] The three professors were sent back to Jerusalem to ensure that their research and life's work was not undone, and all that they had taught to the gentiles was

---

29. Acts 10:10–16, 17–48.
30. Gen 17, 34; Acts 15; Rom 4; 1 Cor 7:19.

not dismantled, because the church leaders in Jerusalem were trying to physically circumcise Titus and all gentile believers.

Paul concludes his discussion on this topic of his dissertation in Galatians 1:10–2:21. He stated that he was given by Christ, as told to Ananias in Acts 9:15–16, the responsibility to preach Christ to the gentiles, just as Peter, James, and John were given that responsibility to preach it to the Jews. My point is that the "Was Not" dissertation process, all the way through Paul's successful defense, occurred in Paul's life prior to, and "Just Before," his first trip to Jerusalem to spend fifteen days with Peter. Then, he was sent out to Antioch, in order to preach and teach the Gospel to "save many."

Finished the Course

Thus, when Paul was in a Roman jail, after preaching the good news to the gentiles on two extended missionary journeys, he began writing to his son in the gospel in 2 Timothy 1–4. Also, by now, Paul had already spoken to kings and high priests. He had declared himself a Roman citizen and was preparing to speak with Caesar, the Roman emperor.[31] The timing as recorded in Acts can be confusing without the supporting documentation found in the Pauline Epistles, as well as other corresponding historical writings.

As Paul discusses the fact that he had finished the course, he was not preparing for "Was Not." No, Paul had lived and fulfilled his kingdom purpose, that purpose for which he was trained and tested, as well as the purpose for which he had progressed through the entire dissertation process, learning to depend on Christ with each successive step. This occurred during those three years in Arabia and Damascus. There in Arabia and Damascus, he went from prospectus to proposal to final defense and graduation.

After that, for Paul the apostle of Jesus Christ, "Was Not" occurred during the time when he, along with his fellow professors, went to spread the good news of Jesus Christ. He did this by taking the gospel to the gentiles. He also ended up defending his research in front of the high priest.

Then, after declaring himself a Roman citizen, as the Roman soldiers were tasked to whip him at the behest of that high priest and the Jewish high council, he was thrown into a Roman jail. After that, he took

---

31. Acts 22–28.

a journey wrought with peril on the way to Rome, as he wrote to Timothy for a second time. This time, asking for a coat, his books, and his papers, because everyone else had abandoned him, he knew that he had completed his task.[32] "Was Not" was finished. His work was done. Time to go home to be with Christ.

THE WALK-UP: TO AND THROUGH QUEEN ESTHER'S "WAS NOT"

I am going to resist the temptation to repristinate the entire story of Queen Esther, in an effort to remain true to the title of this chapter. I will do this by focusing the majority of our attention on Queen Esther's "Was Not." You should read the entire story, in a modern translation, if you have never read it or have not done so in awhile.

If It Was Going to Happen Anyway

I will begin by asking a question regarding Queen Esther's cousin and surrogate father, Mordecai. This question is relative to his famous speech to her which ended in "for such a time as this."[33] This speech served as the launch point for her "Was Not."

First, a little background: Mordecai and Hadassah, or Esther as she was called in the kingdom of Persia, were cousins. They were exiled and captured Jews. Esther's father had died, and Mordecai was an older family member and cousin of Esther's deceased father. He served as a surrogate dad to Esther.

As it happened, the king of Persia at the time, Xerxes, requested the presence of his then queen named Vashti. She refused to appear in front of him and his nobles who were having a banquet which lasted six months. They had a lot to celebrate, I guess. The nobles and other military officers recommended that he depose Vashti for her affront, lest, all other women (i.e., their wives) behave so "offensively" as to not want to be used as a dancing girl in front of the king and his official homies.[34]

---

32. 2 Tim 4:6–18.
33. Esth 4:14.
34. Esth 1.

So, they searched the kingdom for a new bride for the king. Esther won the king's affection, attention, and hand in marriage. She was now Queen Esther.[35]

Haman's Plot

One of the King's officials had been named as the head of all of the royal earls. His name was Haman, son of Hammedatha the Agagite. If the name Agag sounds familiar from its use in this book, it should.

Agag was the king of the Amalekites, who King Saul spared alive when God told King Saul, through Samuel the prophet, to eradicate or "sanctify" everything in Amalek. Ultimately, Samuel chopped Agag to pieces after declaring to King Saul that he would no longer be king of Israel because of his disobedience. Haman was Agag's descendant. Thus, he hated the Jews.[36]

Well, following Haman's promotion to the position of chief of the nobles and most powerful man in the Persian Kingdom, save the King. Haman noticed that Mordecai would never bow down to him—thus, not paying obeisance to his title as was required of the other Persian officials.[37] Mordecai was one who sat at the king's gate. As such, Mordecai was an important official in Persia, himself.

Haman learned from the other nobles that Mordecai never bowed when Haman, and likely his royal entourage, passed by. Specifically, when they passed the king's gate where Mordecai served. The other nobles found out that Mordecai was a Jew. Haman hated all Jews, because of his Great-Grandfather Agag.

Haman plotted to kill all of the Jews because killing Mordecai alone would not fully satisfy Haman's lust for vengeance. Haman paid off the king's royal treasury in an exchange of sorts, in order to get King Xerxes to agree to allow Haman to kill all of the Jews. The king agreed and lent his signet ring to Haman in order to ensure that killing the disrespectful Jews who resided any and everywhere throughout the Persian kingdom became the law of the land.

---

35. Esth 2.
36. Esth 4.
37. Esth 3.

Mordecai's Mourning

Mordecai found out that this order had been issued and sealed by the king who told Haman, "It is your money, do what you want with these people."[38] Xerxes obviously did not know the heritage of his wife, thinking he had no personal stake in the matter. Haman was a powerful, and affluent man who obviously bore great influence in the Persian kingdom. When Mordecai found out about Haman's plot;, he publicly went into mourning.

Esther was told by Mordecai earlier not to tell anyone that she was a Jew, particularly not while she was in the candidate pool to become the next queen.[39] Esther found out that her cousin and father figure was in mourning, so she sent some of her royal staff to bring Mordecai a change of clothes. His pain deeply concerned her.

Mordecai sent a copy of the decree to Queen Esther. He begged her to go and speak with the king on behalf of her people, the Jews. She explained to her "father" Mordecai that, as queen, essentially no one, not even her as queen, has any right to just go and see, much less talk to or even enter into, the king's inner court and presence—not unless the king expressly invites them to visit.[40] Mordecai replied back to her.

"But Why?"

Mordecai essentially told her, "Do not think or carry the expectation for one second that the fact that you are the queen and are in the palace will afford you protection from this edict to kill all Jews in Persia." He goes on to say that God will deliver us, but you will be found out and killed along with the rest of us. Thus, you need to go and speak with the king on our behalf. Who knows, Hadassah? You may have been chosen by God "for such a time as this."[41]

Now, before I move on to Esther, this is the part that makes me think and wonder if God will deliver the Jews from the edict initiated by, brought by, and paid for by Haman, then why again does Esther need to risk her neck by going into the King's presence uninvited? Her surrogate

---

38. Esth 3:11.
39. Esth 2:10.
40. Esth 4:10–14.
41. Esth 4:13.

father Mordecai sent Hadassah in to see King Xerxes, thereby possibly sentencing her to death with the hope that Xerxes' love for his wife was strong enough not to depose her as he did Vashti or have her killed.

Mordecai apparently believed that Xerxes was so in love with her that he would have (gladly) permitted her to come into his presence uninvited and would extend his golden scepter, signifying that she may indeed have audience with the king. Now, obviously Mordecai believed that Esther would not be killed because he believed God would extend grace and favor toward Esther, and deliver all of the Jews from Haman's plot.

However, my question and slight problem with his logic, which I am questioning here as unsound, is if you are good as you say you are, then you are "good," right? Meaning, if God will deliver you guys "anyway" then, why risk the life of your "daughter," Queen Esther? I do not get it.[42]

Actually, I understand. The man was under terrible distress. However, I just noticed the wording and sequence after reading this again.

God Uses All of It

The truth is that Mordecai, though he uttered some very important words relative to history, was just the herald. God used his words to motivate Esther, even if the thought preceding the "such a time as this" statement, as conveyed, was a bit of circular logic.

It was critical for Esther to take this step in faith, and to go before the king, her husband, advocating for her people, the Jews. God had orchestrated the sequence such that the confluence of events would allow Esther to enter into her "Was Not" moment.

Presently, the king had not sent for Esther nor requested her presence with him in thirty days. The man had an extensive harem. Or maybe he was busy planning his next six month bash, complete with an unrequited regal dancing girl. However, if Queen Esther went to the inner court of King Xerxes uninvited, she would be killed. Unless the king extended his golden scepter . . .

Upon receipt of Mordecai's reply, sent via Queen Esther's eunuch and personal attendant, assigned to her by King Xerxes, Esther would spring into action. She was a prepared leader.

She was deeply grieved to learn of her "father" Mordecai's distress. However, she was also a queen who knew her place, one who knew the

---

42. Esth 4:12–14.

laws that governed Persia as well as, more specifically, the palace. On the surface, she made the right call. Of course, what is also at play here is that Mordecai told Esther not to reveal to anyone that she was a Jew, such as not to disrupt her chances of becoming queen.

Divine Favor & Beauty

Divine favor and her beauty allowed God to make her queen. She was also graced to take each step through the long process that it takes for the king to vet potential mates. This, after deposing his previous Queen Vashti essentially for treason.

Esther had made it—she was queen, by the plan and purpose of God. But no one was aware, other than Mordecai, of her national origin. Mordecai, on the other hand, allowed anyone and everyone to know that he was a Hebrew.

Esther had to go through years of beauty treatment, behavioral lessons, education, and training to qualify to gain initial audience with the king, along with all of the other candidates.[43] These were Esther's steps. They searched the kingdom from India to Ethiopia for the most beautiful women in each province.[44]

The plan was to invite them to the capital city in Susa, endure the rigorous training program, be added to the King's harem, and qualify to gain audience with the king. They would all have a chance to stand out. God's grace, her beauty, and her ability to successfully interact with people helped Esther rise to the top of her class. Additionally, her capacity to learn from the eunuchs in charge of training (who also provided beauty treatments and education to the harem candidates) aided her pursuit.

She had made it through her stepwise-dependent progression. She had remained obedient to her cousin Mordecai. She stood apart from all of the other candidates by a wide margin. She was selected to become the next queen. Then, that typical waiting period began.

OK God, Now What?

There comes a point on the final step when you inevitably say, "OK, God, now what?" You think to yourself, if you are like me anyway, "OK God, I

---

43. Esth 2:12.
44. Esth 1:1.

have been obedient. I have done all of the blind faith dangerous stuff that you commanded me to do, while headed to a place that you will 'show' me." At this point in my journey, I obey without hesitation. My friend, Queen Esther, had a small reservation, but still.

The Masters Thesis vs. the Dissertation Defense

One might think that Esther's ascension to the crown was the moment of dissertation defense and graduation for her. Some royal fanfare followed by another huge party, Persian style, I am sure. The land has a new queen. Hadassah . . . I mean Esther. Queens really do get their own band and theme music.

After her selection and coronation process, she entered a life pertaining to the normal queen of Persia. The king had not called to see her in a month's time. If that was when Esther entered her "Was Not," now what?

"What was the grand purpose? What was all of that training and subterfuge about? What am I supposed to do now? Where are the fruits of my labors? All dressed, and crowned up with no place to go? Has God forgotten about me? Did he prepare me *not* to use me?"

This is That

All of her questions were about to be answered with a request: a test of her faith in God, issued by the God who had allowed her to enter into her current position of prominence.

Sometimes, God will promote us like Joseph. Sometimes, he will prosper us like Job, and then, seemingly, the heavens go silent and we start singing "What's It All About?" (I have no idea who sang that song.)

The Carrot We Chase

Everyone who commits themselves to God wants to be used for a kingdom purpose. That's the carrot we are inherently designed to chase. It has always seemed illogical that when we reach the last step, "Just Before" dissertation defense and "Was Not," we are now begging god to work.

Like Joseph ("Just get me out of here"), we tend to forget, in times of crisis, that we are simultaneously walking in at least one, probably more, of our callings.[45]

However, it does not have to occur while working for Potiphar. Actually, please do not let it be working for Potiphar. Anywhere else.

I can interpret dreams, God's business, with the best of them. I can become the managerial leader, manifested-interpretation for your vision, and for any organization. Look at my CV or resume. I can do these jobs with the best of them. Just give me a chance. After all, I am, in Esther's case, already queen. What gives, Jehovah, the self-existent one?

The Kiss is Still Coming

What gives is, at times, the promotion and the prosperity were just a part of the walk-up. They happen during the "Just Before" on the last step, not as a part of the comprehensive exams. You finished those and prospered. This is the proposal defense. You're not done yet.

You still have to go into the room and face Lord Vader, the emperor, and the stormtroopers shooting at your face. That which you just endured was just the prelude. The kiss is still coming. You were prepared, promoted, and prospered for purpose, not for your purpose, for his larger purpose. You were sent there for such a time as this.

Everything that you learned, seemingly out of order, will all flood back to you and you will use every item, instrument, and bit of knowledge gained through the process, through the tests, during the steps and stages. All of this, in order to gather the strength to, for Esther, go before the king. At times, you will do this by taking your life into your own hands, knowing that if you go to see Xerxes uninvited, you do so under potential penalty of death. We know that Queen Esther was well-trained by God, based on her response. She had passed every test at every stage in the process.

She sent word back to Mordecai and to her people, the Jews. She said, "Start fasting and praying for me,"[46] because I know I will be doing the same. In three days, come what may, I am going in to defend my dissertation. If I die, let me die.

---

45. 1 Cor 12, Eph 4:11.
46. Esth 4.

Although the stakes were much higher for Queen Esther, just like the day before your dissertation defense, don't try to do what you have already done. If you have already over-prepared throughout the process, then trust the process.

Trust the God who has prepared you for your big moment on stage. He has likely told you, (as He tersely told me in response to my query regarding "when I would be admitted to, and be able to begin my doctoral program?") "When I need it."

It's in There

Now, Friday, you are three days out on your defense. You defend on Monday morning; you can do no more. The study is "in the can," as they say in the movies. The PowerPoint slides, all eighty of them, are finished. The dissertation itself has been written, professionally edited and vetted by your chair and the committee. Although they left out all of the stuff that they would ask about while shooting at you and swinging their flashy swords at your face.

Prep time is over. You're done. Now, just do it. Time to defeat the empire.

That is exactly what Esther did. She demonstrated her training. She made her final preparations. Three days later, she stepped into the inner court of King Xerxes. Would he extend his golden scepter? Or would he ignore her as if they were perfect strangers, or worse, as if she was the deposed Queen Vashti?

When He Needed It

She entered the inner court as the king sat on his throne facing the entrance. When he saw his queen, he immediately, reflexively, extended his golden scepter. Cue the music . . . but wait, we still have "miles to go before she sleeps, yes, miles to go before she sleeps."[47] Apparently, what had been revealed to Queen Esther while she, her maids, and all of the nation of Israel within her purview fasted was that she needed to invite

---

47. Robert Frost, "Stopping by Woods on a Snowy Evening," https://www.poetryfoundation.org/poems/42891/stopping-by-woods-on-a-snowy-evening.

her husband and Haman to dinner.[48] It was all part of the plan. That is, if the golden scepter was extended.

God had given her grace and favor, not just to ascend to the crown, but to be used at the time when he needed it. In this case, "it" is her role as queen of Persia. Xerxes loved her. He extended his open-ended invitation to her right away. He followed it up by asking her what she needed and wanted. He said that he would give her anything that her heart desired, up to half of his kingdom.

God Knew When He Needed It

Esther simply invites the king and Haman, the chief noble, to a dinner that she planned to host that evening. Surely, she would reveal her request for mercy and favor for the Jews there, right? Nope. She doubles down and invites them to another dinner, the next day. This, after the king reiterates his offer to give her up to half of his kingdom.

He really loved her.

Meanwhile, Haman had his chest puffed out a mile wide. He had just been invited to dinner by the king and queen of Persia. Twice. After the first banquet, Esther promised the king that if he came tomorrow, she would make her request known. All part of the plan.[49]

Haman left dinner the first night in a celebratory mood. To celebrate, he plotted to kill Mordecai. Now that he had the order to avenge his grandfather's, King Agag of the Amalekites, death at the hand of Samuel the prophet.[50] He now could go directly after Mordecai for his blatant disrespect.

After all, not everyone had been invited to two royal banquets by the queen of Persia to dine alone with the king and his beloved queen. Dude was feeling safe. Now he could turn his attention squarely on to Mordecai. Haman and his fellow earls prepared a seventy-five foot pole which they would use to impale Mordecai, the disrespectful Jew.

---

48. Esth 5.
49. Esth 5–8.
50. 1 Sam 15:32–33.

Guess Who's Comin' to Dinner?

Meanwhile, divine providence, (there goes that word—used in proper context—again) was at work in the palace. No, not with the scheming Haman and his jackbooted thugs. Rather, with the king.

King Xerxes could not sleep. So he had the royal records brought in and read to him. He learned that, awhile ago, a man had foiled a plot to assassinate the king. That man was Mordecai, the disrespectful (to Haman) Jew. He decided to honor and thank Mordecai, not knowing that he was his queen's cousin and surrogate father.[51]

The king asked his attendants what was done for Mordecai, since he foiled the plot to murder the king, hatched by two of his eunuchs who guarded the king's sleeping quarters. The answer: nothing had been done. Then, guess who is coming to dinner (or at least to the palace)? Sidney Poitier. Actually, Haman.

The king asks Haman, "What do you think should be done for a man who truly pleases the king?" Innocuous enough of a question. It could be mistaken by a narcissistic, self-centered, murderous chief noble to make him think that he, of course, was the pleasing party in question. So Haman suggests all of the things that he would like done for him.

Haman suggested that the king dress that man up in royal robes, put the royal seal on his head, put him on a horse, and parade him around in front of all of his underling (digi-brained) earls . . . I mean, in front of all of the nobles in Persia. The king then says, "Great. Go and do that for Mordecai." For who? Mordecai the disrespectful Jew, that's who.

Then, "We will see you back here for the banquet." Stunned silence. Haman slinks home after obeying the king's orders. His wife now warns him, "Do not cross Mordecai, not after all of that. It is a suicide mission at this point."[52]

Esther's "Was Not"

At the banquet, Esther enters "Was Not." When the king extended his favor toward her and permitted her into his presence, she had begun her defense. It continued that night at the first banquet. It would conclude

---

51. Esth 6.
52. Esth 6:13–14.

tonight when she would hear the king's reply to her, as yet an unrevealed request.[53]

However, she was not asking for up to half of the kingdom which had already been granted to her at her behest. Even if you do the math, there were a lot of her people throughout Persia. However, they did not constitute half of the population of the Kingdom, nor did they occupy half the land mass of the kingdom—nor was Israel, the home of the exiled Hebrews, half of the kingdom.

But the king said it, and he would be more than happy to deliver it to her, had she desired. The king and Haman would not even need to kick Queen Esther out of the room in order to talk about her.

Yet, there were some tense moments. There still existed the possibility that the king may not be able to countermand his decision. After all, he had given the royal seal to Haman, and the bribe money from Haman was in the bank. The fate of the Jews was effectively sealed, Esther included. Although the king did not know it at the time. She had to finish strong—run on—to see what the end would (or gonna) be.

Queen Esther Drops the Bomb

Queen Esther finally made her request known at the behest of the king.[54] She asked him to spare her life as well as the lives of her people. The king, outraged, asked "Who would dare touch my queen?" She replied, "The evil Haman the Agagite."[55]

Queen Esther: classy to the end. There was no need to shout. However, the king left the room in a fit of rage. The queen, following a harrowing day, week, actually, retired to a couch.

Haman fell to his knees and clutched Hadassah. He began begging and pleading with the queen to spare his life. At that very moment, the king returned.

"Could Not": That was the Way of Things

The king saw Haman grabbing his beloved queen. Haman was sentenced to be impaled on the same pole that he planned to use to kill

---

53. Esth 7.
54. Esth 7:1–10.
55. Esth 7:6–8.

Mordecai the disrespectful Jew. The king went on, after calming down and executing Haman the Agagite, to say that he could not reverse his royal edict. That was the way of things.

If it had been so ordered, not even the king could reverse his own order, sealed with his signet ring. However, he would provide every means to even the odds. King Xerxes would allow every Jew in his kingdom to defend themselves.[56]

They would survive. What Haman had planned as the terminal fate and complete annihilation of the Jews throughout all of Persia "Was Not" to be, because Queen Esther "Was Not."

WHAT TO LOOK FOR "JUST BEFORE WAS NOT"

No matter when your "Just Before Was Not" occurs, you should see your version of the baker and the butler. There will likely be an antagonist or hindrance. This person, or possibly situation, will be used to push you forward and to challenge you.[57]

As I considered Haman the Agagite and how he was used to push Queen Esther through her "Just Before" stage onto the big stage, I began to realize that this negative person is always there.

Joseph had one during his "Just Before" stage although it lasted much longer than Queen Esther's. Joseph had the butler—actually, the butler did not push him, per se, rather, circumstantial frustration pushed Joseph.

However, the butler showed up, along with the baker, to serve as the embodiment of person sent to impede the extension of God's grace, favor, and mercy to be used in our lives "Just Before Was Not." Through that grace, favor, and mercy bestowed on us by God, we will be used to "save many."[58]

The two men, the baker and the butler, as you remember, ended up in jail under Joseph's care.[59] They apparently did something, likely tantamount to treason. Although the Bible does not specify regarding their suspected or actual crimes.

---

56. Esth 8.
57. 2 Cor 12:7.
58. Gen 45:5, 50:20.
59. Gen 40,

All we know is that, after their dreams, which were told to Joseph for interpretation, one was released and one was impaled on a pole. This pole was similar to Haman's seventy-five foot pole, constructed for Mordecai but used on Haman.

The idea is that, at times, a couple of people may randomly show up in your life. People who arrive, in order to signal to you that you are amid a "Just Before Was Not" season on this journey. Like Queen Esther, you are about to defend your dissertation and enter into the promised land of Dr. "Was Not." Samuel's mother, Hannah, had a similar "Just Before Was Not" experience where Peninnah served as her Haman.[60]

We should become aware of the randomly or unusually placed people and storms that appear in our lives. Particularly when we know that we are on the final step of our journey. We will begin by discussing the antagonist and then we can discuss the protagonist figure.

Advisor to the King

Not many people seem to discuss the fact that the cupbearer is an essential figure and advisor to the king during the time of Joseph and, later, Queen Esther. Joseph's forgetful butler was the cupbearer or wine steward to Pharaoh. This is why he was in the room two years later when Pharaoh had his own dreams, God's business, that none of his advisors could interpret—none except for the incarcerated but forgotten Joseph.[61]

Most of the ministers do not mention how critical the chief cupbearer was to the king. They totally obfuscate and miss the fact that Nehemiah held the same position, a few hundred years later, under King Artaxerxes of Persia.[62]

The butler actually fulfilled a dual role in Joseph's life. He was both antagonist and protagonist. But how does the baker factor into "Just Before Was Not"? The baker was most likely the one who got both men thrown in jail, in order to meet Joseph the dream interpreter.

While in the dungeon, under the care of Joseph, the butler and advisor to Pharaoh conveyed his dream to Joseph first. Joseph told him that, in three days, he would be restored to his position upon receiving his

---

60. 1 Sam 1.
61. Gen 41:9–13.
62. Neh 1:11–2:1.

release from the dungeon.⁶³ The baker, seeing how well the first interpretation went for the butler, then told his dream. Although he was also likely the guilty party responsible for their incarceration.

I say this because both of them had dreams. God's business, as described by Joseph, and a man who is about God's business, does not usually end up getting impaled on a pole. Mordecai did not, Haman did. However, the baker took a shot and decided to convey his dream to Joseph as well.⁶⁴

Joseph told the baker that, in three days, Pharaoh will have you impaled on a pole and birds, possibly filthy ravens, will finish you off. However, without the baker's likely treasonous act against Pharaoh, neither man gets thrown in the dungeon. Thus, Joseph would not have had the opportunity to meet the butler, Pharaoh's advisor, and this man could not promptly forget Joseph for two years, which served as Joseph's "Just Before" season.

The Extension of God's Grace, Favor, & Mercy

The role of the antagonist, relative to "Just Before," is the attempt by a person or circumstance to impede the extension of God's grace, favor, and mercy toward the person being prepared for "Was Not." In Joseph's case, the butler would have never met Joseph, if not for the crime most likely committed by the baker.

Had Joseph asked for clemency two years later (not that he ever had to ask because God had the steps ordered), that would have been just the right moment,⁶⁵ the moment which was the preordained conclusion of "Just Before Was Not" for Joseph. Yes, the right time for Joseph would not occur for two years. However, his "Just Before" began when the butler was restored to Pharaoh's employ.

Now, I believe that it took a supernatural act to cause the butler to forget the guy who correctly predicted, to the second, that the butler would not die in the dungeon,⁶⁶ rather that he would be exonerated and restored to his post as Pharaoh's advisor. It was the same supernatural act that jogged that man's memory, at just the right moment for God's grace,

---

63. Gen 40:16.
64. Gen 40:8–23.
65. Ps 37:23.
66. Gen 40–41:1–13.

favor, and mercy to be extended to Joseph through Pharaoh. Such that, Joseph could be used to "save many" as he was exiting his "Just Before" season and entering "Was Not."

Next up was Queen Esther. We just discussed her antagonist, at length: a man named Haman the Agagite. He tried to impede the extension of God's grace, favor, and mercy to Queen Esther via the hand and scepter of her husband, King Xerxes of Persia.

The grace, favor, and mercy of God was immediately extended toward Esther. Thus, she could enter into her "Was Not" and be used to "save many." As a reward for his antagonistic efforts, primarily extended toward Mordecai, but actually toward all Jews in Persia, Haman was impaled on a pole similar to Joseph's baker.

Advisor to the King (Part 2)

The man who we do not spend much time discussing in this book is Nehemiah the chief cupbearer and advisor to King Artaxerxes. Nehemiah held the same position, in a different kingdom and time, as the butler held during Joseph's time. Similar to Queen Esther, Nehemiah found himself in a position to need to draw upon the favor, grace, and mercy of God, extended to him through the king of Persia. King Artaxerxes was the third son of Queen Esther's husband.[67]

Nehemiah was burdened by the receipt of the news that returned to him in Susa via his brother Hanani and others.[68] This news was in regard to the disparate state of the wall around Jerusalem. The Jews were allowed to return to their homeland from exile, to rebuild the wall and Jerusalem, yet they would remain a province within the Kingdom of Persia.[69]

The distressing news was returned to Nehemiah, who could not contain his grief in front of the king. The king and queen really valued and cared for Nehemiah, who had never appeared before the king to serve him looking sorrowful. The king noticed right away, just as Joseph noticed his charges's faces, the morning following their dreams.[70]

---

67. Wikipedia, "Artaxerxes I of Persia," https://en.wikipedia.org/wiki/Artaxerxes_I_of_Persia.

68. Neh 1:1–4.

69. Neh 1–12.

70. Gen 40:6–7; Neh 2:1–20.

The reason that I have not discussed Nehemiah at length in this book is because the first time we see Nehemiah, he is already upon his "Just Before" moment leading into his "Was Not." He had his antagonists, times three. Their names were Sanballat the Horonite, Tobiah the Ammonite, and Geshem the Arab.[71]

Nehemiah was asked by King Artaxerxes why he looked sad, and he told the king about the news that he had received from Jerusalem. The king, with his queen sitting right beside him, asked how he could help his trusted advisor and chief cupbearer, Nehemiah. Nehemiah requested to return to Jerusalem to oversee the rebuilding project himself. The king asked him how long he would be gone. Nehemiah told him such.

Immediately, Yahweh Yireh, the Lord will provide, extended Nehemiah, through King Artaxerxes, the grace, favor, and mercy that he requested and required in order to help "save many" during his "Was Not."[72] Nehemiah also requested letters and supplies of the king. Such that he could travel safely from Susa to Jerusalem through the many Persian provinces that he would pass along the way. When he arrived, he would have all of the necessary resources on hand required to begin to rebuild the wall around Jerusalem. That's when the fight broke out.

The three antagonists did not hinder, in Nehemiah's case, the initial extension of God's grace, favor, and mercy. However, as Nehemiah passed through the territories of Persia and all the way into Jerusalem, these three men antagonized Nehemiah and the rebuilding project.

Tobiah the Ammonite was so bold as to bring "the Fox" into the discussion in a negative way. Only I can antagonize "my muse, the fox," Tobiah was not talking about my version of "the fox"; he was being much more antagonistic toward Nehemiah.

The three unwise men tried to hinder Nehemiah's journey by questioning his motives for rebuilding the wall around Jerusalem. They implied that Nehemiah had abused his relationship with the king, and that he planned to incite treason against the throne of Persia by fortifying Jerusalem.

They accused Nehemiah, who was to become governor of Judah for a time while overseeing the wall's rebuild, of trying to undermine the king, the same king who genuinely cared for and was concerned about Nehemiah relative to the king expressing grave concern over a sad look

---

71. Neh 2:1–4:9.
72. Gen 22:14.

on the face of his trusted advisor. This was the same Nehemiah who the king extended unprecedented grace, favor, and mercy to help along his people, the Hebrews. Tobiah stated that the wall that they were rebuilding could not stand up under the weight of one fox walking atop it.[73]

Nehemiah pressed all the way through the attacks levied by Sanballat the Horonite, Tobiah the Ammonite, and Geshem the Arab as Nehemiah went about completing God's business. In Nehemiah's case, the challenges to hinder the extension of God's grace, mercy, and favor occurred both "Just Before" and during Nehemiah's "Was Not." However, perseverance, endurance, and a lot of clever work aided Nehemiah in his quest to rebuild the wall of Jerusalem and help to "save many."

GRADUATION DAY: "WAS NOT"

Graduation day, for me anyway, was anticlimactic. It was for photographs. Some who attended would later turn into my personal version of Joseph's brothers and a "mother"/Lady Potiphar. However, in the end, God used all of those experiences on my way to "Was Not," too. I only attended my doctoral graduation in order to get the high distinction medallion. I was hooded by a very nice man, one who I have referred to as "the serpent who stood upright" in this book.

My chair could not make it to the, now rained out, rescheduled graduation ceremony. Those who have gone through the doctoral dissertation process know that graduation day is for pictures. You "earn your stripes"—those on the sleeves of your robe and your hood, expressly, when they invite you back into that room, the same room that, fifteen minutes to eternity ago, they just kicked you out of (the dissertation defense conference room where they just talked about you).

If they address you as "Mr. Jones," turn out the lights—the party is over.

The loser game show music plays in your head and your heart sinks. Then it beats out of your chest. If they call you "Dr. Jones," that's when you enter "Was Not."

That moment is when you are truly on stage, the moment when you succeed because you have learned *all* of your lessons well. And you can successfully defend them.

---

73. Neh 4:3.

Maybe you fail, and you have to go back to the drawing board to learn some more.

The final step is not when you are promoted and prospered. I experienced both of those, albeit through many difficulties, tests, and steps (most while I was in the employ of the various kingdoms of the digi-brains).

It is God's good pleasure to give you the kingdom.[74] "Was Not" happens when you have used all of your training and steps. Synchronously, under the power, grace, anointing, and authority of God, you are led all the way to "Was Not," the moment when you get into position, the moment when you fulfill your purpose, destiny, and calling.[75]

---

74. Luke 12:32.
75. Rom 8:18–23.

10

The End & the Beginning of the Journey: The Promised Land of "Was Not"

THE END: PART OF ME REALLY WANTED TO STAY

AS YOU COME TO the end of the last step, you are completing the final exams, or defending your dissertation. As one of my students, the one leaving my classroom that day bearing the weight of 1,000 elephants or beluga whales (I love beluga whales), said when preparing to graduate, "My last final for life." We will see . . .

Anyway, approaching your final exams, the last ones before you graduate, you are reasonably sure that if you do not simply forget everything that you have learned along the way, you will pass them. Thus, you are reasonably certain that you are headed toward graduation or "Was Not."

An Odd Time

In the true context of this book, you know that you are about to end the stepwise progression and you are about to enter into the purpose (or at least one large and overarching portion of it, one where the other gifts and talents that you are aware of, and some unexpected ones, can be cultivated by the Holy Spirit).

This is an interesting time because, at this point, you have developed a close and dependent enough relationship with the Holy Spirit that you know that many, many more challenges lie ahead. However, those challenges are not going to be geared toward your development as it relates to becoming the submitted, faithful, willing, and obedient person that God needed to mold and shape you into becoming. God prepared you before you entered the promised land of your "Was Not," such that, you could properly fulfill his destined purpose for your life. These new challenges are going to be related to continued advancement and making steady progress within the promised land.[1]

The Velvet Rope Now Locks You Out

The "end" can be a peculiar time in your life.[2] Most everyone reading this book can relate to the time when they graduated from high school, left one job and headed toward another, and/or graduated from some particular degree program in college. I remember when a high school student who went to my church discussed that week-long or so period when the seniors had finished high school.

However, the other students were still in school. The former seniors had to return for graduation rehearsal. They had cleared out their lockers, and when they returned to the school, they were almost treated like strangers.[3]

They knew the school like the back of their hand. They knew where their lockers were once located. Though now, they were empty. Your locker, as a student, is kind of your sanctuary and safe space. You feel at home there.

All of a sudden, they were being marshalled down the hallway, the hallway leading to their former lockers—it had been roped off. They were told that they had to "stay in the part of the school where the auditorium was located, only."

I am sure that each of them felt inside, "Are you nuts Principal Whose-It? I run this joint." Alas, you *used to* run this joint. This joint now belongs to the rising seniors (the juniors, who are finishing their finals and last week of school). You have been displaced.

1. Matt 11:12.
2. 1 Pet 2:9–10.
3. Ps 137:4, Matt 11:12.

Remold Your Mind from Within: Feelings Are like Buses

You may experience similar feelings, remembering that feelings are like buses: there will be another one coming along in fifteen minutes to take you to the same place, and your heart does not have a brain so do not try to supplant thinking with feelings. At the end of the stepwise journey to "Was Not" you are now "perfect and complete, lacking nothing." You have to adjust your thinking and your feelings in order to completely move into purpose.[4]

"Through Place" Was Not "New Place"

You have to let go, emotionally, and really in all other ways, of the attachments, dreams, ideas, etc., that caused you or me to mistakenly attach the dream to a "Through Place," as I have called it. You have to prepare yourself mentally and emotionally, which seems easy though the transition is not, to let go of and to forget those things that are (as well as those things that you are about to leave behind) and prepare yourself to press and step by faith. Then, you must move presently, by tangibility and by sight, into the things which are ahead.[5]

What More Was Left to Learn?

I will give you another example from my life. I knew that I had been placed on the last step; I had no idea how long it would last. Of course, I assumed that it would be a short stay.

After all, what more could I, the hero of 10,000 digi-brain kingdom days, possibly still have left to learn? Sarcasm, of course (yet not so far removed from my actual thought process). I had been "in the way" for quite some time. This is how Saul the Pharisee referred to the Christians of his day while persecuting them.[6] Alas, of course, it lasted much longer than I thought, and I had a lot more to learn about learning to walk by faith.

---

4. Matt 5:48; Rom 12:2; Jas 1:2–4.
5. Phil 3:13–14.
6. Acts 9:2.

Nouns

When I knew I was finally nearing graduation, I knew because God kept telling me in my spirit that the time for "New Place" is eminent. Also, he had already revealed the physical location of "New Place" to me, and delineated it from "Through Place" awhile ago. However, as I prepared to go, and had prepared those around me who knew major parts of the journey, purpose, and the real story, God led me to tell them that departure was eminent, so I did. Also, I had to deal with my own separation anxiety.

I am not one who ever experiences any form of separation, or any other kind of, anxiety. I do not allow myself to attach to most people, places, or things. In other words, I do not attach to the nouns. Remaining emotionally detached is both a part of the objective advisor and counselor that I have trained myself to be, as well as the person that I know I have to be in order to be capable of helping.

Honestly, I do not like to be hurt. So I have trained myself to avoid attachment while actually allowing people to know enough of me so I can help fulfill purpose. I do this under the complete direction of the Holy Spirit.

However, in spite of my personal code of conduct, I have had, through many steps and through a major part of my adult professional life, grown accustomed to a certain location—that location included people with whom I had developed significant and lasting relationships. I developed these specific relationships knowing inside that I was never at "home" in this location. However, I also knew that they were home to stay. Personally, I knew that I had one more move to make.

I had left many places. I had physically left many significant relationships in times past. I did not have much problem with that part. I had maintained the relationships that would endure as an ongoing part of my life. With equal alacrity, I was able to let go of once significant relationships that had ended, primarily because the people had revealed their true selves.

Love Gave, Love Gives

Honestly, if relationships end, you can bet everything that you can locate one commonality: someone in the relationship, or both people, refuse to pursue godly emotional healing—at least not to the extent required to submit all of their ways to God.

I always use the verse, "No greater love has man than a man who would lay down their life, or the things that are most important to them, these also being their highly guarded emotional hurts and roadblocks, which lead to walls, and intransigent places in their lives. No greater love has a man than one who would lay those things down, in an effort to allow the Holy Spirit to heal them, such that they can keep their friend."[7]

There is another applicable scripture. This one we all know: John 3:16. It can be boiled down to two simple words: "Love gave. Thus, love gives."

If you find the loss of relationship, you find a lack of Christ's perfect love, which casts out fear and intransigence; you find an inability to give your whole self, described briefly two paragraphs above, over to the Lord.

Then, you find one, or both people, stopped short of giving that same love to their friend. That lack of love will stop the Holy Spirit from touching that infected wound in their emotional psyche. Love gives, but people protect themselves by trying to take and require for themselves. It is perfectly simple.

I had become quite accustomed to, and adept at, letting go of those kinds of relationships. People do not like to look in the mirror.[8] Also, they do not like the light.

Yet I do have a blind spot relative to this topic. That is, I am completely unaware how, or the manner(s) in which, that light inside of me impacts others who I encounter. I can tell that the gift inside of me pulls strongly at those hurts, hidden behind those walls that the person has erected to protect their infected wounds. Consequently, the intensity oft becomes too hot. Thus, many relationships end, irrespective of the nature of that relationship's conception.

Unfinished God's Business

However, this time, I was in a situation where I wanted to stay, or at least a part of me did. I am an ENTJ and a creature of habit, regarding decision-making. I can overorganize anything, and I am a perfectionist.

As God was telling me it was time to leave, I was still walking by faith, pursuing the end of the last step. Simultaneously, I was trying to complete all final requirements, defend my dissertation, and graduate to

---

7. John 15:13.
8. 1 Cor 13:9–12.

the "Was Not" and "New Place" purpose that he had shown me. Yet, now, I had some trouble letting go of what I was to leave behind.

I was more than ready to move ahead. However, I did not know how long the final stages of the last step would last. So I started to look for ways to stay a little while longer in order to make the transition easier. I had already been snatched out of some relationships and familiar places via God's aforementioned "scorched earth policy," but he reinserted me back into the lives of a few of those who I had left in order to complete some unfinished God's business.

Bargaining to Stay & Begging to Go

I began to say and pray, "God if you want me to stay for X period of time, then open these doors." There was a part of me that hoped that he would open them. "Through Place" was as good as any to transition from, and to remain at until the timing relative to "New Place" had fully come. "Through Place," almost felt like home, which is why I thought it was "New Place" at least until I first set foot in "New Place." Then, I knew that I was home, and that "New Place" was to become my permanent home and final step.

The actual "Through Place" was a university. However, it was also associated with a familiar region. I thought, planned, hoped, and dreamed, though not a God's business dream, that I would settle down and remain there for the rest of time, fulfilling purpose there. I thought "Through Place" was "New Place." I thought that it was the proverbial "third move" that I also mentioned earlier in this book.

Alas, it was all part of the second move, or move two and a half. But the picture was cloudy and unclear as it was first revealed to me. I just had pieces, like Joseph's two dreams.

I started doing what many in traumatic situations do: I started bargaining with God, "I will stay if you really want me to," not realizing that I was trying to make decisions with my heart and feelings (no brain in the soul and ego), instead of with my spirit and brain.

I also knew and felt burdened in my spirit that there was still so much work left at "Through Place," as well as in the region. This was work that this sad cop still wanted to do. I also knew that when God said, "Go,"

I was to, just go. I would not look back. Detach and let go.⁹ I was conflicted and bargaining.

I really wanted to leave, deep in my heart. That's the carrot chasing the real dream and vision. You just run toward the light. However, "Through Place" was a very "Familiar Place."¹⁰

Another Confounding Factor

I experienced one more really confounding factor. Detaching is not a problem for me—never attaching in the first place, sans Doc and the Liberian ninja, is not a problem for me. But this scripture has cost me a great struggle to get through the emotion affiliated with this verse: if people can't see what God is doing, they stumble all over themselves; but when they attend to what he reveals, they are most blessed.¹¹

At this point in my faith walk, I just needed that confidence which came from seeing God. I needed to know that there was a plan, in order to continue confidently walking and pressing forward. I needed to see that he has answered, or at least provided me, with a deeply confirming "second or third witness" in my spirit so that there remains a definitive vision. This is still it. I cannot explain it any better than that.

Mind Snap

What usually happens is God shows me the vision. I am, humbly and gratefully, in a position to hear and see the overarching vision, albeit I see it dimly.¹² I realize that it is a fuzzy, cloudy picture by this point in the journey.

However, if I cannot see how God is at work, and see the confirming evidence that we are making progress, I lose it. I stress and I'm an emotional mess. I call these times: having a mind snap.¹³

---

9. Gen 19:26, Luke 17:32.
10. Phil 1:20–26.
11. Prov 29:18.
12. 1 Cor 13:9–12.
13. Isa 26:3.

Conversely, when I can see,[14] and when I know in my spirit what the Lord is doing, I am walking tall in the Spirit. I am like Caleb in that I can whip any giant who is occupying my promised land.

I am, inside, what most people who know me outside think I am. However, when I cannot see the vision clearly enough for my personal level of spiritual satisfaction, I stumble all over myself. I am not seeking comfort, just spiritual confirmation.

I need to know that he has not left me during my darkest and most difficult times.[15] I can take all of the bullets, as well as the tests. I will rarely, outwardly, reveal that I am in any pain. No one will know that I am in pain (sans that beloved and sly Liberian ninja).

The Publishing Contract that "Was Not"

I started bargaining with God because, at times, during the final step, I could not always see the vision. Maybe a part of me desired the comfort of the familiar. Then God decided midway through the final step to confirm that vision through one huge item and to answer to one of three major prayer points that he gave me on this final step. I have failed to mention, clearly, that you will be required to push through to "Was Not" while God also makes you pray your way into your promised land.

God decided, midway through the final step, to offer me a publishing contract. However, a few months later, through a series of highly questionable (some might say) Simeon- and Levi-like activities on their part, I lost the same contract (these were activities that I discovered relatively quickly).[16] But in my spirit, I was uncomfortable with these changes and requested alterations long before I threw my proverbial shoe and the dead fish on the negotiations table with this publishing house.

I can set things straight with the best of them, and talk about relentless. Embarrassingly so, at times.[17] Through an act of God's divine providence (once again, the correct application), and with the assistance of a stellar legal mind (a friend from college), it was finally straightened out.

In the beginning, when first offered the contract, I thought that this was the manifested vision relative to the dream that said, "Do not

---

14. Hab 2:1.
15. Matt 28:20.
16. Gen 34, 49:5.
17. Phil 3:5–6.

self-publish your first book. I AM will allow a reputable publisher to pick the book up." Then, it was gone—all within the span of about six months.

However, after all of the struggles with them over things that were actually able to present a legal problem, I was relieved that it was over.

Now, of course, I enjoyed the fight, but it was also frustrating and confusing because they were taking a clearly illogical position while simultaneously ignoring my and my lawyer's attempts to rectify the real issue. At the end of the day, I simply could not allow them to do what I knew was spiritually, academically, and intellectually lacking in integrity.

I wondered if they were insistent upon pursuing their course of action just to sell books and reap their return on investment (ROI) from their desired, and from my perspective, fearful primary target market. Also, they were doing this to the exclusion of secondary and tertiary markets that I suggested. In short, I could not allow them to "do that thing and sin against my God."[18]

I entered this entire endeavor without any desire to ever become an author, but when God births something inside of you, it is something that you have to see through to its conclusion, irrespective of whether or not you ever wanted to become a father or mother to that vision which you are carrying. You have to see it through to Elohim's desired conclusion, such that it can be used to "save many."

With the promised publishing deal all gone, though relieved, I was back in search of the confirmation of the vision. Now I was between the devil and the deep blue sea. I was too far along in the progression.

I knew that the time of the move to "New Place" was eminent. Thus, my concern and confusion was focused around the idea that I was leaving soon. Then the Lord sends me back to the drawing board. Now? Are you serious?

I know that you are real, and I do not doubt what you say to me. If I had doubted your voice, then I would have opened my mouth and fought those digi-brained queens, knowing that I could have easily remained in "Wrong Place" while knowing that you, Jehovah, the self-existent one, had moved on, thus disobediently staying in "Wrong Place" because it was the safe thing to do, according to ungodly logic and reason. But God, now, I cannot see the vision, although I can feel it inside in my spirit.

Yes, friends, the end can be an odd place, indeed.

---

18. Gen 39:9.

TOOLS IN THE TOOLBOX

I wanted to clean up one issue before the end of this book. I have spoken a lot from my particular frame of reference—metaphorically and allegorically, using my doctoral dissertation as an analogy to help me frame the process associated with walking by faith, with God, on a stepwise journey to "Was Not."[19] While using the entire dissertation process to exemplify the last test, which occurs at the end of the final step, that was in no way an encouragement from me for you to rush right out and get a doctoral degree.

Please do not do that to yourself of your own and personal accord. Obey God. If he wants you and needs you to have an MD, PhD, ThD, or whatever doctoral degree that you would pursue, only do it if you are led to do so by the Holy Spirit. Others in the body of Christ feel and have been given the task of encouraging as many to pursue doctorates as are willing to do so. I am not in that number, and I do not have that calling or burden. I think it to be blithely-applied unwise advice.

I will tell people all of the time, and in all situations, "You have to be led." If he says get it, then get it, and I will help you in any way that I can. But if he does not say pursue, then you need to stay yourself home in the stronghold of Ziklag.[20]

God gives us everything we need that pertains to living a godly life.[21] I equate a doctorate degree with a tool in the toolbox. If I need a hammer, God gives me a hammer because I will work in his kingdom with a hammer. Notice I have yet to mention nails. If I do not need nails, I will not have them (nor should not run off to find some.)

I was called to work in higher education—first as a part time digibrain and lecturer, and now as a full-time teaching professor.

Whoa & Sic 'Em

In order to get into and through those doors that God called me to enter, while living on purpose, I needed that doctoral degree tool. From the beginning of time and creation, God hard-wired this kid from a

---

19. Matt 28:20.
20. 1 Sam 30:8.
21. 2 Pet 1:3.

housing project in Pittsburgh to be a perfectionist, one who was overly competitive.

This was a kid who God would have to say "whoa" to far more often than he would have to say "sic 'em." To my knowledge, he has yet to say "sic 'em" to me. This was a kid who was also hard-wired to love to fight, and to pursue every fight with an intensity previously unknown to mankind. And yes, one who was overly intelligent for the size of his head.

Your Servant has Struck Down the Lion and the Bear

That kid would grow to be a man of God who would love his sheep, i.e., his students, with all of his heart.[22] He would love them with a godly intensity and care previously unknown to mankind.

That kid grew to be a man who would fight for his student against any and all ruling classes of the digi-brain nobility, irrespective of fiefdom or kingdom, that were attempting to derail his students from their pursuit of purpose, no matter the cost.[23] This man would rather lose everything than disobey or sin against God.[24]

Author nor Christian Author

God used that hammer to open academic and other intellectual doors, such as publishing doors. These doors were opened for a guy who never wanted to be, and still does not want to be, an author—much less a Christian author. That title and anointing brings a spotlight, one that this man does not control,[25] one that he did not shine on himself. However, based on his learned obedience, submission, and pursuit of purpose, it is one that he would quickly embrace at God's behest.

You have what you need. If you keep walking you will acquire the rest—not what you want, not to keep up with the Joneses, nor with Jones. I do not want your resume. I am no one for anyone to compete with. I do not compete with people. Rather I just compete to attain perfection.[26]

---

22. 2 Kgs 4:27.
23. 1 Sam 17:34–37.
24. Gen 39:9.
25. 2 Kgs 4:2; Matt 5:16.
26. Matt 5:48.

Please, get the tools that you require to complete your interpersonal and intimate stepwise dependent journey.

THE WORST THING I COULD DO: SUFFERING WITHOUT SUCCESS

That line, in part, comes from a song in a favorite childhood movie of mine. It is associated with what we will call misunderstanding and mislabeling your suffering. All people born into this world will suffer hardships.[27] However, there is a huge difference between suffering because you were obedient and submitted to God, and suffering because you were born into a fallen world.

The saddest thing, in my opinion, for people to do is to attend church every week, and yet allow themselves to be constantly misguided and misled by their circumstances. When I entered the last step of my journey to "Was Not," with many trials and tests still remaining ahead, I fully acknowledged that everything that comes during this stage would be a result of what came before. That means that what occurred on the last step is as a result of my obedience and submission to what I knew was the voice of God.

Chosen for Trouble

I chose to embrace this path. Yes, I obeyed. However, I have free will. Many, many doubted and tried to control me, those who I allowed to have intimate access to some of the information relative to my life and journey. God had concurrently sent me to them in order to pave the way for them to receive inner healing, and to, hopefully, choose to allow perfect love to cast out their fear of exposing their hidden emotional wounds. These folks are presently on the same course as Lady Potiphar and Joseph's brothers.

Abigail

Simultaneously, some helped me, in ways previously unimagined. They truly blessed me with their support and blind faith. Lastly, some, one in

---

27. Job 14:1–2.

particular, a certain Liberian ninja, took care of me during a very vulnerable time. I do not do vulnerability unless forced into it. That's all I am permitted to reveal in print.

Obedience & Success Suffering

I got here via my own obedience. At one specific point, when the last step began, God told me to "open not my mouth."[28] I could have completely derailed his plans if I had disobediently done what an associate viceroy in the kingdom of the digi-brains begged me to do. I might add, if I also had done what comes naturally i.e., fight, if I had fought the transparent lies told about me by a few feudal serfs in that fiefdom of the digi-brains.

These lies were used by the very emotionally damaged, formerly feigning "mother" and penultimate queen of the digi-brain fiefdom, the one who violated God's anointed because the light of God in her "former son" ultimately made her and her newly-coronated queen of the digi-brained fiefdom extremely uncomfortable.[29] Yes, they have to deal with God regarding their decisions, but I had to deal with the results of the test.

This meant, just like Joseph, I was soon to encounter a long season of righteously-incurred suffering. However, I embraced that suffering because, of course, I knew I was both obedient and right. Remember, I do not sit around wondering if I am wrong. So, come what may, I chose to obey and trust God all the way.

Sin's Fleeting Pleasure

So, I suffered a great many untold things. I was hurt by many people and betrayed by many more, some who were close to me. As attached as I allow myself to become, I can still become quite bewildered when Christians behave like heathens, and when self-ascribed mothers like Lady Potiphars. I should not expect integrity. However, at times, I still do. I know that it comes from intransigence, hurt, and an unwillingness to allow God to, usually through me, touch and heal the hurt.

But there are those, my friends, with whom I once walked closely. Some not so much. Yet some with whom I may have, or do now, work

---

28. Isa 53:7.
29. 1 Chr 16:22; Ps 105:15.

with, am related to by lineage, and some attend the same churches.[30] They can take their present suffering, mix it with the message of this book, and assume that they are headed toward a promised land. However, it is a land that God never assigned to them. This is the worst thing that they could do.

Eyes Fixed on the Reward

Job was obedient and would neither curse God nor die, as his wife suggested.[31] Joseph was obedient. He chose to tell Lady Potiphar that he would not sleep with her, even if that was the easier choice filled with a temporary, albeit comparably diminished, joy.[32] I am sure that Enoch faced many critical life decisions during his three-hundred-year walk.[33] Each man had to make the decision to stay with God, come what may.

What came for Job was boils, the death of all of his children, and the loss of everything that he had, but he still had his integrity.[34] Most importantly, he preferred to suffer those horrible things and occurrences over the fleetingly pleasurable path where disobedience leads. Job had a "come what may" mentality. I choose to serve God.[35] Same for Joseph. Same for Enoch.

Prove It

If God has told you to make a specific move, one that you can support via a witness in the form of a passage expressly taken from God's word;[36] if you are willing to accept the consequences of your actions, come what may; and if God has concurrently or previously shown you a picture, a vision, a dream, Chazown, God's business, and a purpose for your life then, by all means, pursue him and do everything that he tells you.[37]

30. Ps 55:13–14.
31. Job 2.
32. Gen 39; Heb 11:25–26.
33. Heb 11:5–6.
34. Ps 26.
35. Josh 24:14–15.
36. 1 Thess 5:21.
37. John 2:5; 1 Cor 13:9–12.

However, if you have chosen to make poor life decisions, life decisions that God neither confirms through his word, nor did he lead you to make, you can neither expect him to bless you in the beginning, middle, nor at the end of your suffering. As a matter of fact, outside of his grace, knowing that if you have indeed observed lying vanities, you have forsaken your own mercies. In these cases, inevitably, you will continue to suffer interminably until you decide to submit to God and obey his will for your life.[38]

CONSTRAINTS & THE BIGGEST KEY

If, in the format of a stepwise progression, or rather regression, which is a mathematical model, you can assume some things as constant or already existing, I can tell you what I believe to be the biggest key—this is the key that is required to reach and unlock the door to "Was Not."

If we can assume that you have read this book, in its entirety, sans the last few pages to come, we can reasonably hope, assume, and/or guess that you have a real and genuine relationship with Jesus Christ. You know him both as Savior and as Lord of your entire life. No one is asking you to already be perfect,[39] nor can they ask you to be perfect on this journey. Just have the relationship and keep walking.

Though, of course, we also more than allow for those of you who do not have that relationship with Christ to continue reading. That is fine, too. Read on.

Further, if we can assume that you have entered into that relationship to such an extent that you have a developing dependence on God and you have an emergent faith in God, then you likely have an understanding about both what faith is and what it is not. Again, you have also read this book and have obtained at least a little better understanding of faith, I pray. Once you know what faith is, we can discuss the biggest key to continuing to walk until you reach "Was Not."

Obedience

The biggest key is obedience, including submission. I have already discussed the scriptures associated with the topic, at least some of them.

38. Jonah 2:8.
39. Matt 5:48.

You can learn to blindly obey. It is difficult even if you have a relationship with Christ. I mean a real relationship, not just something like, as I always say, "You know where we keep God, and you might slide by there from time to time on Christmas, Easter/Resurrection Sunday, and maybe on Mother's Day, if you live where momma lives."

If you are deeper than that, and betimes, when you need him, even when it rains, you slide by him in prayer.[40] No, not that mess. Sorry, but you actually have a formed relationship with him, prayerfully, in some small ways, especially regarding the intimately close bond that you should develop with the Holy Spirit.[41] It may be comparably similar to one that you have with someone you love, romantically.

If you have that kind of relationship with Christ, sans perfection and sans your human standard, which guilt, at times, tries to force you to diminish the reality thereof, then you likely also have a reasonable-to-good grasp on what faith is and is not. If you have both, then obey. That is the key element.

I Chose This

Now, as I just explained, your submissive obedience will come, at times, with severe consequences. This will depend on the purpose that God has for your life. Irrespective of the calling, all suffering is painful, but if you can walk as I do, knowing that, "I chose this," then you freely and confidently can proceed on the journey.[42]

Based on my relationship with God, as well as the knowledge that he is a rewarder of we who diligently seek him,[43] we know that he will come right on time. He will bring "Was Not" to you."[44]

Furthermore, we know that he has a plan and a purpose for each of us. However, only those who choose, of their free will, to obey will: see, reach, and actualize the clarified and abundant manifestation of his purpose in and for their lives.[45]

---

40. Rev 3:16.
41. 1 Chr 28:9; Song; Amos 3:2.
42. Heb 11:1 (adaptation).
43. Heb 11:5–6.
44. Luke 12:32–33, Phil.
45. Heb 10:37; 2 Pet 3:9.

We can also have confidence in the fact that he will never break or delay his promises. However, only through submission and obedience, will you be able to see, realize, and actualize all that God has promised to you. Only through obedience will you reach the promised land of "Was Not."

WHAT HE WILL TELL US TO DO VS. WHAT HE WILL DO

On this stepwise journey to "Was Not," God will give all sorts of directions. As an extension of my first publishing contract example: I wrote my first book, the first draft anyway, in four days of intensive binge writing. When I was nearing the end, in my heart and probably with my mouth, I was asking God, "Now what?"

What do you want me to do with this? That is when he told me not to self-publish. Self-publishing is a perfectly acceptable avenue for many people who have dreamed of writing books all of their lives.

Remember, I was not one of those people. I never wanted this job. I knew it would happen. I think I did anyway. Thus, I sort of accepted it. I had heard it revealed to me that I would begin to write.

While I believed it, I was opened to the idea of looking at that one darkly and dimly.[46] "Whatever you want, God" was my attitude toward actually writing. With a couched wink and a nod, "However you want it Father."

First Publishing House

God told me to send the first book to a secular publisher, one that I had worked with as a lecturer. I did. They rejected it.

I was fine with that. The best way I can describe it is to say, I did not much care; I did not want to be an author, nor to be published, anyway. I only cared as much as I did, which turned out to be a lot, because I knew that God had told me to send it to them. However, I mistook, "send it to them" to mean "they will publish it."

So, I did what I always do. I fought. I asked them, "Why won't you publish it?" They actually explained. I told that first contact liaison to please send it to another person within the company, one in a different

---

46. 1 Cor 13:12.

department and division, one who represents a different, yet still major, theme of that particular manuscript.

When you know, as I did, that you did not write this manuscript and you know that only via God's grace and revelation could this be written, then you realize that you must ensure that his message, the author and finisher's message, get out to the people who were supposed to receive it.[47] That fact pushes you past your, in my case, lack of desire to become a published author.

I was rejected by the second person at that first publishing house as well. However, this publishing house would send me a quote that I would later use as I submitted manuscript proposals to other publishing houses.

This first publisher liked the book, however, they believed it too "specialized" for their readers. That stuff, as I learned, was big with publishers. No, not publishing good books. Rather, will our specific demographic of primary readers buy this type of book?

I was a business professor so I got that part. They were a for-profit corporation. Thus, their only goal, in a capitalist economy, was to maximize profits and shareholder interest. It was not to sell nice, divinely-inspired, God-breathed books by Jones.

I took that to mean that there was way too much Christian or religious content in it. I had become quite accustomed to the world of academia and the inherent conflicts between those of different faiths, as well as with those who do not believe.

Let Willy Be Free

I did not, and do not, care what you believe. If you are a Christian, I expect a standard and integrity. If you are not, I and *we* have no right to hold you to our standards as outlined in the Bible.

You do not believe it, or you believe that it is up for interpretation as a spiritual matter—not a legal, natural, or physiological matter as it relates to humans. I know that the word of God is not up for interpretation.[48]

If we find and have common grounds, as well as similar general senses of integrity, then we can enjoy ourselves together. I understand the difference. I am led by the Holy Spirit, not by my human urges and

---

47. Rom 10:17; Heb 12:2.
48. Matt 5:18; 2 Cor 1:20; 2 Tim 3:16.

predilections. I chose that. You may not have. God made us all with free will. So, let Willy be free—free to choose what Willy wants to do.

And That's When the Fight Broke Out

I started sending this manuscript, still in first draft form, to Christian publishers, in addition to other secular publishers that I had worked with. I did this through that plague on professorial humanity called the college book salesman—sales weasels, who I used to hide from. But everyone needs a purpose and a job. I say this knowing that someone will likely be selling my books to professors with the same intensity. Get 'em, guys.

Anyway, fast forward a year or so: I still had my book on the desk of Christian publishers. The secular ones had returned rejections with more alacrity, and I still had God's business relative to this book. A year in and I still had no real desire to be an author. All of this occurred as the bombs went off in other areas of my life and as the Lady Potiphars got into full swing.

I heard some promising news from a few publishers from time-to-time, but the list was narrowing. Then a self-publishing house, a major one, contacted me as a result of a forward from a major Christian publishing house who rejected it.

More months went on and I had a real offer from a vanity or "co-publisher." This is, essentially, self-publishing, with fewer strings attached. They were a reputable, if not huge, publisher. Earlier, a reputable Christian publisher contacted me. My friend had to tell me that they were reputable because I do not read. I used the quote from the first secular publisher and the offer from the co-publisher to help me negotiate with this reputable Christian publisher.

As time went on, I had a contract to publish the book. I had to add new material, as well as complete many other publishing tasks. Also, I had taken that first manuscript through many editing jobs, adding new material on my own. I had never done this before, so I could not over organize this venture. I had to be led every step of the way. Then, I had a date set for publication—and that's when the fight broke out.

Judge Me on My Integrity

They violated all of my principles of integrity: academic integrity and my Bible-fed, Spirit-led, godly integrity.[49] They did so in a way that made me look at them and literally say, "Have any of you people ever attended college or at least taken an elementary statistics course?"

Ask my publishing advisor friend, or ask the college friend, who eventually became my lawyer. I was astounded by *some* of their requests. Then, I began to notice and recognize the Joseph's brothers' duplicitous nature associated with the first publisher's requests and demands. Did I mention that this was a "Christian" publishing house?

Mind Snap (Part 2)

Well eventually this, bane of my existence, publishing contract ended. I had a bit of a mind snap. Now, as I am headed toward purpose on the last step, figuratively prepping the dissertation defense, I continued to hear God tell me, "The time to depart is eminent." I wonder if Joseph heard that just before being called to Pharaoh's palace.[50]

God had manifested and fulfilled one of three dreams for me. He did this in the form of telling me not to self-publish and insisting that a reputable, traditional publisher would publish it.

Mjölnir & Some Lightning

I knew that I was eminently headed back to the classroom in a secular university. This time, never to come out. After all, I had (been tricked and thus I) promised.

That author business, on the other hand, was not on my radar. I accepted the fact that I would publish bighead articles for journals, as a job requirement, when the time came. Also, I had published a few articles in the past.

I had just lost the publishing contract. Well, some may say that I took Mjölnir and some lightning (my lawyer). We blew the thing up! Scorched earth policy at its finest! I pushed it with my lawyer's astute council until they blew it up. She's a genius!

---

49. Job 1:1; Ps 26:1, 119:1; Prov 10:9.
50. Gen 41:1–14.

I am back to promises. I can no longer "see what God is doing, and I am stumbling all over myself."[51] But, that is the difference between what he tells us and what he does with it.

JONES' IF I HAD NEVER . . . STEPWISE ORCHESTRATION

If I had never . . . awakened that morning, my birthday actually, after some bunker buster bombs had gone off in my life and heard God say: "this is how you write that book! The one that you have been musing for some years! And then, put aside for a while." He gave me the missing piece!

If I had never . . . gotten up and began to binge write a book in four days, completing the first edition. And then get it in the mail by close of business the fifth day.

If I had never . . . gotten that pull quote from the first rejection email. The one from the first secular publishing house where God told me to send it. When I asked Him: OK omniscient one, it's finished, now what?

If I had never . . . taken their "too specific" comment to mean that I needed to also send it to Christian publishing houses. After I was slightly devastated, because they rejected it as "too specialized;" rather because I had lost sight of the vision I knew that I had heard from God, and did a Kingdom "magic trick" never attempted before by Jones, i.e. binge write a manuscript for publication in four days. But what actually happened was He said, "send it." While I (thought that I) heard; "they will publish it!" And through that, you will put me back into the classroom, now that I have the doctorate, that doctorate that I was not released to get until "When I AM Needs It!"

If I had never . . . decided to move forward and send the manuscript proposal to Christian publishers as well as to the secular ones, accepting what it might be, to whosoever I AM wills to publish it. Although I still do not want to be an author, much less a Christian author.

If I had never . . . continued on through many rejection letters, fueled by the singular desire to get this book. A book that, actually "I never really wrote (a book). Rather, it was like taking dictation. I was given things to say." So, I knew I had to get it out to the people. Because He "Said it!" Not because I wanted to become an author. Much less a Christian author.

---

51. Prov 29:18.

If I had never . . . received emails from the self-publisher. The first one. The one which had my manuscript forwarded to them by the only other traditional publisher with promise.

If I had never . . . eventually, amid my miserable dungeon experience, received interest from another traditional publisher, the one to ultimately sign the book. However not until I heard from a co-publisher, the one who wanted to publish it, with very few strings attached. The co-publisher who sent the most reasonable, though still not higher class-self publishing offer. However, I could now use that offer to negotiate with the one remaining traditional publisher left who was still interested in publishing the book, though they were taking their time. And, like Joseph . . . I wanted out!

If I had never . . . waited, on the Lord, by force! Believing that He told me not to self -or co-publish.

Then, I would have never . . . signed my first publishing deal.

If I had never . . . gone to college as an undergrad, majoring in marketing, which was just "aiight!"

If I had never . . . taken an elementary statistic class as well as a quantitative business statistics class as an undergrad, much less come to actually understand levels of statistical significance at an obnoxious and ridiculous degree of specificity, upon completion of my masters and doctorate.

Then, I would have never . . . noticed the true plans and desires of my version of Joseph's brothers Lady Potiphar, i.e. the first "Christian" publisher. Oh, Wait! Rewind these, "If I had nevers ..."

If I had never . . . loved counseling and advising so much, though I was a marketing major in undergrad because I was told to do so by a career exploration test to become said marketing major, and I stayed because I liked parts of marketing, but not all of it. I also stayed because I had taken too much of it. Too many credits. Too many business and marketing major courses to ever turn around at that point. Again, and like Joseph, on this step, I wanted out!

If I had never . . . eventually realized or had revealed to me that I was only good at one thing: college people.

I would have never . . . studied the material that became the foundational subject matter for that first book, which also led me to be in a position to teach marketing, only teaching marketing, such that I could also do what my heart truly desired. That being: advise academically at-risk college students.

If I had never . . . advised those students, I would not have developed enough expertise with academically at-risk/proactive advising to write a dissertation about it and obtain a God's business doctorate for doing so. And that dissertation would have never been downloaded over seven hundred times to date. Downloaded on six of the seven continents around the world. A fact that I still find absolutely hilarious. Why? Because I never wanted to be an author. Much less a Christian author.

If I had never . . . listened to God. Because, at this point, my "fateful first Christian publisher," who still has apparently never taken a course in elementary statistics, was now ignoring all of my email requests and demands to make the necessary changes. Changes, required to maintain my, if not their, Godly-elevated sense of academic and spiritual integrity.

If I had never . . . listened to God when He said; "Direct message your lawyer friend from college" and see if she can help. And she was more than happy to do so. And she is a genius!

I would have never . . . with her help, gotten them to end that contract.

If I had never . . . ended that contract, with the astute assistance of my college friend and lawyer. However, after the contract was terminated, once again, I would not be able to "see what God was doing." Thus, I would be left saying; "God, now what?" First you manifest one of the three Chazown or Dreams, only later to drop us back to zero out of three? Keep walking by faith? On this last step? With departure imminent? Yet, there was another side to this.

If I had never . . . negotiated and subsequently signed that contract with the first "Christian" publishing house, then I would have never written at their behest And subsequently learned to love the new material that they asked me to include in the first book. Of course, I initially resisted adding new material, because I wrote what I wrote, and saw that it was good. And I do not sit around wondering if I am wrong! However, this new stuff, which I initially resisted writing, was very good. But I was also skeptical in my spirit about something else. Something elusive, relative to the request for the new material. Later I understood that I was skeptical and resistant because it was "too much Christian material" and it did not fit my misinterpreted Chazown for the book. However, as a result of writing it, rather more like taking more dictation, I added it. Then I altered it. As led! And as the true vision for that first book came into clear focus! So, I subsequently embraced it. I loved It! It was very, very, good!

If I had never ... done all of that; I would have never ... learned to embrace one simple fact:

I am purposed to be a Christian author. Oh my goodness! Also, I am purposed to be a teaching (and research) professor, one who is called to be back in the classroom, never to come out once he gets back in. Although, the Master Teacher had actually gotten me back into the classroom at "Through Place" as well as at "Other Places."

If I had never ... gone to "Other Place" for the conference after skipping out on it the previous year, because it was not yet time for me to go. And I almost skipped out on a big meeting with those from "Other Place," during the first year of my relationship with them, while I was beginning the journey on my final step, this time to go fishing. However, God said, just like "Through Place," you must need go to this meeting. And to this conference.

If I had never ... gone to the conference, a little while later, at "Other Place." A "Place" that I had never ... visited before. However, I had some six degrees of separation connections via various people in my past, and via a random teaching professor application that I had sent while ABD on a previous step a while before I had reached my final step.

If I had never ... attended that conference, fishing or not, I would have never found The Real "New Place!"

The Immutable Reality of "Was Not"

If I had never ... done all of those things.

Then I would have never ... embraced the Immutable Reality of "Was Not." That Immutable Reality states that:

> I was purposed and promised to be a Christian author and a professor at a secular university. I resisted one. I actually resisted the other, if you remember, but I was destined to be both at the same time, and never the twain need to actually meet. Although I thought that they were destined to meet, but I saw a cloudy vision, dimly. [52]

And, if I had never ... done all of that, and a million other things, completed out of obedience, faith, relationship, intimacy, and submission.

---

52. 1 Cor 13:12.

THE END & THE BEGINNING OF THE JOURNEY

Then, I would have never . . . allowed God to wake me up on another morning, shortly after my birthday a while later and write this Christian book, by a Christian author (oh my goodness!).

Jones' Stepwise Dependent Progressive Journey: Seven Steps to "Was Not." Orchestrated by the Master Teacher, Himself!

THE BEGINNING: WALKING IN "WAS NOT"

I really wanted to stop and drop the mic there, but I am obedient. Thus, I will conclude this odyssey by saying that this book is more about walking toward "Was Not" than it is about describing what "Was Not" looks like, or living in "Was Not." Prayerfully, it is an encouragement to those who are going through their own unusual storms, trials, and struggles on the way to their own God-breathed promised land. It is much more that kind of book than one about "what it is like to Walk in your Promised Land." Thus, it was similarly named by this Christian author: "Was Not."

After all, Enoch walked with God and he "Was Not" because God took him.[53] We have no idea what heaven looked like for Enoch. We have no idea what being taken from the metaphysical world and translated into the very presence of God looked like for Enoch.

Thus, we used Joseph, Job, and many other biblical leaders', as well as one Christian author's, journeys to help us see and understand—not only what the walk up to "Was Not" looks like, but we used their stories to help us understand what progressing toward the promised land, while remaining here on this planet, looks like for each of us. There are many more trials and perils awaiting all of us in the promised land.

However, we can know, with blessed assurance, that everything that we have endured, persevered through, and sought God diligently to make it through has been divinely orchestrated in order to prepare us to do all of the things that we are called to do.[54] We have been equipped to do exceedingly beyond all of those things that we can ask, think, or conceive of doing and becoming.[55]

---

53. Gen 5:24; Heb 11:5.
54. Phil 4:13.
55. Ephesians 3:20.

Like Caleb, we are well able to overcome any and all obstacles. If we are willing and obedient, we will eat the good of the promised land.[56] Also, God will use us to "save many."[57]

So please, let go of and forgive all of your Lady Potiphars, Joseph's brothers, Job's fateful friends, and all of those unnamed people that Enoch encountered during his three-hundred-year odyssey to "Was Not." Know that, when the time is right, we will graduate from our final step. Be assured that the Master Teacher has brought together this stepwise dependent progressive journey as only Jehovah, the self-existent one, could. Thus, at such a time as that we will finally step into our version of "Was Not."

---

56. Num 13:30; Isa 1:19.

57. Gen 45:5, 50:20.

Epilogue

A Dissertation Presented in Partial Fulfillment of the Requirements for Graduation from the Final Step into "Was Not"

www.ingramcontent.com/pod-product-compliance
Lightning Source LLC
Chambersburg PA
CBHW050845230426
43667CB00012B/2149